W9-COG-021

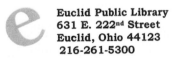

SEX AND THE
FOUNDING FATHERS

In the series *Sexuality Studies,*
edited by Janice Irvine and Regina Kunzel

ALSO IN THIS SERIES:

Colin R. Johnson, *Just Queer Folks:*
Gender and Sexuality in Rural America

Lisa Sigel, *Making Modern Love:*
Sexual Narratives and Identities in Interwar Britain

SEX
AND THE
FOUNDING
FATHERS

———

The American Quest for a Relatable Past

———

THOMAS A. FOSTER

TEMPLE UNIVERSITY PRESS

PHILADELPHIA

TEMPLE UNIVERSITY PRESS
Philadelphia, Pennsylvania 19122
www.temple.edu/tempress

Copyright © 2014 by Temple University
All rights reserved
Published 2014

TEXT DESIGN BY KATE NICHOLS

Library of Congress Cataloging-in-Publication Data

Foster, Thomas A.
 Sex and the founding fathers : the American quest for a relatable past /
Thomas A. Foster.
     pages cm. — (Sexuality studies)
 Includes bibliographical references and index.
 ISBN 978-1-4399-1102-0 (cloth : alk. paper) — ISBN 978-1-4399-1104-4
(e-book) 1. Founding Fathers of the United States—Sexual behavior—United
States—History. 2. Presidents—Sexual behavior—United States—History.
3. United States—History—1783–1815—Biography. I. Title.
 E302.5.F668 2014
 973.4092'2—dc23

                                        2013020501

♾ The paper used in this publication meets the requirements of the American
National Standard for Information Sciences—Permanence of Paper for Printed
Library Materials, ANSI Z39.48-1992

Printed in the United States of America

2 4 6 8 9 7 5 3 1

For Marlon

CONTENTS

ACKNOWLEDGMENTS ix

INTRODUCTION: REMEMBERING THE FOUNDERS: SEX AND
THE AMERICAN QUEST FOR A RELATABLE PAST 1

1 GEORGE WASHINGTON 11

2 THOMAS JEFFERSON 45

3 JOHN ADAMS 77

4 BENJAMIN FRANKLIN 97

5 ALEXANDER HAMILTON 119

6 GOUVERNEUR MORRIS 143

CONCLUSION 165

NOTES 169

BIBLIOGRAPHY 201

INDEX 213

ACKNOWLEDGMENTS

ALTHOUGH MY NAME ALONE appears on the cover of this book, I could never have written this volume without the time and effort that were contributed by a humblingly large number of people. What follows is my acknowledgment of a mere portion of the help I received. The earliest idea for the book came from conversations with John D'Emilio, to whom I am most grateful for his mentoring and encouragement. The support and guidance of Mary Beth Norton have sustained me throughout not only this project but also my career.

A long list of individuals generously contributed in various ways, providing important feedback, reading drafts, and writing letters for grant applications. I especially thank Lauren Berlant, Frances Clarke, John D'Emilio, Toby Ditz, Carolyn Eastman, Estelle Freedman, François Furstenberg, Lori Glover, Annette Gordon-Reed, Nancy Isenberg, James E. McWilliams, Robin Mitchell, Rebecca Plant, Elizabeth Reis, Lisa Sigel, Roshanna Sylvester, David Waldstreicher, and—for making a trip to Mt. Vernon so enjoyable—Wayne Wheeler. I am also grateful to Jordan Stein, who provided timely, insightful, and encouraging words at a very critical point.

I thank Dr. Gerard Gawalt, in the Manuscript Division of the Library of Congress, who granted me access to Gouverneur Morris's original diaries. Numerous other individuals helped me understand Morris's world, including Dena Goodman, Catherine Kudlick, Jeffery Merrick, Melanie Miller, and Ben Mutschler.

I am grateful to Marello Harris for his initial research at the University of Georgia; to Ramiro Hernandez and Katarzyna Szymanska for their help with various projects; and to DePaul University's College of Liberal Arts and Social Sciences Undergraduate Research Assistant program for supporting the labor of Sandra Sasal, Zachary Stafford, and Katie Suleta. DePaul University has provided me with not only a reliable livelihood but also supportive colleagues and engaging students. I received additional financial support from DePaul in the form of a DePaul Summer Research Grant, a fellowship at the DePaul Humanities Center, a Competitive Research Grant, and travel funding.

As the book took shape, it benefited from the feedback and support of a small army of editors, peer reviewers, and even potential agents—but especially Debbie Gershenowitz, Gayatri Patnaik, and Janet Francedese and the team at Temple University Press.

Over the years, I honed my arguments and gained new understanding from the responses of audiences at the Gerber-Hart Library, the University of Northern Iowa, Purdue University at Calumet, and the University of Mary Washington. I was also fortunate to have the opportunity to discuss the work at a number of conferences, including the American Men's Studies Association Annual Conference, Creating the Past: Early American Museums between History and Edu-entertainment, the European Early American Studies Association Biennial Conference, the Newberry Seminar on Women and Gender, Queering Paradigms IV, and (Re)Figuring Sex: Somatechnical (Re)Visions.

Finally, I express my gratitude to New York University Press, *Disability Studies Quarterly*, the *Journal of the History of Sexuality*, and the corresponding anonymous peer reviewers, who provided useful feedback on portions of this project that I developed into essays published in these academic journals and in an edited volume published by New York University Press.

INTRODUCTION

REMEMBERING THE FOUNDERS

---◈---

Sex and the American Quest for a Relatable Past

IVING AS WE DO in an era in which public figures are subjected to extreme scrutiny in the form of media intrusions, we tend to think of our interest in reconciling public images with private sexual conduct as uniquely postmodern. In fact, Americans have long invested national heroes with superior moral status and at the same time probed into their private lives. If the Founding Fathers seem remote to us now, that distance persists despite the efforts of generations of biographers who attempt to take their measure as leaders and tell us what they were really like in their most intimate relationships. From the early years of the Republic till now, biographers have attempted to burnish the Founders' images and satisfy public curiosity about their lives beyond public view. At the same time, gossips and politically motivated detractors, claiming to have the inside track on new information, have circulated scandalous or unpleasant stories to knock these exalted men off their pedestals. Looking back at the stories and assessments that have proliferated in the two and a half centuries since the Founders' generation, we see the dual nature of these accounts and how they oscillate between the public and the private, between the idealized image and actions in the intimate realm. We see how each generation reshapes images of the Founders to fit that storyteller's era.

On the one hand, the Founders appear desexualized. The images of the Founding Fathers that we regularly encounter—as heads on money, as reference points in discussions about political ideology, and as monuments at tourist sites—assert their status as virtuous American men. They typically appear either disembodied—as heads or busts—or in clothing that reminds us of their political or military position. Their flesh is covered from neck to wrists, with only hands and face exposed. Typically, the men are frozen in advanced age—generally gray-haired, if not topped off with wigs—further confirming their identities as desexualized elder statesman for generations of Americans who associate sexual activity with youth.[1]

On the other side of the coin, curiosity about their "real" lives has continued seemingly unabated into our own time. In 1810, Mason L. (Parson) Weems, originator of the cherry-tree myth, emphasized the importance of discussing George Washington's personal life. Weems argues that "public character" is no "evidence of *true greatness*" and calls for a spotlight to be shined on his "private life." Weems gives the compelling example of Benedict Arnold, who could "play you the *great man*" "yet in the *private walks of life*" reveal himself to be a "swindler"—including not only his political deception but his use of the "aid of loose women." For Weems, the Founders' intimate relationships should not be off-limits for Americans: "It *is* not, then, in the glare of *public*, but in the shade of *private life*, that we are to look for the man. Private life is always *real* life." To truly know them, their conduct in that realm is an important piece of the puzzle.[2]

By tracing how intimacy has figured in popular memory of the Founders from their own lifetimes to the recent past, *Sex and the Founding Fathers* shows that sex has long been used to define their masculine character and political authority and has always figured in civic and national identity.[3] Each generation has asked different questions about the Founders and their private lives, but Americans have consistently imagined and reimagined the private lives of the Founders through the lens of contemporary society. As Michael Kammen and others have argued, countries "reconstruct their pasts rather than faithfully record them" and "do so with the needs of contemporary culture clearly in mind."[4] Gore Vidal has referred to our selective national memory as "The United States of Amnesia."[5] It is true that we tend to embrace the national narratives that we desire and "forget" those that we prefer to hide away. Stories about the Founders' lives have always been told in ways that make use of the norms and ideals of the time period. Founders can never be embraced in their late-eighteenth-century context, for, as the saying goes, the past is a foreign country—and the Founders lose their cultural utility when viewed as foreigners. Americans want to see themselves in their images, because these men, the men who created America, are by their actions the embodiment of the nation and of our national identity.

Scholars have shown how the Founding Fathers have been central to our sense of national identity. The Founders created the nation and can never be divorced from our understanding of it. They embody the nation, its principles, and even its founding documents. In this sense, they are unchanging and can always serve to connect Americans with American identity.[6] Today, the Founders generate both vast book sales and daily reference by politicians, jurists interpreting the Constitution, schoolteachers, and ordinary citizens—each of whom holds up the Founders' historical significance because of their roles in establishing the political structure of the nation and in shaping our national identity.[7] By examining how their most intimate thoughts and actions figure in popular imagining of the Founders, we are able to deepen our understanding of how sexuality and gender are important components of civic and national identity.

Today, Americans still trade in stories about the sexual escapades of the Founding Fathers. The topic is often used to draw a contrast between distinct private and public worlds.[8] Consider the following examples. A farcical article, written in the straight-faced style of The Onion, reports on the recent discovery of raunchy letters written by Washington to a woman he desired;[9] the article is accompanied by a lurid portrait of Washington with a grotesquely large bulge in his pants. A popular author visits The Daily Show with Jon Stewart to promote his recent book on Thomas Jefferson: "It's a book about our founding fathers as if they had penises," he tells the audience. "Most founding-father books omit the cock. I put it in."[10] Such self-consciously irreverent cultural expressions draw on the assumption that the authors are making a compelling contrast by placing that which is sexless (historic, public, proper) alongside open sexuality (modern, private, crude). They rely on a particular notion of the Founders as popularly repressed and mock our culture for denying them, and all Americans, their sexuality.

Some authors have focused entire studies on the intimate lives of the Founders.[11] Journalist Thomas Fleming has published a collection of biographies on the "intimate lives" of the Founding Fathers as a way to personalize them for a modern audience.[12] But he is certainly not the first to do so. Historian Charles Tansill published his book on the romantic lives of the Founders in 1964, basing it upon lectures he gave to his students as a way to "humanize" the political leaders of the American Revolution. Others have included chapters on the Founders in their books on the "sex lives" of the American presidents.[13] Hustler publisher Larry Flynt has teamed up with historian David Eisenbach to write a book that argues that the presidents' sex lives have, in fact, shaped the development of the nation. Management consultant Wesley O. Hagood has written a book on the sex lives of presidents in part to contextualize President Bill Clinton's impeachment trial. Michael Farquhar has similarly written his best-selling collection of "American scandals" in part so that "the first three centuries of American scandal" could "put a little perspective on the relatively minor sins of recent memory."[14]

Many Americans are already familiar with anecdotes about the Revolutionary War era's leaders' sex lives precisely because they are the topic of a long-running discussion. To provide two immediate examples, Jefferson's long affair with Sally Hemings and Benjamin Franklin's "flirtation" with Parisian ladies during his tenure as diplomat continue to fascinate. At the time of the nation's founding, political enemies used such information to smear the Founders' characters. In cultural memory, many Americans use such stories to emphasize the flaws, foibles, or vanities that make the Founders more fully three-dimensional and relatable.

Recent studies have shown that Americans today embrace history but "reject nation-centered accounts" that do not allow them to "build bridges between personal pasts and larger historical stories." Americans want to "personalize the public past."[15] As Lois W. Banner points out, the lives of the Founders "have become sounding boards for what the nation thinks of itself."[16] The National Constitution Center in Philadelphia, just steps away from the Liberty Bell and Independence Hall, promotes this kind of personal connection in an online eleven-question quiz titled "Which Founder Are You?" The landing page for the website declares that the Founders had "many different personalities" and encourages the Web surfer to "Discover which Founding Father you're most like!"[17]

Every generation likes to say that it has finally learned the truth about the Founders and that by examining their private lives, their loves, and their desires, it has exposed the real men. With few exceptions, revelations do not come from the discovery of new documents. The "breaking news" that authors like to assert is most often based on (sometimes) novel interpretations of familiar sources, the diaries and letters that we have regarding the Founders' loves, families, and marriages. More often, new interpretations are possible because of gaps in the record that conveniently have lent themselves to readings that suit generation after generation of Americans seeking themselves in their Founders. In general, academic historians are rigidly tied to the rule that claims must be directly supported by existing documentation that is analyzed by understanding the historical context in which it was produced. Academic historians are more accepting of the fact that history is full of unanswerable questions, of nuanced and contradictory settings, and of holes in the record. In contrast, popular biographers and filmmakers are often compelled by their respective media to fill in those gaps.

By proffering new readings of old men, popular biographers are, of course, able to create straw men that allow them to sell their books as something fresh—but more than just this strategy is at work here. By claiming to lift the veil for the first time on the private life of a Founder, they enable us to feel that we are getting closer to the perceived truth about ourselves and the nation. And by believing that the private man is being revealed for the first time, readers can see themselves as modern, having made a true break from the past. Sex is central to this understanding of modernity, as is evidenced by our understanding of modern sexuality as being somehow more liberated than the sexuality of previous times.[18]

Museums and popular biographers, if pressed, might concede that they use sex opportunistically; a titillating message draws in a wider public for the real history that they want to teach. In my view, the role of sex in history should not be so easily dismissed. The element of sex heightens interest in the histories of the Founders because learning about their intimate lives also personalizes abstract notions of political citizenship and connects Americans to their nation and their own identity as Americans. Current stories increasingly use *sexual personalizing* of the Founders not simply because sex is more openly displayed in the media but because Americans increasingly need to know what is American and see themselves in that definition. Many Americans get that reassurance from the Founders.

To understand how popular memory takes shape, this book makes use of a wide range of materials, including print sources, such as books, magazines, newspapers, poetry, published songs, eulogies, cartoons, and caricatures, as well as portraits, statues, memorials, popular films, musicals, websites, and museum exhibits.[19] Because of their immense popularity in the past and today, popular biographies are also an ideal source for looking at changing ideas about sex and the Founding Fathers, and they make up the core of the book. Throughout American history, biographies have remained the most important source for communicating to Americans information about the personal lives of the Founding Fathers. "Phenomenally popular" in nineteenth-century America, biographies were "regarded as a method of moral teaching."[20] Today, exposure to biographies is still one of the main ways that most Americans learn about history.[21] In contrast to academic histories written to shed light on the past on its own terms, popular biographies are usually written with an eye toward showing how a life story can resonate with present concerns. These "life stories" can tell us a great deal about the cultural moments that produce them. Together, all these sources, through their circulation and as products of the thinking of their time, both popularize and reflect understandings of sex and masculinity.

We can recognize the contours of the history of sexuality in America in the chapters that follow.[22] Each chapter begins with an examination of public discussion of the personal lives of the Founders while they lived. The Founders often cultivated their own public reputations around sexuality in response to cultural norms of the day. In the personally charged political climate of the early Republic, the press operated in what today would be considered a tabloid style, making hefty use of rumor and innuendo and relying on the public's thirst for sordid details and voyeuristic thrills. This approach meshed well with political standards of the day, which, as Nancy Isenberg reminds us, indicated that "political figures were expected to virtually embody the well-defined traits of republican virtue in their personal and public demeanor, speech, and lifestyle."[23] The sexually charged, scandalmongering political climate of the American Revolution and early Republic also generated public discussion about personal lives. Americans did not exempt the Founders from this examination, discussing Jefferson as a slaveowner who indulged in intimacy with enslaved adolescent Hemings, Alexander Hamilton as a repentant adulterer, and John Adams as a prickly prude.

As the Founders passed from life into memory, their public reputations lay entirely in the hands of Americans. The sexualized political climate of the early Republic waned. By the nineteenth century, public memory of the Founders struggled to reconcile Victorian modes of sexual morality with the elite sexual cultures from which the Founders came. The earliest biographies written about the Founders seek to establish a permanent respectability for the individual political leaders of the Revolution and nation's founding. In the hands of biographers, many of the Founders serve as role models for American boys and men. To accomplish this goal, of course, life details are handled carefully, because many of today's most revered Founders suffered from early scandalous reputations: Franklin was branded as immoral, abolitionists labeled Jefferson a child rapist, and Gouverneur Morris's private life had to be whitewashed for Victorian audiences.

The sexual revolutions of the 1920s and 1960s breathed new life into sexual and romantic details of the Founders' lives. Throughout the twentieth century, sexual desires increasingly became viewed as a psychologically healthy part of a man's life. As the writings of Sigmund Freud and his ilk have made their mark on American culture, sexual expression has become an important part of being "normal," and the Founders are no exception. In addition to being ever more sexually explicit, American memory also yokes nationalist concerns about domesticity to our image of the Founders, and writers push ever harder to depict the Founders as exceptionally happy in their marriages and homes, despite the lack of evidence to support such claims.

In the twenty-first century, we have seen best-selling books about the Founders and a renewed interest in the moral and virtuous exceptionalism of the Founding generation. A changing political and demographic world has increasingly made the Founders—slave-owning, elite white men—seem irrelevant, but Americans have used sex to relate to them and connect in a way that parades itself as universal. From museums to political stump speeches, the Founding Fathers are as publicly prominent now as they have ever been. American memory in this moment uses sex to connect eighteenth-century men with contemporary concerns. Jefferson, for example, has emerged as a multicultural hero, Washington is seen as a virile father, and Morris and Franklin are considered as delightfully modern in their approach to sexuality.

The book is organized into this introduction, six numbered chapters, and a conclusion. Chapters focus on specific political leaders of the American Revolution and Founding of the nation. Although the term "Founding Father" was coined in the early twentieth century, even in his own lifetime, Washington was called the "father" of the nation.[24] Different generations have quibbled over who belongs in the pantheon, but few would dispute that the men featured in this book—Washington, Jefferson, Adams, Hamilton, and Franklin—are some of the most significant of the group. Morris, although less well-known, operates in the book as a prime example of how the connections between sex and manliness in cultural memory of the Founders are not limited to the top tier. Indeed, many others will come to mind for readers as a good fit for this study—Benjamin Rush wrote about masturbation; James Madison, hardly considered an ideal model of masculinity, fathered no children with Dolley yet is remembered as the father of the Constitution; and Aaron Burr, who shot and killed Hamilton in that famous duel, was early vilified as a libertine and seducer, only to be recently recast as an early feminist. The list goes on.

Structuring the book along biographical lines rather than topically allows it to engage with the construction of public memory of these individuals as well as to consider the ways that biography itself participates in defining manliness and appropriate sexualities more generally. We can see how over time reputations shift, as the public emphasizes aspects of a Founder's biography that have been ignored and dismisses others that have loomed large in earlier tellings. We can see too how one generation's portrayal is no more or less "true" than another's and how each shapes the narrative to fit its cultural moment. Chapter 1 examines how Americans have remembered Washington's virility. As the "father of the nation," Washington invokes a masculine ideal and has done so for as long as Americans have been remembering him. That he fathered no children of his own puts particular pressure on cultural memory to shore up his image as a model of heroic manhood. Chapter 2 examines Jefferson's legacy, which today is most notably associated with his intimacy with Hemings. By examining how his portrayal morphs from that of a chaste widow to that of a man with passionate relationships, we can see just how important the sexualizing of his image has been for laying the groundwork for today's understanding of him as a man with two families, black and white. Chapter 3 examines how Americans have remembered Adams. In his own lifetime, he wore his moral code on his sleeve and did not hesitate to castigate his fellow Founders for their sexual immorality. The extraordinary number of surviving letters between him and his wife, Abigail, has led many to cast them as uniquely matched and "modern" in their loving bond. Today, Adams is also uncomfortably embraced as a prickly, cranky, prude—a man who embodies the Puritan core of American national morality. The avuncular elder statesman, Franklin, is the focus of Chapter 4. Franklin is today remembered as the nation's "foxy grandpa," and his sexual appetites have become celebrated in a way that puts the lie to a line between sex and political life.[25] Chapter 5 focuses on Hamilton, the man on the ten-dollar bill, who is most famously remembered for being killed while in office as secretary of the Treasury in a duel with then–Vice President Burr. Less often recalled is Hamilton's extramarital affair and the very public pamphlet that he authored to fully explain the circumstances. Chapter 6 examines the least-known of the men in this book, Morris, who has recently been called the "rake who wrote the Constitution."[26] A bachelor for most of his life, Morris is the only Founder for whom extraordinarily revealing sources came to light long after his death. His detailed diaries remark on sexual intimacies with married and unmarried women, providing a treasure trove for some biographers and an embarrassment for others.

The Founders lived in a world that fit neither the stereotyped image of a Puritanical past nor a more modern sexual culture that makes them "just like us." The problem with using sex to make the Founders relatable is that sex is not transhistorical: It can't be used in this manner any more than medical or racial understandings of the day can be used to connect readers from early America to today.

Remembering the intimate lives of the Founding Fathers with simple tropes, hyperbolic superficialities, and meaningless romanticized generalizations prevents us from meaningfully engaging with eighteenth-century sexual variance. Doing so also trivializes sex, perpetuating our own discomfort with the topic, a discomfort with a long history. Superficial glosses relegate the subject of sex to the status it held in previous generations—one of titillation, shame, and humor—all of which rely on a certain assertion of the transhistorical or *human* understanding of sexuality. But the ways in which Americans have ordered their sexual lives and their sexual identities have changed greatly over the centuries. Viewing the Founders' intimate lives and identities as somehow accessible to us through surface descriptions, such as "love at first sight" or "healthy sexual appetites," prevents us from taking historical sexual identities and sexual expressiveness seriously. By focusing in a sustained way on the manner in which Americans have asked and answered their own questions about sexual intimacy and the Founders of the nation, we can examine how Americans have both broached and obscured sexual realities and the cultural connections between sex and nationalized masculinity in the public memory of these men.

Collectively, these stories show how gendered sexuality has long figured in our national identity via the public memory of the political leaders of the American Revolution. By tracing these histories of public memory, we are confronted with how blurred the line has long been between sex and politics in memories of the Founders and how sex has helped tie an ever-diversifying American public to a handful of staid, elite, white, eighteenth-century men.

1

GEORGE WASHINGTON

O F ALL THE FOUNDERS, George Washington (Figure 1.1) is at once the most familiar and the most mythologized. As the unwavering general of the colonial army and the first president of the Republic, he cuts a commanding figure in American memory. When we see Washington in our mind's eye, we recall the iconography that depicts him as a gentleman, a hero, a paragon of personal and civic virtue; we see the very picture of American manhood at its best. The persistence of such too-good-to-be-true images says something about the ongoing project of national mythmaking and a common belief in the idea of an essential national character.

Take Emanuel Gottlieb Leutze's painting *Washington Crossing the Delaware* (1851), for example. Washington stands tall and firm near the prow of a crowded boat in rough waters; only the tousled American flag behind him stands taller than he in the fierce wind. He is resolute and powerful, leaving no doubt about who is in charge. Small wonder, then, that this painting has been used in so many accounts of the nation's difficult birth and Washing-

Figure 1.1 (*above*). Portrait of George Washington. (*George Washington, the First Good President, 1846*. Gilbert Charles Stuart. Oil on canvas, 1797.)

ton's emergence as its hero. We have seen it so many times that we sometimes fail to really *see* it, just as we lose sight of its mythic properties.

In 2006, a Pulitzer Prize–winning account of General Washington's early military campaign in the Revolution dazzled Americans with its heroic story. The attractive book cover, featuring a version of Leutze's famous nineteenth-century painting *Washington Crossing the Delaware* (Figure 1.2) painted by one of his students, Eastman Johnson, captures in vivid color the richness of the story.[1] The central figure of the general standing at the front of a small boat illustrates the valiant image of Washington that is described within the book's pages. The painting itself is a national treasure. Eastman's version of Leutze's masterpiece is an interesting choice; it alters a variety of aspects of the original, including a detail that most might not know—the omission of Washington's ornamental watch fob, which in the original painting is gold and red, dangling closely to his crotch (Figure 1.3). Presumably, for Eastman and for contemporary audiences, the object risks taking attention away from the man and the gravitas of the moment and instead bestows it on something trivial and irrelevant, even unseemly.

Eastman Johnson's copy is perhaps more in circulation today than Leutze's original. A 2011 special issue of *Time* magazine devoted to the life of George Washington contains a centerfold reproduction of the famous painting, again with the fob missing.[2] Georgia school administrators might have saved themselves a headache had they been able to ensure that the publisher of their textbooks went with the Johnson version instead of the original Leutze: In 1999, a Georgia school district instructed teacher's aides to erase the image of the fob by hand-painting twenty-three hundred fifth-grade textbooks. In another county, they tore the page from thousands of copies of the book. In 2002, several editions of an American history high school textbook that contains the image of Leutze's nineteenth-century masterpiece were also altered because administrators feared that it would draw attention to this private area of Washington's body or, worse, might actually appear to be his manhood, exposed.[3]

It might strike some readers as odd for me to begin a book on sex and the Founders with a chapter on George Washington. The depiction of Washington as a desexualized statesman is certainly familiar to Americans. He does not come to mind immediately when one tries to think of anecdotes related to sex and the Founding Fathers—certainly not in the same breath as Benjamin Franklin or Thomas Jefferson. Yet inquiry into the private life of Washington is centuries old, and the discussions highlight how sex has long been a component of American masculinity. Moreover, while the stories themselves are interesting, they also reveal to us the long-term interconnectedness of sexuality and national identity in public memory of the Founders.

Sex Scandals of the Eighteenth Century

Sexual interruptions to Washington's stately image did not originate in the twenty-first century's sex-saturated media-driven culture, in the Sexual Revolution of the 1960s, in the Victorian era, or even in the early nineteenth century. In his own lifetime, Washington was no stranger to sex scandals.

Born in Virginia in 1732, Washington was a surveyor and planter before becoming a lieutenant colonel in the French and Indian War. After the war, he resumed his life as an elite planter and married the wealthiest widow in Virginia, Martha Custis. During the American Revolution, he served as general of the Continental Army. He became the first president of the United States in 1789 and served two terms before stepping down. His retirement was lauded as a pivotal moment in the establishment of American democracy, as history was rife with military leaders who assumed positions of political power and remained unwilling to relinquish their authority. Washington died in 1799 at the age of sixty-seven.[4]

During the American Revolution, Washington was subjected to a variety of sexually charged public attacks on his personal reputation. These were designed to attack not simply his character but the larger political project that he represented. British satirists, for example, lampooned Washington as a cross-dressing woman. The emasculating slur was then captured in an engraving that ran in a London newspaper. Captioned "Mrs. General Washington Bestowing Thirteen Stripes on Britania [sic]," it depicts Washington with his general's tricornered hat, his familiar profile, in a long dress while exclaiming, "Parents should not behave like Tyrants to their Children."[5] The image was typical of the cross-dressing satire of London's late-eighteenth-century print culture. Sexual satire in London and America was common, and leaders bore the brunt of it. Images were not as common as clever verses and prose, but Washington's stature no doubt warranted the extra expense for the printer.

During the American Revolution, other sex scandals surrounded Washington. Some writers alleged that Alexander Hamilton, who had become a close aide, was his illegitimate son. This claim has become one of the enduring myths of the era.[6] Another tale came from a pamphlet that was published in London, supposedly reprinting captured records of New York trials of Tories. Included in the testimony was a charge that Washington made secret visits to a Tory woman. Still another rumor named Washington as

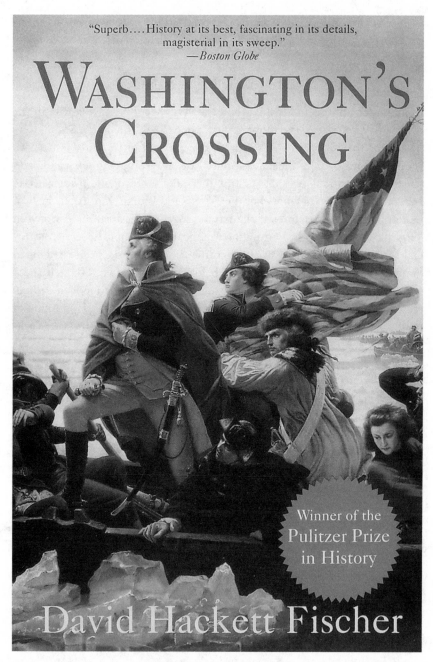

"Superb....History at its best, fascinating in its details, magisterial in its sweep."
—*Boston Globe*

WASHINGTON'S CROSSING

Winner of the Pulitzer Prize in History

David Hackett Fischer

Figure 1.2. Cover of David Hackett Fischer's *Washington's Crossing*, featuring an Eastman Johnson version of Leutze's masterpiece, which eliminated the gold and red ornamental watch fob that dangles close to Washington's crotch in the original painting. (David Hackett Fischer, *Washington's Crossing* [New York: Oxford University Press, 2004].)

Figure 1.3. Detail from *Washington Crossing the Delaware*. (Emanuel Leutze. Oil on canvas, 1851. Metropolitan Museum of Art, Images for Academic Publishing. Copyright © Metropolitan Museum of Art.)

the father of a neighbor's son.[7] Yet another, from a pro-British newspaper account, alleged that he had a relationship with a servant girl while in Philadelphia.[8] In the Revolutionary era, he was smeared with many unsupportable charges, as was the tactic of the day.

As a member of the Freemasons, the fraternal order that was founded in London in the early eighteenth century, Washington may have enjoyed the esteem of the brotherhood but would almost certainly, too, have been the subject of occasional whispers by those who were deeply unsettled by the all-male secret society. In eighteenth-century newspapers, the Freemasons were mockingly associated with homoeroticism. In the mid–eighteenth century, for example, the *Boston Evening Post* ran an engraving and poem suggesting that Freemasons were overly interested in socializing, drinking, and dancing with one another. The satire went a step further by accusing the men of engaging in anal penetration with wooden spikes used in ship building.[9] Clearly, the desexualized Washington has long been accompanied by a twin—one sexualized in the public sphere.

Today, perhaps the most obvious sex "scandal" surrounding Washington is that he never fathered any of his only wife's children. This was certainly unusual in the eighteenth century. Consolidated families, stepchildren, the raising of other people's children and extended family, and multiple marriages due to the death of a spouse were all common in the eighteenth century. Not siring any children, however, was decidedly rare.[10] In some colonies, one of the only grounds for divorce, in addition to adultery and abandonment, was sexual incapacity at the time of marriage. Some women in New England, for example, divorced their husbands for being impotent or sterile. Divorce was more difficult to obtain in Virginia, but as an elite woman, Martha certainly would have had options for separation if she so desired and could demonstrate that her husband was dysfunctional. She would almost certainly have been aware of the negative cultural view of men with sexual inability. The language of the household medical literature of the period deems infertile husbands as lesser men.[11]

In his lifetime, however, Washington played the role of consummate general, head of household, and father to his wife's children and suffered no scathing commentary about his manhood with regards to having no children of his own.[12] The issue was raised perhaps in closer circles, going undocumented and now lost to us. The only surviving mention of the issue comes from a letter written by Washington to his nephew Augustine. In the letter, Washington reassures his nephew that he could develop lands that he would eventually inherit from Washington, because Washington would not be having any other heirs. "If Mrs. Washington should survive me," explains

Washington, "there is a moral certainty of my dying without issue; & should I be the longest liver, the matter in my opinion, is hardly less certain; for while I retain the faculty of reasoning, I shall never marry a girl; & it is not probable that I should have children by a woman of an age suitable to my own, should I be disposed to enter into a second marriage."[13] As this chapter shows, Washington's positioning himself as capable of having children has been taken at face value by biographers concerned with developing an explanation for his having had no children. But we would do well to heed the reminder of early American scholars, such as Karen Lystra, who notes that understanding historical subjects "by reading their mail is neither as simple nor as straightforward as it sounds."[14]

Having no son meant that he had no heir to inherit his political dynasty. Even at the time, commentators remarked that this helped the Republican transfer of power and authority. As historian Gordon Wood points out, "So prevalent was the thinking that Washington resembled an elected monarch that some even expressed relief that he had no heirs."[15] Such relief may not have been unwarranted. John Adams's oldest son, John Quincy Adams, became president. Fortunately, Washington, James Madison, James Monroe, and Jefferson did not have sons of their own, or, according to some, the Virginia dynasty may well have threatened the democracy in its infancy.[16]

By having no children of his own, the version of Washington memorialized is free of paternal attachments. As people have long noted, this perception leaves him able to directly serve, without competition, as the father of the nation, a view that would only strengthen through the nineteenth and twentieth centuries. One early-twentieth-century biographer envisions that having no children also allows Washington to be "father" of the development of the capital city. He declares, "Denied the satisfaction of children of his body, Washington put into the Federal City, child of his brain and heart, his hopes and ambitions for the future of his country."[17]

Only recent biographers have become explicit about the issue of his childlessness and evidently feel the need to explain the cause. But for generations, writers have been implicitly compensating for this chip in his otherwise flawless masculine façade by crafting a depiction of Washington that demonstrates manliness in his personal life on par with his extraordinary military and political achievements.

Domestic Ideal

Washington's absence of children positioned him dangerously close to unmanliness both in his own life and in national remembrances of the man, given the endurance of this measure of manhood. Being childless could raise symbolic questions about one's favor with God; procreation is seen by some as divinely ordered (go forth and multiply) and also as nature's approval of one's lineage. But far from being a problem for Washington, being childless positioned him well. Indeed, to early commentators, it seemed almost providential that he had no children of his own. The childless man would either be out of favor with God or, in rare cases like Washington's, closer to God-like himself. In her history of nineteenth-century schoolbooks, Ruth Miller Elson describes the depiction of Washington in many books as near Christ-like, being delivered from Heaven for the salvation of the nation.[18]

This view of Washington as "father" of the nation dates to his own time. In his funeral oration, Gouverneur Morris notes that Washington was, indeed, both a faithful and loving husband and the father of the nation:

> Bound by the sacred ties of wedded love, his high example strengthened the tone of public manners. Beloved, almost adored by the amiable partner of his toils and dangers, who shared with him the anxieties of public life, and sweetened the shade of retirement, no fruit was granted to their union. No child to catch with pious tenderness the falling tear, and soothe the anguish of connubial affection. . . . AMERICANS! he had no child—BUT YOU—and HE WAS ALL YOUR OWN.[19]

As mentioned in the introduction, in 1810, Mason Weems emphasized the importance of discussing Washington's private life, calling it "*real* life." Sex was a component of this aspect of life, as we can see in his reference to Benedict Arnold and his experiences with "loose women."[20] In the hands of biographers, Washington has served as a role model for American boys and men. Historian François Furstenberg points out that the focus on Washington's private life had important early national implications as well as an impact on how he was viewed: "Because Washington's fatherhood was understood so literally—and because it served as such a powerful means of uniting Americans—the eulogies dwelled on the details of his private life to learn about the precise nature of his paternity." A host of early-nineteenth-century publications dwelled on Washington's personal life and, as Furstenberg notes, such connections had resonance at the level of national identity. Furstenberg concludes, "By focusing intensely on Washington's private life, such texts made Washington's family a matter of great political significance."[21] Indeed, his domestic self would serve to unite the nation much as his public actions in the military and government had done.

Washington's earliest biographers craft the image of a man with extraordinary virtues, an image that would serve many authors in their pursuit of extolling the morals and qualities that all Americans should seek to embody. In nineteenth-century schoolbooks, Washington serves as a "paragon of virtue." Schoolbooks of this era specifically use his biography to teach the value of "filial obedience, prudence, modesty, courtesy, [and] charitableness."[22] Illustrating this function, one begins a chapter on his domestic life with these words: "I am now to present Washington to the contemplation of my young readers in a character not less worthy of their admiration, and in which they may all imitate him if they please."[23] Weems's and John Marshall's books were the most widely circulated early biographies of Washington. The earliest of biographers also eroticize his image and establish that Washington was physically appealing to women—far beyond what the average man could boast. "Happy was the fairest lady of the land, who, at the crowded ball, could get Colonel Washington for her partner," writes Weems.[24] Library records show a waiting list of people wanting to borrow Marshall's 1807 *Life of George Washington* in the early nineteenth century.[25] And though Weems had his critics (even in 1810), his biographies were the best-selling of any in the early decades of the nineteenth century.[26]

Although many Americans wanted even more of an emphasis on private life in the nineteenth century, the broader cultural goals of the writers tend to the nationalistic more than to the private. Marshall's *Life of Washington* was criticized because it mentions Washington very little in the first volume and focuses on American history rather than Washington's biography in the other volumes. Marshall's account "cover[s] his entire early life in a page and a half." Later accounts would spend more time on his development and youth.[27]

Washington's body was also scrutinized and displayed for evidence of personal masculine integrity that could be yoked to national Republican identity. The body of a Greek god Washington may not have had, but that did not stop some nationalized imagery from insisting on this aspect of his physique, albeit in symbolically depicted statuary. In 1832, to commemorate the centennial of his birth, the U.S. Congress commissioned a statue of Washington that now sits in the Smithsonian Institution (Figure 1.4). It depicts him as a toga-wearing, half-nude, classically muscled figure, returning his commission as general of the army. The statue naturally raised eyebrows at the time of its 1840 unveiling, and some considered it unbefitting to so embody the former commander in chief.[28]

In 1837, Jared Sparks published an early biography of Washington. Professor Sparks, a respected popular historian of the American Revolution, was for a time president of Harvard, and his *Library of American Biography*

Figure 1.4. Washington as a toga-wearing, half-nude, classically muscled figure, a rendering that some nineteenth-century Americans regarded as inappropriate. (*George Washington.* Horatio Greenough, 1840. Courtesy of the Smithsonian Museum of American History.)

was the most respected and well-read biographical series at the time. Sparks believed biography was a legitimate genre of historical writing and based his works on documentary evidence.[29] But early biographers, such as Sparks, wrote with the purpose of "adulation, not disinterested scholarship." And as we know, although he relied on documented sources, he did so by selectively editing or destroying those documents that he believed would threaten his biographical subjects' reputations.[30]

By using documentation, Sparks was one of the first to set in motion a long practice of reading love letters for evidence of early emotional attachments. In his biography of Washington, he mentions one Mary Philipse as an early crush of Washington's, and he also discusses Washington's writing about another young woman. Couching this as an early love, he explains that Washington had in his youth "felt the influence of the tender passion." "At the age of seventeen," he writes, Washington "was smitten by the graces of a fair one, whom he called a 'Lowland beauty,' and whose praises he recorded in glowing strains, while wandering with his surveyor's compass among the Allegany [*sic*] Mountains."[31]

Sparks writes little about these early romances and only marginally more about Washington's marital relationship with Martha. After discussing the transfer of wealth and assets and the assumption of guardianship for Martha's children, Sparks assesses the relationship and concludes, "This union was in every respect felicitous."[32] His relatively sparse comments on Washington's early romances and marital life are undoubtedly the product of his research method: Very few personal writings of Washington exist to shed light on love and marriage in his life. But Sparks's reticence would not have been disagreeable to his readers, because early-nineteenth-century biography does not pay close attention to the lives of wives, nor does it (yet) extensively highlight romantic sentiments. Washington's earliest biographer, Marshall, describes George and Martha in ideals befitting of the period: "Not long after his resignation, he was married to Mrs. Custis; a young lady to whom he had been for some time attached; and who, to a large fortune and fine person, added those amiable accomplishments which ensure domestic happiness, and fill, with silent but unceasing felicity, the quiet scenes of private life."[33]

Sparks's depiction of Washington's private life is not unlike the mid-century version authored by Washington Irving, famed author of the "Legend of Sleepy Hollow." He, too, has little to say about the relationship of Martha and George. As it was sufficient to only discreetly establish domestic tranquility and a pattern of romantic love, Irving tersely writes of Washington's early "love" for Philipse and the unnamed "Lowland Beauty." Although not greatly elaborated, for Irving, such incidents reveal Washington to have an "early sensibility to female charms" and demonstrate that "with all his gravity and reserve, he was quickly susceptible" to them.[34]

The inclusion of such information, therefore, was vital, and many in the nineteenth century believed that "private habits, not public deeds, gave the truest measure of character, and that biography should emphasize individual character over national history."[35] The broader cultural goals of the writers, however, tend to emphasize the connections between the individual romantic life and national concerns. For Irving, for example, the relevance of highlighting Washington's early interest in girls is explained in his preface, where he asserts that "all his actions and concerns almost from boyhood were connected with the history of the country" and therefore, even seemingly "apparently disconnected" topics have "bearing upon the great drama in which he was the principle actor."[36]

Washington's list of loves, however, would only grow through the century as the capacity for romantic love increasingly came to matter. One of three letters that Washington wrote to one Sally Fairfax also briefly contributes to the nineteenth-century depiction of Washington as a man of powerful romantic inclinations and illustrates the emphasis on documentation to support interpretations of personal life and its association with masculine character. One letter first surfaced in 1877 in one of the largest newspapers in the country, the *New York Herald*. The newspaper headlines the letter "A Washington Romance: A Letter from General Washington Acknowledging the Power of Love." It reads, in part:

> 'Tis true, I profess myself a Votary of Love—I acknowledge that a Lady is in the Case—and further I confess that this Lady is known to you.—Yes Madam, as well as she is to one, who is too sensible of her Charms to deny the Power, whose Influence he feels and must ever Submit to. I feel the force of her amiable beauties in the recollection of a thousand tender passages that I coud [*sic*] wish to obliterate, till I am bid to revive them.—but experience alas! Sadly reminds me how Impossible this is.—and evinces an opinion which I have long entertained, that there is a Destiny, which has the Sovereign Controul of our Actions—not to be resisted by the Strongest efforts of Human Nature.[37]

In addition to publishing the text of the letter, the newspaper notes that it was "never before made public" and describes it as a letter to a woman to whom "George Washington once offered his hand but was refused for his friend and comrade, George William Fairfax." The newspaper is not forthcoming about the timing of Washington's alleged expression of love for Fairfax, which, according to the letter, would have taken place *after* his engagement to Martha. Indeed, the newspaper remarks on portions of the letter that declare love for Mrs. Custis as unintended and incorrectly reports that Mrs. Custis was still married at the time and therefore could not be someone he was romantically interested in while expressing love for Fairfax. After this very public debut, the auctioned-off letter was secretly and anonymously archived. Yet as this chapter shows, the revelations it allegedly exposes would be scrutinized by biographers for generations.

For nineteenth-century Americans, it was relatively easy to see that Washington had a healthy interest in women and that he had successfully married and established himself as head of a prosperous household. The issue that became somewhat thorny, however, was his lack of children. No early account hides the fact that he had no children of his own. But nineteenth-century writers do not dwell on this aspect of his life, leaving some readers to their own devices to determine this aspect of his private family life. When Weems includes at the end of his biography excerpts from Washington's will, he singles out his "affection" for Martha, as indicated by Washington's leaving his estate to her "during her life." He also mentions that "having no children," Washington left much to his nephews and nieces.[38]

Writers in the nineteenth century could not anticipate that readers would ever expect an answer to the very personal question of why he had no children. Such speculation would have gone beyond the bounds of delicacy and intruded on the privacy of George and Martha. Typical accounts declare the childlessness and leave it at that: "No children had blessed the union of George Washington and Martha Custis," writes one late-nineteenth-century biographer, leaving the question of why unasked.[39]

Washington may have had some influence in establishing a view of his home life as normative, despite having had no children of his own. In an early authorized biography, portions of which Washington had reviewed and approved, David Humphrey states, "Though he has no offspring, his actual family consists of eight persons: it is seldom alone."[40] At the end of the nineteenth century, one writer describes him as a "devoted husband, [who] gave to his step-children the most affectionate care."[41] Another writes that Washington "fathered" Martha's children.[42]

Even more popular and more broadly consumed than biographies were the images of Washington that were widely reprinted. The popular engravings and paintings of Washington that depict him as properly domestic reflect the portrayal found in early biographies. And while rumors abounded that highlighted Washington's virility and his early biographers were giving little attention to the reason for his childlessness, artists and printers did their part by busily fashioning an ideal head-of-household and father figure, befitting of the nineteenth-century domestic ideal. Washington alone could serve as an individual role model. The Washington household, of which he was head, could also operate as an American icon. And, indeed, scholars have noted, "Their marriage came to serve as a model union for mid-nineteenth-century Americans."[43]

Contrary to the contemporary claim that Washington has always been disembodied and only recently humanized, even the earliest images emphasize both his domestic life and his military and government successes. Echoing the biographies of the day, some nineteenth-century images also establish Washington as the romantic man. Early images include his courting of Philipse.[44] Other nineteenth-century images focus on his courtship of and marriage to Martha. Many of these were often widely reproduced and copied. In addition to portraying his relationships with women, and especially his wife, painters, engravers, and other nineteenth-century images disseminate the view of Washington as the idealized father figure and head-of-household. Many images focus on Washington as the family man (Figure 1.5).

Virtually no writers in the nineteenth century raise any questions about Washington's manhood. Biographers then move away from the early emphasis on using only documents and an approach of objectivity (an emerging

Figure 1.5. Washington family portrait. (*The Washington Family.* Edward Savage. Oil on canvas, 1789–1796. Andrew W. Mellon Collection. Courtesy of the National Gallery of Art, Washington, D.C.)

concept in history) to begin including "oral lore" to supplement lacking documentation. This approach opened up the possibility of telling additional stories that could be folded into the public memory of Washington's personal life, which would only shore up his reputation as properly and successfully masculine in his private life.[45] Indeed, a rumor in the 1870s, for example, suggested that Washington had actually fathered a son, but not with Martha. The *Cincinnati Daily Commercial* published a statement that relied on the "fact" that many people believed that one Thomas Posey was Washington's son, although no documentation was provided.[46] Posey's parents had lived as tenant farmers on one of Washington's plantations. According to the story, after Posey's mother was widowed, she and Washington had a son whose education he oversaw. In 1886, a newspaper in St. Louis, where Posey was buried, similarly reported that everyone in southern Illinois believed it to be true.[47] Another undocumented rumor, this time regarding his death, also irreverently underscored Washington's sexually charged image in public memory. This story explained that Washington's death was the result of a cold he caught from leaping out a window, pants-less after a romantic encounter with an "overseer's wife."[48]

Late-nineteenth-century biographies assert that Washington lacked no romantic interests in women. Like other early biographers, Woodrow Wilson, a historian by training who published several biographies before embarking on a successful career in politics, mentions Washington's early courtship of Philipse in New York. But by the end of the nineteenth century, biographers like Wilson were increasingly linking sexual interest in women to an emerging concept of normative desire and heteronormative masculinity. Wilson writes, "Mary Philipse had but taken his fancy for a moment, because he could not pass such a woman by and deem himself still a true Virginian."[49] For Americans, the message was clear, and their Founder served as the delivery system: Real men desire beautiful women. Other late-nineteenth-century biographers echo this point. Writes one, "There can be no doubt that Washington during the whole of his life had a soft heart for women, and especially for good-looking ones."[50]

By the late nineteenth century, even those biographers who write largely political accounts of his life also broach the subject of his personal life: Using the nation's first president as a model of virtuous manhood necessarily entails examining his life beyond his public accomplishments. In 1897, noted historian and senator Henry Cabot Lodge authored a two-volume biography of Washington that includes a chapter entitled "Love and Marriage." In the chapter, Lodge explains that "by the time he was fourteen he had fallen deeply in love with Mary Bland of Westmoreland, whom he calls his 'Lowland Beauty'" and as he matured—"a gentleman writing of a Mrs. Hartley, whom Washington much admired, said that the general always liked a fine woman."[51] Indeed, Lodge writes that Washington fell in love in Philadelphia as a young hero of the French and Indian War.

Echoing the sentiment articulated by Weems almost eighty years earlier, for Lodge such stories reveal the true man: "How much this little interlude, pushed into a corner as it has been by the dignity of history,—how much it tells of the real man! How the statuesque myth and the priggish myth and the dull and solemn myth melt away before it! . . . One loves to picture that gallant, generous, youthful figure, brilliant in color and manly form, riding gaily on from one little colonial town to another, feasting, dancing, courting, and making merry."[52]

Sally Fairfax in the Early Twentieth Century: A True Man Emerges

Early-twentieth-century writers depict Washington's private life in essentially the same way as do portrait artists of the nineteenth century: Virtually all of them present an image of manliness that speaks to virility, fatherhood, and marriage. Even without children, Washington's image cultivates the manly ideal. At the turn of the century, a series of biographies with "True" in the title focuses on private life.[53] *The True George Washington*, for example, includes discussion of his relations with women, among other personal anecdotes.

The volume of writing on Washington's personal life increased exponentially through the century. The rumor that he had fathered Posey, for example, continued to spread. An encyclopedia entry referring to Revolutionary soldiers buried in Illinois describes Posey as "reputedly the natural son of George Washington."[54] No doubt, such stories led many to assume that he was not childless in his own marriage. In part, this is because of a broader cultural shift that occurred with regards to sex in American society. In the early twentieth century, American culture underwent a sexual revolution. In the 1910s and 1920s, the Victorian silence surrounding sex and romance withered in the face of a new emphasis on open public expression of erotic desires and feelings.[55] As love and desire became openly celebrated in song and dance, so too, did biographies begin to emphasize in greater detail the loves of Washington. Most notably, this focus gave rise to the presence of Fairfax in biographies on Washington. The view we have of Fairfax today is that his "love" for her "was a lengthy torment" and an "impossible infatuation."[56]

In the early twentieth century, three brief letters from Washington became central to building a case for an intimate connection to Fairfax. As we have seen, one was published in the *New York Herald*. It was one of two letters that were written in 1758 before his marriage, and they are flirtatious. The third letter comes from later in Washington's life, when, as one biographer puts it, he "confessed to an elderly Sally that she had been the passion of his youth, that he had never been able to forget her." The key sentence from this letter is one that declares that he had not been able to "eradicate from my mind those happy moments, the happiest in my life, which I have enjoyed in your company."[57] In the absence of additional evidence, little more has been revealed or written about by biographers. Yet the flirtatious letters generally have been read as expressions of sincere and deeply felt life-long love. (It is notable that they are never read as indicating the less-virtuous lust—which in the late eighteenth century could have been expressed in the same politely flirtatious manner.)

The controversy over how best to interpret such letters has been generally overlooked by popular writers, who typically accept such letters as historical artifacts or documents to be taken at face value and read with modern sensibilities in mind. Academic historians and literary scholars, however, have long argued that eighteenth-century letters are anything but transparent and, as was the approach of the day, often inflect popular literature as well as the style guides published in letter-writing manuals. Moreover, as one scholar reminds us, "Letter reading, as opposed to writing, was until quite recently an entirely social affair." Letter writers would typically indicate which passages were to be kept private, and, as letters between John and Abigail Adams illustrate, writers would often hold back for fear of public exposure of private sentiments.[58] The later letter is referred to in nearly all twentieth-century biographies of Washington.[59]

A 1926 biography, subtitled *The Human Being and the Hero*, mentions not only his attraction to a "Lowland lady" and to Philipse but also his involvement with Fairfax. Rupert Hughes includes a chapter entitled the "Mystery of Sally Fairfax," in which he calls their lost love a "tragedy." He derides Wilson's handling of the Fairfax attraction, charging that by not mentioning her by name, he is able to "evade direct mention of the most pathetic and baffling incident." Critical of those who deny the interpretation of the letter as proof of the engaged Washington's love for the married woman, Hughes writes, "Sally Fairfax can not be ignored in Washington's life-story. She ought not to be. She deserves the honor of having a profound influence on the formation of his character. She stirred his heart more deeply than any other woman ever did."[60] Others biographers follow suit. Despite emphasizing "love at first sight" between George and Martha, another account points out that "Martha was not George's first love, nor his third, nor yet his fifth; nor was she ever, perhaps, his real love."[61] Still another 1920s biography, after discussing the Lowland Beauty and Philipse, turns to Fairfax, who is identified as "the grand passion of Washington's life." This account views the letter written just a few months before Washington married Martha not as scandalous but rather as something that tells readers that "he was human enough to love in such a way." Echoing popular ideas of the day about masculine prowess, the author notes, "George Washington had courage to face sentiment as he had courage to face his foes, and, in both *love* and *war*, his unusual tactics made him victorious."[62]

These observations rang true at a time when Sigmund Freud's influence was making its early and initial impact on American culture by highlighting the centrality of romantic and sexual desires to human existence and personal development.[63] Washington, Hughes writes, may well have been "cold" and "silent" and "under almost perfect self-control." "But," he continues, "he could love. He did love." Critical of his nineteenth-century predecessors, specifically Sparks and Weems, Hughes writes that his biography is "a study of the man." And he laments that in previous generations, Washington's memorializers have so obscured his personal life that "he was a man of whom it may almost be said that he had no private life."[64]

Striking a similar tone, Eugene Prussing published *George Washington in Love and Otherwise*, explaining that his early-twentieth-century account corrected an earlier generation's avoidance of Washington's intimate life— "This is what Washington meant to be and was." Prussing includes a chapter entitled "In Love" alongside his coverage of Washington the "Engineer" and "Captain of Industry." Setting Washington's personal life on par with his professional self, Prussing explains that "the most difficult test of character" for men and women is "their conduct when in love." Like Hughes, Prussing publishes the letters to Fairfax and reads them as evidence of a "startling confession" of love for her. And he does so with the explanation that Washington had done "what nearly every man has done at some time"—that is, he told "a woman he has no right to tell, that he loves her, whom he has no right to love."[65] Another account similarly emphasizes the normativity of Washington's desires, commenting on the Fairfax letters that his "romantic strain . . . will not be unfamiliar to many men who can honestly recall their youth."[66]

Underscoring his view that one's conduct in love could reveal much about the individual, something espoused by Weems but now laden with new psychological meaning, Prussing writes about Washington's turning away from Fairfax and deciding to marry Martha: "Such was Washington's romance. He had firmly removed it from his path when it became dangerous." He continues, "In place of it he had put a wholesome plant, which he carefully and faithfully tended."[67]

Washington's mid-twentieth-century definitive biographer, Douglas Southall Freeman, includes the full text of the Fairfax letter in his seven-volume biography. He acknowledges that no original exists, that it came to be known only after being published in the *New York Herald* in 1877, and that some biographers discredit the letter because its existence has not been verified. Weighing in on a debate about its authenticity, he notes that in style and writing, he believes it to be authentic. Moreover, he argues in a footnote as a matter of "interpretation not a statement of fact" that it should be concluded that "he was going to marry Martha but was in hopeless love with Sally and wished above everything else to know whether she loved him."[68]

Some biographers read the letter to Fairfax in a different light. John C. Fitzpatrick, author of a multivolume publication of Washington's writings, in his biography expresses discomfort with the interpretation that most would come to accept. For Fitzpatrick, the letter is clearly an expression of love for Martha and for her alone. If it is not, Fitzpatrick remarks, Americans would have to think of Washington as a "worthless scoundrel." The letters written to Fairfax while Washington was encamped during the French and Indian War, he explains, were prompted by a "bored state" and "to claim more than this requires an imagination unresponsive to the niceties of honor and good breeding." Fitzpatrick sees these desires as elements of normative masculinity but believes that Washington's writings are best interpreted as stemming from "the tendency of youth to exaggerate personal romance."[69]

Regardless of how his interpretation stands in contrast to the popular notion of the story of a young Washington deeply in love with, and never able to have, Fairfax, what is underscored by his discussion is the extent to which biographers, academic or lay, have had to deal with the public's knowledge of and interest in this story of one of Washington's early loves.

Twentieth-Century Happy Family

In addition to the importance they attach to the Fairfax story as evidence that Washington was capable of deep love, twentieth-century biographies also depict his household as a happy one. For much of the century, biographers downplay his childlessness and emphasize his paternal nature, which was demonstrated by his fatherly emotions and material care that he gave to the children that Martha brought from her previous marriage.

Although the 1926 title *The Family Life of Washington* might lead us to expect a discussion of his childlessness, readers receive only two phrases that assume knowledge of his childlessness—and are never offered any explanation or reason for it.[70] Another biographer explains, "They kept hoping for children" but offers no more than this claim on the topic.[71] Similarly, another notes that his "faithfulness and lifelong devotion to Martha Washington were not rewarded, as we think they deserved to be, by children, to carry it on."[72]

The view of Washington as the ideal family man gained new currency in the twentieth century, and many biographies emphasize that his was a household that raised children. Thus, Charles Moore, for example, asserts that Washington was "naturally affectionate to the point of indulgence, and dearly loving children." And on his not having "offspring," he writes, "he made up for this lack by fatherly care of his wife's children and grandchildren and his own nephews and nieces."[73] On taking in the grandchildren, one author writes, "He and Martha were a childless couple who loved children."[74] Even books that focus on the domestic life of the Washingtons take this approach. One notable exception is an early-twentieth-century account that insinuates that the childlessness was Martha's responsibility, stating that his life might have been quite different if he had married Philipse: "There might have been children if she had been Washington's wife," the author postulates, "to gambol on the green slopes of Washington's childless home."[75]

In the nineteenth century, childlessness was relatively rare, happening in less than 10 percent of married families. Through the twentieth century, however, shifting contexts would contribute to the issue of Washington's childlessness as being one that begged for more explanation—and perhaps compensation. At the turn of the twentieth century, Theodore Roosevelt famously talked about "race suicide," drawing attention to the alarming drop in the birth rate for white, middle-class, native-born families. This comment was explicitly linked to concerns about American manhood becoming weakened and sexually degenerate.[76] Historian Elaine Tyler May discusses the "pressure to procreate" that white middle-class families felt in the early decades of the twentieth century. Yet, for the most part, few early-twentieth-century writers venture beyond the above statements, perhaps to avoid raising questions about Washington's potency, which was becoming an increasingly important element of American manhood.[77]

By mid-century, however, infertility became more of an unavoidable topic, occurring in some 20 percent of couples. Thus, it was perhaps more of a cultural concern in the mid–twentieth century than at other times. This factor would be one of many that would drive discussions of Washington's infertility in the later twentieth century. A post–World War II baby boom and the "rise of compulsory parenthood" were linked to patriotism that continued in the early years of the Cold War. Post–World War II fatherhood "was an important responsibility and evidence of maturity, patriotism, and citizenship." Childlessness was linked to subversiveness, to "pinkos" and "homos," and anticommunism nurtured the notion that it was patriotic to have a nuclear family. Washington's lack of children had to be addressed, and for some, his fathering of stepchildren and extended kin would be one way to fit the bill.[78]

The emphasis on happy families in the twentieth century also gave rise to greater degrees of speculation about the marriage of George and Martha. Despite the reservations of one biographer, who reminds people that "little is known" about Washington's marriage or courtship and that "the stories of this part of the lives of George Washington and Mrs. Martha Custis are nothing but gratuitous, imaginary pictures," a romanticized view of the marriage of Martha and George grew through the twentieth century.[79] An early-twentieth-century account imagines a scene where George and Martha, "infatuated with love at first sight, talk the moon down and the sun up."[80] Some biographers, such as Moore, argue that the letters written to Fairfax indicate Washington's deep love for Martha and are not evidence of love between him and Fairfax. If Fairfax "ever sacrificed either time or affection for his sake," contends Moore, "that fact has not appeared."[81] A 1926 account repeats the characterization of George and Martha's bond as "love at first sight."[82]

Freeman's mid-twentieth-century biography takes issue with the argument that Washington courted Martha too soon after her husband passed and underscores that she selected him above all others. Washington, he argues, began his courtship at the "earliest" nearly a year after she was widowed, and, as she was only twenty-six and very wealthy, she could have married any number of eligible men.[83] Many biographers acknowledge the utility of the union but imagine that it was also privately satisfying. It was a "prudent engagement," writes one, but there is no reason to assume a "marriage of convenience."[84]

In the middle decades of the twentieth century, George and Martha could plausibly serve as fodder for books penned in the style of romantic novels. Such accounts continue the appealing image of Washington and imagine his marriage in idealized romantic terms. *Martha Washington: Our First Lady*, published by author and photographer Alice Desmond in 1942, depicts the couple as perfectly matched and in love. In a chapter entitled "Love at First Sight," the meeting of Martha and George is wrapped in the gauzy headiness of early romance novels. Desmond imagines Martha, then still married, at the theater when she sees George for the first time. As she scans the crowd, she notices "a man—a young giant of about twenty-four, in the blue uniform of a Virginia soldier. He was an unusually noticeable figure, more than six feet tall, broad-shouldered, yet of a slender and athletic build." Even the man whom she asks about his identity admires him, commenting, "Isn't he a fine-looking man?" Martha suddenly recalls having met him years before: "Who could forget that commanding presence? That handsome head poised on broad shoulders? That face with the rather large nose, ruddy cheeks, firm lips and chin?" The image of an attractive young Washington gives way to the still-appealing older president: "His face was so handsome," Desmond writes, "that many a lady's heart fluttered as she curtsied to him. Always distinguished-looking, George Washington, nearing sixty, was even more striking in appearance than in his youth."[85]

When mid-century smiling nuclear families in their domestic bliss symbolized the American Dream, the romantic imagining of George and Martha's relationship would take center stage and endure for decades.[86] In 1969, best-selling romance novelist Mary Higgins Clark published *Aspire to the*

Heavens.[87] Washington is the idealized masculine hero of romance novels in this account. Women flirt with him and find him charming. He dances, banters, and is full of manly appeal. And the chemistry between Martha and George is evident at their first meeting.

Romantic Man for the New Millennium

In their efforts to depict a more appealing and approachable Washington, contemporary biographers position themselves in opposition to what they argue is an older, starched image. Writing in an era that has popularized the stories of ordinary men and women and viewing with a critical eye the unsullied images of elites, biographers often note that Washington has been disembodied and dehumanized. He comes to us, they lament, as a marble bust in a museum, a statesman in an early American painting, an enormous head on Mount Rushmore, on the dollar bill, and on the quarter. We see Washington everywhere, they say, but nowhere do we Americans connect with the *man.* More than for any other Founding Father, modern biographies of Washington have had to struggle with portraying their human subject while still presenting the embodied symbol of the nation itself. Washington's face and name have become iconic symbols of the United States of America, not merely images of one of its Founding Fathers. Asserts one recent biographer, "For more than two centuries, artists and historians have portrayed George Washington as cold, stern, and distant. . . . But the real George Washington—the private, personal George Washington—was human to the core: laughing, loving, and living life to the fullest."[88] But, as we have seen, it has become a centuries-old cliché that he is always disembodied through nationalized imagery that makes the identity synonymous with his portrait.

In the late twentieth and early twenty-first centuries, writers have drawn on older legends and depictions of Washington as the charming general. This redoubled emphasis is, in part, a reaction to the perceived wisdom regarding how the public feels distanced from Washington, viewing him as inaccessible and elite—as "dull but perfect," to quote Gore Vidal.[89]

In the twenty-first century, biographers have continued to emphasize what they see as Washington's deep passions; says one, "George was always susceptible to women."[90] A 2009 biography on the "intimate lives" of the Founding Fathers largely repeats early-twentieth-century tales and similarly concludes that as a young man, "George was powerfully attracted to the opposite sex—hardly surprising for a healthy, vigorous teenager."[91] Similarly, journalist Willard Sterne Randall concludes, "Washington was capable of being a great romantic."[92]

In popular biographies in the new millennium, gone is any hesitation about interpreting the letters Washington wrote to Fairfax. Long gone is the defensive view that he wrote as a "votary of love" for Martha, despite the letters' being penned for Sally. For many today, the letters written to Fairfax, a young woman who has been described in romanticized terms as having "large, steady, wide-open eyes" and "a mouth that was a cupid's bow," serve to make Washington personable by emphasizing sex, love, and romance.[93] Best-selling author Joseph Ellis explains, "The titillating 'consummation' question is almost as irrelevant as it is unanswerable. The more important and less ambiguous fact is that Washington possessed a deep-seated capacity to feel powerful emotions." He adds, "Only someone dedicated to denying the full import of this evidence could reject the conclusion that Washington was passionately in love with Sally Fairfax."[94] For another writer, the Fairfax letters reveal a romantic man: "There's no credible way to read the letters he wrote in the fall of 1758 other than as those of a young man suffering from a forbidden love; they're practically incoherent, the outpouring of a sorely troubled heart."[95] Popular writer Thomas Fleming waxes even more romantic, calling the later letter evidence that Washington and Fairfax "were lovers that destiny had tragically separated."[96] Another brief biography identifies Fairfax as "his first love," and a recent biography takes the position that she was his one true love in life.[97]

Many accounts exhibit a near fetishistic fascination with his body. Speaking of his wedding gloves, as though anticipating this later development, Desmond writes to an earlier generation that they are "still treasured in the Masonic Museum at Alexandria, Virginia, and they are huge."[98] The emphasis on eroticized depictions of Washington's body has blossomed in the new millennium.[99] *Mount Vernon Love Story* begins by establishing that Washington was a "giant of a man in every way."[100] In his best-selling biography of Washington, Pulitzer Prize–winning writer Ellis similarly exclaims, "He was the epitome of the man's man: physically strong, mentally enigmatic, emotionally restrained."[101] Wood also depicts Washington in this manner. Washington, he writes, had "all the physical attributes of a classical hero. He was very tall by contemporary standards, six feet three or so, and was heavily built and a superb athlete. Physically he had what men and women admired."[102] Likewise, Randall describes him as a "giant" whose "209 pounds were spread over a taut six-foot-four-and-a-half-inch frame."[103] Fleming links Washington's build to his father, Augustine Washington, whom Fleming describes as a "huge, muscular man, a sort of rural Hercules famous for his feats of strength."[104] In one final example, readers of David Hackett Fischer's *Washington Crossing* are introduced to Washington's "muscular legs" in the opening paragraph, and they are informed that he, "at forty-two, looked young, lean, and very fit" at the time of his famous crossing of the Delaware River.[105]

Other authors specify that Washington was unusually desirable to those around him. In her preface to the new edition of a 2003 historical novel, the author explains that in her "research," she found that Washington was "the best dancer in the colony of Virginia"[106] A 2006 biographer explains, "His social graces left ladies swooning as he spun them 'round the ballroom."[107] Richard Brookhiser bolsters the tradition of focusing with intensity on the unusual body of the allegedly disembodied first president. He provides the usual description of Washington's body and explicitly links it to sex appeal: "Women also took note of him," he writes. Brookhiser, a journalist, goes one step further. He claims that John Trumbull's 1792 portrait of Washington striking a classical pose after the Battle of Trenton "clearly shows a pair of well-developed thighs" (Figure 1.6). In the absence of the image itself, he mobilizes testimony from an authority to support his assertion: "When I showed it to a body builder, she said: '*Nice* quads.'"[108] That the body builder is a woman sexualizes the assessment. Similarly, a recent biography of Martha Washington views George from his wife's vantage point. "What did Patsy [Martha's daughter, Martha Parke Custis] see when George Washington walked into her parlor?" asks author Patricia Brady. "Towering over most men by half a foot, George was exceptionally tall for the time" and "exceptionally athletic, powerful and graceful." The depiction of such a body is not just about sex appeal, of course—culturally, it speaks volumes about the man's qualities and character. Thus, Brady follows her description of Washington's body with the phrase "bespeaking the leader rather than the fop."[109] Writer Fleming remarks that "there were undoubtedly a great many women in Virginia who would have felt shivers" "at the thought of being embraced" by Washington.[110]

Such phrases as "he had an athlete's body" raise the question of what imagery this calls to mind for Americans today.[111] This type of language likely conjures up an appealing physique, not simply a capable one. As women's historians have noted, physical ideals for the female body have changed over time. Even in the context of the twentieth century, this is obvious when one compares the voluptuous physique of Marilyn Monroe to the waif models of the early twenty-first century or the Hollywood hunks of the 1950s with today's more muscular leading men. Physical ideals have changed over time for both men and women, so modern readers may well impose their twenty-first-century athletic eroticized ideal on an aging eighteenth-century military officer. Washington may have been strong, but according to many

Figure 1.6. *General George Washington at Trenton.* (John Trumbull. Oil on canvas, 1792. Courtesy of the Yale University Art Museum.)

accounts he had an ungainly frame, was disproportioned, was "wide across the hips," had a concave or "flat" chest, and would certainly not have been toned or taut in a currently idealized way.[112] The increased emphasis on crafting an appealing body for Washington can be illustrated by comparing one author's descriptions over time. Twenty-one years after publishing the description that includes the phrase "wide across the hips," John Ferling changes it to "broad shoulders," "muscular arms," and "small, flat waist," with no mention of the wide hips that many associate with femininity. He also emphasizes instead that Washington "exhibited the striking look of what we would expect today in a gifted athlete."[113]

Accounts and images depicting his size and athleticism create a man who stands alone. Washington himself may have had a hand in establishing this depiction of his body. In an unpublished authorized biography, drafts of which Washington reviewed and approved, he is described as "remarkably robust & athletic."[114] Such comments about size, appeal, and physical attributes stand on their own and are intended to suggest that somehow nature had endowed him with a physical presence that indicated his superior skills and capabilities and the pivotal role he would play in the founding of the nation. In this way, large hands and big muscles are connected to founding the national government and acting as figure head to a fledgling country.

Modern Marriage

Turn-of-the-twenty-first-century accounts do adopt a slightly more skeptical view of the bond between husband and wife. Certainly many have speculated that it was a marriage of convenience for both. As biographers have long noted, the marriage itself was crucial to Washington's advancement. According to Ellis, "Nothing he ever did had a greater influence on the shape of his own life than the decision to marry Martha Dandridge."[115] It is often noted that his marriage to the wealthiest widow in Virginia catapulted him up the social ladder to the highest echelons of Virginian planter society. For many biographers, the evidence clearly suggests a calculated first meeting. Washington called on the extraordinarily wealthy widow too soon after her husband died—and in a calculating measure to impress left a hefty tip for her servants.

But even those who emphasize this initial motivation highlight evidence that the union developed into something to be envied. Writes one pair, "The marriage may initially have been one of convenience, [but] it seems to have turned out to be an exceptionally happy one on both sides."[116] Still another author asserts, "If the main source of Martha's appeal was initially more economic than romantic, there is reason to believe that the relationship soon developed into an intimate and mutually affectionate bond of considerable affinity."[117]

If some later views are decidedly less romanticized, we still learn that the marriage was a success from a public perspective. Historian Gordon Wood points out that George and Martha had a model marriage. In New York and Philadelphia, Wood elaborates, they operated as "matchmakers," and they did so "with their own marriage . . . as examples." The result was a success in quantity and quality: "He and Martha arranged sixteen marriages, including that between James Madison and Dolley Payne."[118]

Biographers, however, anticipate any of this skepticism that readers may have held about the marriage of Martha and George. Some remind us that Martha was not a great deal older than George, as is often misremembered by a public familiar only with her matronly portrait—indeed, she was only three months older. "The fact that they had no children of their own is almost certainly not a sign that they were sexually incompatible," assures one.[119] "Late efforts to suggest that Washington's marriage lacked passion . . . have all been discredited by most scholars," he continues.[120] "The fact is that George and Martha loved each other deeply," writes another.[121]

Indeed, the skeptics' view of the marriage has been well challenged by romantic accounts. Twenty-first-century romantic depictions of their marriages enshrine the Founders as men far more virtuous than others. One biographer of Martha Washington writes that during the Revolution, George's conduct was exemplary, and his satisfying marriage was a key aspect of this behavior:

> Many British officers entertained themselves in camp with all-night drinking bouts, high stakes gambling, and a plethora of easily available sexual partners. The Puritan strain in American society called for greater discretion in their camp, but some men took the opportunity to kick off—or at least loosen—the marital traces. Not their commander. Whatever George Washington's sexual experiences as a young man may have been, he had never led a dissipated life—even his love for the married Sally Fairfax had been well-nigh respectable. There would be no startling middle-aged outbreak: he was well aware that he set the example for his men, and he genuinely delighted in his wife's company and their "domestic enjoyments."

For this author, the love of husband and wife was not just privately shared. It radiated outward, bolstering the beleaguered American forces:

"Everybody enjoyed being with the Washingtons at headquarters because of their obvious fondness for each other and the good cheer they radiated."[122]

Turn-of-the-century popular accounts rely on lore and speculation as much as the romanticized accounts published a century earlier. The introduction to *Worthy Partner*, a 1994 publication of the letters and writings of Martha Washington, repeats a nineteenth-century account that the courtship was romantic "love at first sight."[123] "After they married," explains the author, "there is not a sign that George was a bored or unhappy husband. They shared a bed throughout their marriage (no separate bedrooms here), and he desired her companionship as often as possible when he was away from home during the war and the presidency."[124] A recent biography by journalist Fleming asserts—without a source of evidence for the claim—that Martha was "the only person with whom Washington could relax and speak candidly." Fleming further emphasizes a chemistry between them by focusing on how Martha must have felt when marrying George on the heels of her first husband, whom he describes as a "rather pathetic" man. "Martha," he imagines, "must have felt a few tremors," as Washington "must have been a breathtaking sight" on his wedding day. He poignantly remarks that upon her death, Martha was "almost visibly eager to join the man she had loved so long and so deeply in an eternity of happiness."[125] Keep in mind that all of these deeply personal insights about the affective bond between Martha and George come from scant few letters to analyze: Martha famously destroyed virtually all of their correspondence after his death.

As we have seen, one of the reasons that Americans today may not know that Washington never fathered children is that there is a long history of portraying Washington as a model father figure—of the nation to be sure, but also of his own household. And any of the negative associations with childlessness—homosexuality, impotence, lack of desirability—have been roundly countered by his memorializers for well over a century.

The desire to create a more approachable Washington has led to a sustained and perhaps increased portrayal of the man as an appealing father and family man. This trend continues today, as demonstrated by biographer Bruce Chadwick and others who emphasize Washington's paternal side by using the terms "stepfather" and "father" interchangeably—and "daughter" and "stepdaughter," in the same manner. In descriptions of certain moments, such as when Martha's daughter Patsy died, the term "father" is used to underscore the bond between them. Thus, Chadwick follows "Patsy died in her father's arms" with "The stoic Washington was too overcome to offer much detail on his daughter's sudden demise."[126] Chadwick is right to characterize the relationship in this manner, but the unintended effect may

Figure 1.7. Washington family statues. Greeting visitors to the Mount Vernon Visitor Center is a group of statues that depict George and Martha striding youthfully alongside two young children. Although the youngsters appear to be members of the nuclear family, the legend identifies them as grandchildren. (*Statue of Washington and Family.* Mount Vernon Visitor Center. Courtesy of the Mount Vernon Ladies' Association.)

be to contribute to a long history of compensating for what some might find controversial about Washington's family life.

Reacting in part to the relatively recent historical inquiry into the lives of ordinary Americans, Washington's image makers have sought to depict him as still relevant for a populace who sees elite, slave-holding men as less and less the central focus of early American history. Thus, the new visitor center at Mount Vernon, in an explicit attempt to "humanize" Washington and connect with contemporary museumgoers, returns to the image of Washington the family man with a set of four statues in the welcome area. The statues that greet visitors are of George and Martha striding youthfully, accompanied by their grandchildren (Figure 1.7). The effect is to recreate an image of the nuclear family. To many visitors, the children could appear to be their own.[127] But on the floor, engraved in the stone tile at the foot of each statue, not set off by any color or distinguishing features, is a name and age, and each of the children has "grandson" and "granddaughter" presented for those who would closely inspect.

At the same time, by the end of the twentieth century, many writers have taken it upon themselves to directly address the issue of Washington not having children. And for the first time, most accounts offer readers what they now want—an explanation. This approach has been taken for at least two reasons. First, the move to make Washington more ordinary and accessible, as typified by all biographies today, includes saying more about this aspect of his life. Second, the contemporary issues around childlessness have become much more public today. If marriage was the central aspect of becoming a man in the eighteenth century, having a child has become one of the measures in contemporary society.

Many contemporary biographers draw on the letter that Washington sent to his nephew to assert that he was sterile. For example, "The conclusion that he was sterile is inescapable," Brookhiser confidently declares. "The act of generation . . . was one he could not perform."[128] Given masculine standards of the day that negatively characterized sexually dysfunctional men as, among other things, withdrawn and weakly, one wonders if Washington were sterile, would he have shared this information with his nephew?

Of course, some writers are more tentative than others but are nonetheless explicit in their speculation. According to the ever-changing popular website Wikipedia, for example, "George and Martha never had any children together—his earlier bout with smallpox followed, possibly, by tuberculosis may have made him sterile."[129] Another biographer notes that, given Martha's children from a previous husband, George was "probably . . . sterile."[130]

Notably, impotence is virtually never suggested, unless it is being ruled out. Washington's award-winning biographer James Thomas Flexner explains to the readers of popular history magazine *American Heritage* that the "evidence presents a very strong presumption that Washington was, although not impotent, sterile."[131] "There is nothing in his behavior," writes another biographer, "to suggest that he was impotent, or that his sexual nature caused him any deep uneasiness."[132] Another portrays Washington as a man who was clearly performing his husbandly duty beyond question and claims that Washington was "mystified why, year after year, he and Martha could produce no Washington heir."[133] Most recently, a 2009 biography also does not raise impotence as a possibility, declaring that "reasonable speculation suggests two possibilities. . . . Martha may have had difficult deliveries . . . that left her unable to conceive again, or Washington's bout with smallpox . . . may have left him sterile." This account also seems to suggest that impotence was not at work, as Washington never expressed guilt or self-consciousness. Indeed, the author infers that Martha was the problem in his explanation that George was filled with "forbearance" and "understanding" as he "tried to help Martha deal with her almost uncontrollable maternal anxiety." (This interpretation is based, it seems, on the one brief surviving letter that we have from Martha to George in which she comments on a "rainey and wett" day during which she expressed feeling "sorry" that he would "not be at home as soon as" she had "expected.")[134]

The inquiry into Washington's childlessness is not just limited to popular biography. In a medical journal, John K. Amory publishes his conclusion that Washington could not likely have been impotent given what we know about him as a "healthy, vigorous man." Tellingly, the author also rules out sexual infertility as the result of a sexually transmitted disease (despite their commonness in eighteenth-century America), noting Washington's "character and strong sense of moral propriety."[135] We know that erectile dysfunction occurs far more frequently than sterility—although frequency today may not match that of Washington's era. Nonetheless it is striking that writers resist raising the possibility.[136]

A minority of biographers are invested in singling out Martha, mother of two of her own children, as the cause of the Washingtons' childlessness. Writes one pair, "According to a tradition passed down in Masonic circles, Martha Washington would have needed some sort of corrective surgery in order to conceive additional children after the birth of Patsy."[137] In another account, the author imagines Martha accepting blame for the couple's never having their own child: "I never gave you a child of your own and you never reproached me, not once."[138]

On the scale of emasculating sexual deficiencies, it seems that sterility ranks slightly lower than impotence. Sexualized manhood has long been predicated on the ability to penetrate. The colonial-era medical literature, for example, argues that sterile men should not divorce, as they could still fulfill the marital duty of sexual intimacy. The impotent man could not.[139] In the eighteenth century, childless couples could and did consult midwives, physicians, and reproduction manuals, but we have no evidence that George and Martha did any of this—again, perhaps suggesting the problem was not a mystery to them.[140]

For some writers, the question of whether the problem lay with George or Martha is answered by the conclusion that he did, indeed, reproduce—just not with Martha. In recent decades, there has been increasing public attention given to the idea that Washington fathered a child with an enslaved woman. The descendants of a man named West Ford have identified him as a direct descendant of Washington, and, indeed, the evidence seems to suggest that, much like the case of Jefferson, someone in the Washington family was his father. Although oral history has linked him to the Washington family for centuries, Ford is initially identified as Washington's son in print in the 1940s, first in the *Pittsburgh Courier* and later in a book on race in colonial America. As one recent biographer of Washington concludes, "In the matter of West Ford, the documentary evidence is ambiguous, but there is virtually no doubt that he was kin to the first president."[141] A fictionalized history that uses oral tradition imagines how Washington could have been Ford's father.[142] If Washington could be proven to have been sterile or impotent, he would clearly not be the father of either Ford or Posey.

Founding Father

In modern biographies, then, readers learn that, although childless, Washington was decidedly heterosexual, monogamous, and ideally suited for fatherhood. In biography as well as imagery, sleight of hand could lead many to believe that Washington had his own children. The compensatory portrayals of Washington—those that emphasize his masculine sexual appeal, his interest in women, his romantic marriage, and his paternal nature—all dispel any questions about manhood that childlessness could raise. As the next chapter shows, the ability of biographers to use success in private life to balance out perceived deficiencies of masculine virility would play out in the accounts of Jefferson's life as well—although with an unintended consequence.

If we step back from the stories of Washington's romantic life, we can see broad changes that indicate an early shift from an emphasis on the national significance of his personal life to a closer reflection on his personal and individual character. This shift mirrors trends in the nation as well as the emergence of a psychology of sex that highlights the centrality of sexual desires and behaviors for personal character. Yet throughout the twentieth century, the trend reverses; although in the early twentieth century, the focus on sex and individualized personhood deepens, by the turn of the new millennium, sexuality has become so associated with national social and political matters that inquiry into Washington's personal life could speak to a host of contexts, including the emphasis on the history of ordinary Americans and multiculturalism and a reactionary politics that concerns itself with a perceived sexual liberation in contemporary America and a distressing move away from a stereotyped more moral past. The tendency to include more material of a sexual nature in the twentieth and twenty-first centuries is not just a story of decreased censorship and increased liberalism. It is also a story about changing understandings of what is normal and Americans' corresponding desires to remember the nation's first president as desirable and masculine.

The question of not having his own children has been answered by pointing out that he *raised* children. For one recent biographer, Washington's Mount Vernon was teeming with children. In this biography, journalist Harlow G. Unger does not discuss that Washington had no children of his own until the very end of the narrative, when he concludes the book with a final paragraph that begins, "Although George Washington had no issue, well over five thousand descendants of his extended family survive in virtually every state," thus endowing him with the necessary progeny for manhood.[143] Indeed, with this line of thinking, to those five thousand we might add the hundreds of millions of U.S. residents living today—what better counterweight to childlessness than paternity for every living American for the duration, something no other man living or dead, not even the most prolific, could claim? Military hero and successful politician, Washington without question was and is still a model of successful American manliness as a public figure. And, through the careful handling of artists and biographers, in national memory the private Washington, as well, truly achieves manhood without issue.

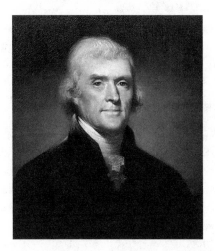

THOMAS JEFFERSON

ON APRIL 12, 2001, President George W. Bush invited both the black descendants of the Hemings family and the white descendants of the Jefferson family to the White House to commemorate the 258th anniversary of the birth of Thomas Jefferson (Figure 2.1). Speaking in the East Room at the White House, to the multiracial crowd that had assembled, he noted that "America sees itself in Thomas Jefferson."[1] This type of gathering would have been unthinkable only a short time ago—for generations, the Hemings family was prevented from attending Jefferson family events. Even today, the view of Jefferson as founder of a multiracial family is contested. But on that day in 2001, the president's words in America's White House indicated just how much things have changed.

Second only to George Washington, Jefferson ranks consistently as one of the most popular and revered of the political leaders of the early Republic.[2] Jefferson, of course, authored the Declaration of Independence—a document that not only gave political birth to the nation but also captured its very essence with the preamble's articulation of "unalienable Rights" of

Figure 2.1 (*above*). Portrait of Jefferson. (*Thomas Jefferson.* Rembrandt Peale, 1800. White House Historical Association.)

equality and "Life, Liberty, and the pursuit of Happiness." He is also celebrated for doubling the size of the young nation through the Louisiana
Purchase and for exploring the West with the famed Lewis and Clark expe-
dition. His face adorns the nickel, his head is on Mount Rushmore (along
with that of Washington, the only other Founding Father), and his marble
monument is one of the top tourist destinations in Washington, D.C.

As if to compensate for Jefferson's very developed philosophical sensibilities, his earliest biographers emphasize love and devotion in his relationships
with women. In the Victorian era, this approach meant focusing primarily
on his marriage, portraying him as a chaste widower after his wife died in
1782 at the age of thirty-three. By the twentieth century, given the increased
emphasis on the centrality of sexual urges, a more passionate Jefferson was
remembered, and increasingly he was portrayed as a man who had a variety of intimate relationships with women before and after his marriage. Of
course, some of these interactions were presented as scandals in the hands
of detractors. But biographers, tending to place their subject in a favorable
light, have almost always, however, emphasized how such interactions reveal
a less cerebral side of Jefferson.

Today, Jefferson is publicly reremembered as the man who had a thirty-
eight-year romantic relationship with his slave Sally Hemings and as the father
of her seven children. The new Jefferson has been identified as Hemings's
lover not only in a range of widely viewed media, including as the butt of
jokes in passing references in popular films, such as *Scary Movie* (when students at a high school gather beneath a statue of Jefferson surrounded by
his African American children), but also, more seriously, through portrayals
with sustained focus in best-selling novels, National Book Award–winning
histories, and popular television movies.[3] If we look back at how Americans
have remembered Jefferson's intimate life, we can see that the Hemings story,
for many, is now the latest in a number of romances that have made this
intellectual Founder more accessible to many Americans; Jefferson's enduring
stature is the greatest testament to the resilience of the Founders in American
national identity and the significant role that sexual personalizing can play in
securing favor, even in the face of controversy. Indeed, for some, his relationship with an enslaved woman bolsters a new perception of him as being ahead
of his time, and for some, he has even emerged as a "multicultural hero."

In His Lifetime

Jefferson was born in 1743 and died, remarkably, on July 4, 1826, the fiftieth anniversary of his famous Declaration. Like Washington, Jefferson was

a Virginia gentleman. He attended the College of William and Mary and became a lawyer. He served as Virginia delegate to the Second Continental Congress and at thirty-three authored the Declaration of Independence. He was the second governor of Virginia and served as the nation's first secretary of state (under Washington), as the second vice president (under John Adams), and as the third president.[4]

In his lifetime, two stories were told about Jefferson's relationships with women outside his marriage, both from political enemies who used the media to attack their opponent. In the first instance, Jefferson was romantically linked to Betsey Walker, the wife of a neighbor and friend, John. The story largely came from rumors in the press in 1802, with most additional information from an 1805 letter from John Walker to Jefferson's political enemy Henry (Light-Horse Harry) Lee. In the letter, Walker claims that during the summer of 1768, he had left his wife and child on official business, entrusting the still-unmarried Jefferson to look after them. During the four months of his absence, Jefferson's "conduct to Mrs W was improper so much so as to have laid the foundation of her constant objection to my leaving Mr J my exct telling me that she wondered why I could place such confidence in him." He also describes two other occasions when Jefferson tried to convince her of "the innocence of promiscuous love."[5]

In the second instance, a political hack also first broke public silence on the sexual relationship between Jefferson and his slave Hemings. Hemings was born in bondage in Shadwell, Virginia, in 1773 and died in Charlottesville, Virginia, in 1835. She came to Monticello as the inherited property of Martha Jefferson, Thomas's wife. Martha's father was alleged to also be Sally Hemings's father. Hemings was his until he died and his slaves passed to Martha, less than two years after she had married Thomas. At Monticello, the Hemings family enjoyed a privileged status relative to the hundreds of other slaves, with virtually all of the Hemings family being consigned to house labor and therefore receiving better treatment.

The story initially appears in print in the Federalist newspaper the *Recorder* in 1802. The article entitled "The President, Again" was authored by James Callender and published in Richmond. Callender was a partisan writer who had fallen out of favor with Jefferson. Angry by the perceived betrayal, he broke the silence on Jefferson's relationship with Hemings. "It is well known that the man, *whom it delighteth the people to honor*," he writes, "keeps, and for many years has kept, as his concubine, one of his slaves. Her name is SALLY. The name of her eldest son is TOM. His features are said to bear a striking although sable resemblance to those of the president himself." "By this wench Sally," he declares, "our president has had several children.

There is not an individual in the neighbourhood of Charlottesville who does not believe the story; and not a few who know it."[6]

In response, a number of articles appeared in newspapers across the country, some denouncing the report as false and scandalous, but others eventually giving credence to the story. The leading Federalist political and literary magazine of the day, *Port Folio*, published the following lines, "Supposed to have been written by the Sage of Monticello," to be sung to the tune of "Yankee Doodle":

> *Of all the damsels on the green,*
> *On mountain, or in valley,*
> *A lass so luscious ne'er was seen*
> *As Monticellian Sally.*
> *Yankee doodle, who's the noodle?*
> *What wife were half so handy?*
> *To breed a flock, of slaves for stock,*
> *A blackamoor's the dandy.*
> *Yankee doodle (etc.)*
> *When press'd by load of state affairs,*
> *I seek to sport and dally,*
> *The sweetest solace of my cares*
> *Is in the lap of Sally.*
> *Yankee doodle (etc.)*
> *Search every town and city through,*
> *Search market, street and alley;*
> *No dame at dusk shall meet your view,*
> *So yielding as my Sally.*
> *Yankee doodle (etc.)*
> *She's black you tell me—grant she be—*
> *Must colour always tally?*
> *Black is love's proper hue for me—*
> *And white's the hue for Sally.*
> *Yankee doodle (etc.)*
> *What though she by the glands secretes;*
> *Must I stand shil-I shall-I?*
> *Tuck'd up between a pair of sheets*
> *There's no perfume like Sally*
> *Yankee doodle (etc.)*
> *You call her slave—and pray were slaves*
> *Made only for the galley?*

Try for yourselves, ye witless knaves—
Take each to bed your Sally.
Yankee doodle, whose the noodle?
Wine's vapid, tope me brandy—
For still I find to breed my kind,
A negro-wench the dandy![7]

The piece is prefaced with the following statement: "Some of our papers have hinted at the amours of a certain great personage, which are said to be of a *dark* complexion." It quotes Benjamin Franklin as saying, "A man may *kiss his cow*" and quips, "Surely a *Philosopher* may *kiss his wench.*" As a jocular but politicized song, the piece immediately interjects derisive humor at Jefferson's and Heming's expense. It approaches a potentially explosive topic directly and with no deference for his presidential status.

A remarkable 1804 political cartoon similarly takes aim at Jefferson (Figure 2.2), depicting him as a rooster and Sally Hemings as a hen.[8] The humorous image suggests serious sexual misconduct with a double entendre that is crudely inescapable. Even more serious is the depiction of human heads on animal bodies; the specter of monstrosity haunts the image, underscoring the perceived unnaturalness of their union.

The story had legs and continued to flourish in the United States and abroad. For example, in 1806, an Irish poet published the following: "The weary statesman for repose hath fled/From halls of council to his negro's shed/Where blest he woos some black Aspasia's grace/And dreams of freedom in his slave's embrace!" In a footnote he is more explicit: "The 'black Aspasia' of the present P******** of the United States . . . has given rise to much pleasantry among the anti-democratic wits in America."[9]

Jefferson never responded publicly to the scandal, and the effect of the rumors was minimal in terms of damaging his revered public image. His earliest biographers would have been aware of these stories, but most choose to draw from stories of his romantic encounters that emanate from their subject, using his personal papers and family legends rather than material from his political enemies.

Burwell, an Early Love

In the mid–nineteenth century, writer and politician Henry Stephens Randall published his three-volume account of the life of Thomas Jefferson. Randall admired Jefferson but wanted to write in response to the earlier biographical trend that portrayed founders as "Goody-Two-Shoes" with no

A PHILOSOPHIC COCK

*Tis not a set of features or complexion
Or tincture of a Skin that I admire*

Figure 2.2. Jefferson depicted as a rooster and Sally Hemings depicted as a hen in an 1804 cartoon with the crude double-entendre title "A Philosophic Cock." (James Atkins. Courtesy of the American Antiquarian Society.)

faults. His account includes personal details and criticizes the earlier account by George Tucker for covering only Jefferson's public life. Randall mentions, albeit not at length, Jefferson's attraction to one "Belinda," whom he identifies as Rebecca Burwell. And the biography notes that she married another, after Jefferson failed to pursue the relationship fully. Jefferson, Randall asserts, was at least desired by young women and vice versa.[10]

In 1871, Jefferson's great-granddaughter Sarah N. Randolph published *The Domestic Life of Thomas Jefferson*, which largely uses family letters and what she calls "reminiscences": "My object is only to give a faithful picture of him as he was in private life—to show that he was, as I have been taught to think of him by those who knew and loved him best, a beautiful domestic character." Randolph expands the discussion of Jefferson's private life and continues a trend of commenting more fully on Jefferson's early connection to Burwell: "We have seen, from his letters to his friend Page, that, while a student in Williamsburg, Jefferson fell in love with Miss Rebecca Burwell— one of the beauties of her day. He was indulging fond dreams of success in winning the young lady's heart and hand, when his courtship was suddenly cut short by her, to him, unexpected marriage to another."[11] Similarly, James Parton's 1878 depiction includes the early connection to Burwell, and a chapter entitled "Jefferson in Love" notes, "He had left his heart behind him at Williamsburg. He had danced too many minuets in the Apollo—the great room of the old Raleigh tavern—with Miss Rebecca Burwell."[12]

By the twentieth century, Americans increasingly thought of him as suitably amorous in his youth and highlighted Burwell as an example of this behavior. One early-twentieth-century account starts with a chapter entitled "Jefferson's Family." It begins, "Jefferson was an ardent and sentimental lover, and his egotism appears in his love-affairs in a most amusing way. He adored several young women from time to time; such behavior is not uncommon among men of his youth; and to one of them,—Belinda,—when about twenty, he confessed his love."[13]

Another early-twentieth-century biographer similarly highlights his romantic life and emphasizes that Jefferson found himself in exciting social circles as a young man, where he "met lovely and refined ladies, felt the pleasure and temptation of social entertainments." He positions Jefferson as normal in his desires and romantic orientation: "In common with the vast majority of young men, Jefferson had known what it was to fall in love with handsome girls. At college he had tenderly nursed a passion for a sweetheart or two, and while he was studying law he had been sorely smitten. Just how many of these adventures the young man had weathered before he met the charming Widow Skelton is not clear, but there were several."[14] Another early-twentieth-century biographer writes, "He did his share of dancing and flirting with the pretty girls at Williamsburg and Rosewell, thought fondly of Belinda, sent gallant messages to Betsy Moore and Judy Burwell, bet a pair of garters with Alice Corbin, [and] pinch-hit as a beau for Sally Nicholas."[15] Illustrating the early-twentieth-century expectation for love and romance, one account explains, "The love affairs of Thomas Jefferson were perfectly normal: he experienced the usual youthful infatuation before the right one came along."[16] This account includes a chapter on Jefferson that describes Burwell as his first love.

Although we know little about her, his early correspondence with Burwell has been mined to speak of an early love that could well have blossomed into marriage. Seven letters written by Jefferson to a male friend, John Page, and several to another, Will Fleming, preserve the interactions that have been read by many as "anguished affection."[17] Jefferson met Burwell in 1762, when he was nineteen and she was sixteen. For his biographers, the letters written to his friend Page reveal playfulness, wit, and anxiety about love. But at least one biographer has long pointed out that "in trying to make up his mind to follow her he was a laggard."[18] Journalist Albert Jay Nock in his biography of Jefferson explains that he could have married an early crush but did not—"Rebecca Burwell did not take the young man's attentions any too seriously. No question she might have married him if she had liked."[19] In the early twentieth century, one biographer sums it up thusly: "His most serious flirtation" during his college years "was with a Miss Rebecca Burwell. . . . [T]he lover was too cool, or the courtship too protracted. . . . Miss Burwell cut the courtship short by marrying another in 1764."[20]

This emphasis on Jefferson as sociable and amorous only increased through the century. One mid-century author notes, "One gathers that he was not so much enchanted with a girl as with girls" and that "the college days of Jefferson were not entirely free from the entanglements of Cupid," adding that he was "a favorite with the girls." This biographer also argues that as Jefferson matured, he became increasingly appealing to women: "That he was a prime favorite among the charming belles in and about Williamsburg we may assume from the record, and he was no stranger to the ballrooms and the flowering grounds of the country seats near-by. . . . [H]e appealed to the young women by his appearance and manner. Physically he was now impressive and distinguished. . . . [H]is ability as a dancer was not lost on the young ladies."[21] Similarly, decades later, another biographer asserts, "Had all the women Jefferson invited to make the tour of America with him accepted his offer, he would have suffered from an embarrassing plethora of female company."[22]

By the mid-twentieth century, this presentation of Jefferson was in overdrive. One author stretches the bounds of his analysis by declaring that Jefferson's healthy sexuality could be determined simply by looking at his masterpiece, Monticello. "Anyone who has visited Monticello," he explains, "realizes that Jefferson had a sharp eye for alluring lines and arresting curves. At times he was particularly interested in feminine architecture. . . . He was always aware of the attraction of a well-turned ankle, a prettily rounded breast, or a soft, inviting voice that set one's nerves on urge. In other words, Jefferson was not only a philosopher."[23] Burwell was the early flirtation that simultaneously blew up into a first serious possible wife (and then at the same time authors almost shrugged their shoulders in disappointment that he failed the test of manly sexuality)—"in Jefferson's courtship of her, caution had replaced ardor."[24] Despite Jefferson's apparently rather awkward approach to her, biographers have seized on this relationship as one of youthful and intense love. In the 1990s, journalist Willard Sterne Randall would also highlight the Burwell story and point to her as evidence of Jefferson's deep passions for women, as well as someone whose "awkwardness" could get in the way of his successfully "courting" her. For Randall, Burwell was a "first flame" of Jefferson's, one who filled him with "infatuation," a girl he was "stunned by."[25] Journalist Christopher Hitchens similarly repeats the lore and crafts it as part of Jefferson's "early instability," when he was a reckless youth who spent his time chasing "loose company."[26]

Martha: Marriage and Loss

As we have already seen, interest in Jefferson's personal life dates back to his lifetime and was expressed in images, poetry, and the written word. Jefferson's very earliest biographers, however, following the style of the day, include relatively little information about his romantic life or even his marriage. In 1826, T.P.H. Lyman only mentions Jefferson's marriage with little comment on the nature of the relationship.[27] Several early publications portray his life primarily through original letters rather than the voice and analysis of a biographer. In such accounts, Jefferson is, however, described as a man with a "mild and amiable wife."[28] By 1843, several writers began to include additional commentary on the marriage. Thus, lawyer, author, and son of the famed first chaplain of the U.S. House of Representatives William Linn remarks that Jefferson married the "daughter of Mr. John Wayles of Virginia, an alliance by which he at once gained an accession of strength and credit, and received, in the intervals of public business, that domestic happiness he was so well fitted to partake and enjoy."[29]

Randolph expands the discussion of her great-grandparents' courtship: "So young and so beautiful, she was already surrounded by suitors when Jefferson entered the lists and bore off the prize." Randolph's account illustrates the Victorian-era emphasis on domesticity and romantic love: "A pleasant anecdote about two of his rivals has been preserved in the tradition of his family. While laboring under the impression that the lady's mind was still undecided as to which of her suitors should be the accepted lover, they met accidentally in the hall of her father's house. They were on the eve of entering the drawing-room, when the sound of music caught their ear; the accompanying voices of Jefferson and his lady-love were soon recognized, and the two disconcerted lovers, after exchanging a glance, picked up their hats and left."[30] The account serves to rescue Jefferson from being merely the rejected suitor of Belinda and establishes him as having bested other suitors for the desirable Martha Skelton.

Randolph also includes an anecdote about the Jeffersons' first arrival at Monticello as husband and wife, in heavy snow, "late at night" after all the "servants" had "retired to their own houses for the night." Having glossed over slave life at Monticello, the account proceeds to depict a charming scene of the young couple, who were "too happy in each other's love" to be bothered by the cold and who quickly, according to Randolph, "refreshed themselves" with wine they found "behind some books," warming themselves with "song and merry laughter."[31]

Virtually all late-nineteenth-century accounts focus on portraying Jefferson in harmony with the Victorian ideals of marriage and family. For example, Parton's 1874 biography includes a chapter entitled "Jefferson in Love."[32] Parton was a newspaperman who "self-consciously defined his identity as America's first professional biographer," insisting that he was not a "hack-biographer" at a time when high-brow/low-brow distinctions were being drawn for the genre.[33] Parton's biography of Jefferson began as a series for *Atlantic Monthly*, a notable popular achievement for the "first modern American biographer" who had already tasted success with biographies of Aaron Burr and Benjamin Franklin.[34]

By 1878, Parton's account had gone through several editions. Drawing on family stories first told to Henry Randall, his *Life of Thomas Jefferson* gives the fullest description of his marriage and loss of his wife. He describes Jefferson's wife as "Martha Skelton, childless, a beauty, fond of music, and twenty-two." Using the metaphor of musical instrument, he playfully notes "how delightfully the piano and the violin go together," adding coyly "when both are nicely touched." Jefferson, he explains, "grew better looking as he advanced in life" and had "now advanced from the bashful student to the condition of a remarkably successful lawyer and member of the Assembly."[35] John Torrey Morse's 1883 account also emphasizes charm and beauty: "The bride had every qualification which can make woman attractive; an exquisite feminine beauty, grace of manners, loveliness of disposition, rare cleverness, and many accomplishments."[36] In these tellings, such qualities reflect as much on Jefferson as they do on Martha.

Parton also includes the cozy story of Jefferson and Martha's first approach to Monticello as a married couple: "No voice welcomed them. No door opened to receive them. The servants had given them up long before, and gone home to bed. Worst of all, the fires were out, and the house was cold, dark, and dismal. What a welcome to a bride on a cold night in January!" This version leaves out the bottle of wine and focuses solely on the couple's exuberance: "They burst into the house, and flooded it with the warmth and light of their own unquenchable good-humor!" Parton remarks, "Who could wish a better place for a honeymoon than a snug brick cottage, lifted five hundred and eighty feet above the world, with half a dozen counties in sight, and three feet of snow blocking out all intruders?"[37] The scene delightfully emphasizes their privacy while providing for the reader an exceptional vantage point from which to view their love.

For Parton, the marriage brought Jefferson great joy: "The year 1772, which was the first of Jefferson's married life, I think he would have ever after pronounced the happiest of all his years." But as we know, the joy would not last forever. Jefferson's painful deathbed promise to Martha is described in detail and yoked to the pleasure of their love: "At last she said that she could not die content if she thought her children would ever have a step-mother; and her husband, holding her hand, solemnly promised that he would never marry again." But Parton adds what would become a romanticized barometer of the depths of his love for his wife, his terrible grief at her passing. Parton explains, "Towards noon, as she was about to breathe her last, his feelings became uncontrollable. He almost lost his senses. His sister, Mrs. Carr, led him staggering from the room into his library, where he fainted, and remained so long insensible that the family began to fear that he, too, had passed away. They brought in a pallet, and lifted him upon it. He revived only to a sense of immeasurable woe."[38]

Other writers read deeply into his wife's death and her deathbed scene, yoking them to his faithfulness to her after her death. Describing the scene in tender prose, one account explains, "Holding her other hand in his, Mr. Jefferson promised her solemnly that he would never marry again. And he never did. He was then quite a young man, and very handsome, and I suppose he could have married well; but he always kept that promise."[39] As Linn writes, the marriage would end in tragedy: "Its duration, however, was but short; in little more than ten years, death deprived him of his wife, and left him the sole guardian of two infant daughters; to whose education he devoted himself with a constancy and zeal, which might, in some measure, compensate for the want of a mother's care and instruction."[40]

In early-twentieth-century biographies, Jefferson's marriage emerges as, above all else, the most important aspect of the view of him as a red-blooded American man. One biographer concedes that "the general poverty of fact and record concerning Mr. Jefferson's early years is threadbare in the matter of his marriage. No one knows how he met his wife or what she was like."[41] And another explains, "He saw to it that no mementos of hers were preserved for posterity. There are many relics of the Jefferson family, but none of Martha—

not one ringlet of her hair, not a garment she may have worn, not a piece of jewelry she may have prized."[42] But many of the same biographers nonetheless claim to know the most intimate and hard-to-document aspect of the relationship—their true regard for each other. One writer captures the essence of how public memory has revered the marriage: "Mr. Jefferson's marriage was one of the most successful known to biographical literature." But the author does not stop there: "In the harmony of the relation between himself and wife there never seems to have been a discord. No shadow ever fell between them chilling their perfect, trustful devotion."[43] Another notes, "The wooing had not been perfunctory nor cold," although we have no evidence either way, and continues, "The profound love that marked their married life makes more than questionable any such conclusion."[44] Through the century, the depiction remains largely unchanged. According to one typical account, "For a decade, all their dreams had come true."[45] Writes another, "They were to remain lovers to the end. It was a happy household."[46] This depiction would only strengthen as the century passed. The 1969 musical *1776*, which was so successful that it became a popular film in 1972, depicts Jefferson and Martha as nearly sex-crazed and utterly in love. Although we know that she was suffering from a difficult pregnancy at the time, in the film they cannot contain their passion: Jefferson is shown actually taking a break from writing the Declaration of Independence to make love. In addition to celebrating his virility, the film suggests that sex not only served as a distraction from his work but also informed his belief in individual liberty and pursuit of happiness. This depiction delighted fans of the musical, who saw the presentation as echoing that generation's view of sexual desire as natural and the censorship of the 1950s as an allegory for Victorianism. The image of the Jeffersons as exceptionally loving has remained constant, and the bond was poignantly underscored by Martha Jefferson's death in 1782 at the age of thirty-three.

In the late twentieth century, many biographers repeat the oft-told story of the Jeffersons' first arrival to Monticello as husband and wife "snug in their picturesque honeymoon retreat" and just at the "start of their domestic life." "Whether it be fact or fiction," explains one author, it "properly conveys the spirit of their marriage."[47]

As is typical of such accounts, an emphasis on her attractiveness helps establish his credentials as a desirable man and as one whose desires were consistent with societal norms. "She was beautiful" writes one author—although we have no contemporary images of her and we should ask the relevance—"better educated than the average Virginia belle of the day and her mind was superior."[48]

Given the general paucity of information about how the Jeffersons met or how their relationship developed, biographers mobilize his reaction to the loss of his wife as evidence of their bond. One turn-of-the-twentieth-century account, typical of most, remarks, "Undoubtedly Mr. Jefferson loved his wife with an extraordinary depth of devotion. It must have been so, for there is a clear record that when she died, he was inconsolable, and that he remained always quietly faithful to her memory, never finding room in his heart for any other woman."[49] A 1960s account notes that he never found another: "Jefferson's affection for Martha was as deep as it was exclusive."[50] By the 1990s, the depiction of Jefferson's love for Martha continues to be evidenced by courtship tales of when they "fell in love," the threadbare lore about their first arrival to Monticello, and the alleged deathbed promise that Mrs. Jefferson solicited from her husband before passing away.[51]

In his review of *The Hemingses of Monticello*, preeminent historian Edmund Morgan writes of the marriage (with veiled contrast to George Washington), "No one believes that dynastic succession was of huge importance to Jefferson. He married for love." He also states, "Fidelity and felicity were the themes of the married life of Thomas and Martha Jefferson. When she died he was utterly undone. It is said, and there is no reason to doubt it, that the happy intimacy of this marriage was so nearly complete that he promised Martha to take no wife in her place. And to that he held."[52] Other academic historians confidently assert the same, despite the lack of complex documentation. "Thomas Jefferson loved his wife with all his heart," assures one historian.[53]

Cosway: A "Legitimate" Object of Affection

Twentieth-century writers also add descriptions of a new romance with Maria Cosway. In the nineteenth century, biographers depict Cosway as a friend, but for most twentieth-century biographers, Cosway is a woman with whom Jefferson fell passionately in love. Jefferson met her while a relatively young widower in Paris, and although their story is generally discussed as a scandal, it is worth noting that she was married at the time of their association. His earliest biographers avoid discussion of Maria Cosway as a romantic relationship, focusing instead on only his wife, Martha. The evidence for the relationship comes to us from eighteenth-century correspondence, and many early biographers, perhaps finding a relationship with a married woman distasteful, dismiss it as "flirtation." Only later would the letters serve as evidence for an entirely new interpretation—that she became his "lover and mistress."[54] Jefferson famously broke his wrist while with Cosway, and (in the absence of any evidence) many paint romantic visions of the scene—his gallantly dashing over a fountain to impress her or leaping a log.

By the 1940s, there is division among biographers about how to treat the relationship—as flirtation or a clear signal of "adultery."

But this omission would end by the mid–twentieth century. Although recent accounts also point out that Jefferson began his relationship with the enslaved Hemings while in Paris, virtually all twentieth-century biographers highlight Cosway as *the* Paris romance. Undoubtedly, this is in part because Cosway was white and Hemings was black. Biographers often assert that this relationship was intensely passionate and punctuate the story with an image of the "beautiful" Cosway. Recently the affair has been unequivocally embraced and sincere love declared. "If ever a man fell in love in a single afternoon it was he," writes one biographer about Jefferson's instant emotional state after meeting Cosway.[55]

Highlighting a relationship with a married woman could have backfired but for the story's ability to compensate for Hemings, lurking in the background, and for the added bonus of its showing Jefferson as besting another man. The relationship with Cosway thus could also serve Jefferson's image in that it could be fashioned to indicate his cuckolding of her husband. Although nearly the same age as Jefferson, Cosway's husband is described as a man whose "foppishness and affectation made him less than pleasing as a man, and his vanity was immeasurable."[56] Brodie notes that he was "mocked for his pretentiousness in dress, especially a mulberry silk coat ornamented with strawberries."[57] Out-manning such a husband might not have been very challenging, but nonetheless his biographers take note of Cosway's eagerness to fall in love with Jefferson, whom they imply cut a sharp contrast to her husband.

In the hands of late-twentieth-century Jefferson image makers, Cosway's being married is far from a liability; the detail is reworked to highlight his attractiveness to women in addition to his superiority to other men. All the women in his life are noted as pretty or extraordinarily beautiful, with Cosway as the pinnacle. That Jefferson outmans her husband in some biographies is underscored through their emphasis on Cosway's desirability. She is always described as an extraordinary beauty. One typical account includes, for example, such descriptors as "very pretty, slender" and "great expressive soft blue eyes that smiled readily, and a great quantity of beautiful blond hair"—"her most noticeable feature."[58] Another describes her as "small, exquisite, and feminine," "a fragile, languorously feminine woman of twenty-seven, with luminous blue eyes, exquisite skin, and a halo of golden curls."[59] Still another describes her as "beautiful" and as "charming, blond, blue-eyed, and lovely."[60] Such references are, of course, loaded with racialized connotations, and these glowing descriptions of hair and eye color are used disproportionately to describe women of European descent.

For biographers, her beauty could shore up his credentials as a properly sexual man—one with healthy, normative desires. One biographer imagines, "Her voice was soft and alluring, and at times it took on overtones that set him all atremble." Jefferson, he writes, felt "many spasms of the heart when he looked at Maria Cosway."[61] Chroniclers through the twentieth century have made use of the Cosway story to highlight the Jefferson's romantic side. As Joseph Ellis explains, "The Cosway affair is significant not because of the titillating questions it poses about a sexual liaison with a gorgeous young married woman but because of the window it opens into Jefferson's deeply sentimental soul and the highly romantic role he assigned to women who touched him there."[62]

Biographers have been gushing over Jefferson's "Head and Heart" letter to Cosway (an extended dialogue between rational and romantic sides) for nearly two centuries now—perhaps because we have so little from him to use. It has been called the "greatest love letter in history." Biographers who discredit the letter and portray it as merely eighteenth-century romantic prose have been taken to the woodshed by others. Jefferson's mid-twentieth-century biographer Charles Tansill, for example, points out that Julian Boyd, editor of *Jefferson's Papers*, is gravely mistaken when he characterizes the "Head and Heart" letter as romantic but asserts that Jefferson had "control of his passions." Taking issue with it as an understatement, Tansill argues, "It is apparent that Dr. Boyd knows little about Jefferson's emotional balance and less about the way of a maid with a man." And he asserts, "Jefferson's October 12 missive to Maria Cosway is, indeed, 'one of the notable love letters in the English language.' It has all the earmarks of sincerity and could hardly have been part of a game of make-believe."[63] Thomas Fleming, for example, in his 2009 collection of biographies on the romantic lives of the Founders describes the head and heart letter to Cosway as "twelve electrifying pages."[64]

As previously mentioned, Jefferson's growing number of romances often lent support to each other—that is, each one became more plausible than the last as a case was made for the depiction of Jefferson as a man of passion and desires rather than merely a bookish, chaste widower. The above interpretation of Jefferson's "Head and Heart" letter illustrates this point once more. The author continues, "If in Jefferson's case the head had really been sovereign, there might never have been the attempted intimacies with Betsy Walker." Here the scandal of Walker works to support the claim of Jefferson as having normal desires and lends credence to the claim that his attraction to Cosway was genuine and had been acted on.[65] In 1993, journalist Willard Sterne Randall continues the emphasis on depicting Cosway as someone Jefferson "would fall in love with" while in Paris—indeed, for

Randall, Jefferson "fell in love with Maria Cosway from the moment he met her" and she became someone with whom he would want to "spend every possible moment."[66]

Popular writer Hitchens similarly declares that "Jefferson carried on a passionate relationship during his time in Paris" with Cosway, even if we "may not be sure about consummation." For Hitchens, the "Head and Heart" letter is evidence of their emotional bond. Repeating the lore that Jefferson broke his wrist jumping over a fence to impress Cosway, Hitchens also asserts that the relationship soured when Jefferson took it too far, inserting a crude sexual reference in one of his letters to Cosway (making references to a nose in a manner that suggested a euphemism for penis), and it was then that Cosway was "displeased" and "the relationship between them cooled." However, for Hitchens, the bottom line here is that Jefferson was "fond of beautiful women," "sexually knowing," "forward," and "eager"—and most important, echoing the assessment of twentieth-century scholars, "without a mistress."[67]

Walker: A Minor Scandal

Although virtually all biographers from the earliest to the most recent mention his lost love for Burwell, not all of his earliest biographers would comment on a connection to Betsey Walker, the wife of a neighbor and friend, John. As we have seen, the story first appears in the nineteenth-century politically charged press. But despite including chapters devoted to "Jefferson in Love," Parton, for example, omits any mention of Walker in his 1874 writings.[68] This omission of Walker continues well into the twentieth century. Writing in 1926, for example, Francis Hirst mentions only Burwell and Martha—erasing any explicit discussion of Walker.[69] By the mid–twentieth century, however, most writers frame the relationship with Walker as both a minor scandal and a revealing romance before his marriage.

By the twentieth century, biographers who write of it mention that early public knowledge of the relationship was the result of political enemies who resurrected this moment in Jefferson's life to slander him. Says one, "The lady was a woman of charm and beauty, vivacious, and perhaps unconsciously seductive, and probably, without considering the consequences, not a little flirtatious." The husband complained that this was not a one-time affair—a year after initial flirtations, "Jefferson had 'renewed his caresses' and slipped into her gown sleeve cup a paper pleading the innocence of adultery." Other charges included that Jefferson had on another occasion "stolen into his room where the lady was undressing or in bed." Jefferson, we are told, "made no reply in public" when the husband told his story to the press.

He did, however, write "a personal letter to two members of his Cabinet. . . . 'I plead guilty to one of the charges,' he wrote, 'that when young and single I offered love to a handsome lady. I acknowledge its incorrectness. It is the only one founded in truth in all their allegations against me.' That this youth of twenty-five, susceptible to women, was not 'pure as light and stainless as a star,' we would prefer to believe. But the rash and persistent pursuit after the rebuff is not in character."[70]

Beginning in the twentieth century, sex scandals have generally worked in Jefferson's favor by portraying him as a more human, more mortal man with a natural desire toward romance rather than a sublimated sex drive replaced with books. One biographer writes of Jefferson's youth, "That at this age Jefferson was exceedingly susceptible to the charms of beautiful women there can be no doubt. It was about this time, in his twenty-fifth year, that he became infatuated with the young wife of an absent friend of the neighborhood and made advances that were repelled."[71] Similarly, Dumas Malone, once considered the most scholarly Jefferson biographer, explains, "It was in the year he was twenty-five that Jefferson made a mistake. He was then unmarried. Full of physical strength and vigor, and for four months his friend was away from home."[72]

The Walker episode, in the hands of skilled biographers, could highlight Jefferson's passionate side, but it could also be used to comment on the strength of his character. In a chapter called "Tangle in a Petticoat," Tansill focuses on the scandal of the Walkers and finds positive things to say about Jefferson as a result: "Jefferson was being harassed by a scandal that might have affected his nerves or frightened him into silence, if he had been a weak man. He met it, dealt with it, put it in its place; but since it charged him with coveting his neighbor's wife, it must have cost him some of the most wretched moments of his life, knowing as he did that the Anglo-Saxon peoples throughout their history have reacted strongly against any accusation of sexual irregularity involving an eminent man."[73] Given that the charge is adultery, this explanation stands out for going to such lengths to bolster the manhood of Jefferson. In his 2009 collection of biographies on the romantic lives of the Founders, Thomas Fleming explains the connection to Walker as follows: "We know only this much: after tantalizing him long enough to send the bachelor into a frenzy of frustration, Betsey said no at the crucial moment."[74] Hitchens uses the tale of Jefferson's "unsuccessful attempt to seduce" Walker because for him it "demonstrates that Jefferson was ardent by nature when it came to females." "Generations of historians," he laments, "have written, until the present day, as if he were not a male mammal at all."[75]

Unintended Consequences

Thus, in the nineteenth century, the famed author of the Declaration of Independence (by then already a "sacred text," one venerated by the nation) could not be, and would not be, memorialized as a man who sexually exploited his young slave girl.[76] His biographers would successfully ensure that public memory of Jefferson's private life fit the domestic ideals of the era. To this end, romanticized depictions of his marriage and his loss would be accompanied only by brief mentions of an early love, Belinda.

For those biographers who created a personal romantic life for Jefferson, the biggest challenge was not the skeletons in his closet but the lack of information with which to work. Writes historian Peter Onuf, "He kept his own secrets, destroying his correspondence with his wife, Martha, and revealing nothing about his long-term relationship with his slave Sally Hemings." And he elaborates, "Jefferson's autobiography (drafted in 1821) is a sketch of his public career, virtually bereft of illuminating details about his private life."[77]

Calling him a "sphinx" or "impenetrable," popular and academic twentieth-century biographers acknowledge that Jefferson's most intimate life is elusive because he wanted it that way. For example, according to one, "No one ever succeeded better than Thomas Jefferson at hiding his inner springs of sentiment. . . . [I]n more intimate matters, especially in matters of affection and feeling, he never spoke out."[78] Mid-twentieth-century biographers continue the characterization. As one notes, "He was extremely reticent about private domestic matters. . . . [T]here is no better way to describe his attitude toward an individual's religion than to say that to him it was as private a matter as his intimacies with his own wife."[79] In the words of another biographer, "Not only he never wore his heart upon his sleeve, but tried to lead the approaches to it through a maze."[80]

One tangible result of this secrecy is a pronounced lack of documentation. Although one would never guess it from the literature, as is the case for many of the Founders, biographers have experienced almost a total absence of documents from which to reconstruct Jefferson's early romantic life. Jefferson's mother's house at Shadwell, Virginia, burned in 1770, destroying nearly all of his letters and papers. As the writer of the best-selling *American Sphinx* concedes, this "ma[de] the recovery of his formative years an exercise in inspired guesswork."[81]

Rightly or wrongly, Jefferson's image has at times been dogged by rumors that he was hardly the model of virile manhood. At least as long ago as when Alexander Hamilton called him "feminine," Jefferson's image has risked suffering from a lack of manly virility.[82] His status as a chaste widower also made him an unusual president.[83] With his wife, Martha, Jefferson had no sons, only daughters, and because his father died when Jefferson was young, Jefferson was both oriented toward women and yet typically (for the eighteenth century) misogynistic.[84] Historian Winthrop Jordan writes, "With women in general he was uneasy and unsure."[85] Of Jefferson, a biographer notes, "In his relations with the opposite sex he was temperate to the point of continence."[86] A later biographer explains, "Jefferson preferred to meet his lovers in the rarefied region of his mind rather than the physical world of his bedchamber."[87] He is often fondly remembered as agrarian—yet, and in despite of how he espoused and idealized the model of the yeoman farmer, he himself was not a farmer, especially in contrast to Washington. Unlike Washington, he gave his State of the Union address in writing and made very few speeches as president. And he tended toward the overly refined. Depictions of him after his wife's death have him "swooning" and "fainting," and he suffered through life from chronic headaches. Others contend that he was no rough-and-tumble man—that he neither gambled nor drank (although he did). In his youth, writes one biographer, "heady, mature conversations, fine dinners, theatergoing, and other gentlemanly activities formed a milieu the young Jefferson loved . . . a life of high culture."[88] Jefferson is famed for his love of architecture and design—most notably as expressed in his own home, Monticello. He is generally not referred to as handsome or especially athletic. Indeed, he was described as gangly, tall, lanky, sometimes awkward—a man who only later grew into his frame, but only just barely.

As the influences of Sigmund Freud and turn-of-the-century sexologists spread, sexual urges came to be seen as a natural part of life, and in particular of a man's healthy libido.[89] Twentieth-century Americans would in turn be less satisfied to portray Jefferson as a model chaste bachelor and widower, and a new generation began to emphasize in greater detail other relationships. Writing in 1952, Howard Swiggett quips, "There is an implication in several books that from 1784 until his death Jefferson lived in chastity and that there was something very noble in doing so. As to this, there is presumably no valid evidence but surely it is as unlikely as the charge that 'he peopled his plantation with slaves' by intercourse with black women."[90]

The developing characterization of Jefferson as a man of great romantic passion eventually had an impact on the handling of the Hemings story. The Cosway and Walker stories gained traction, it seems, only in the absence of the Hemings story. They served as a counterbalance by inserting a proper object of affection and also served to humanize Jefferson in the absence of any other love interests—the image of the chaste widower having long since served its Victorian purposes. In doubt of the view of Jefferson as a chaste widower, a late-twentieth-century biographer asks rhetorically, "Does a man's sexuality atrophy at thirty-nine, especially if he has already demonstrated that he was capable of very great passion?" Establishing him as a man of "great sexual vitality," one who had adulterous affairs and who was capable of great passion, made it easier to eventually also understand him as a man who had a decades-long intimate relationship with his slave Hemings.[91]

The story that Jefferson fathered the children of his slave Hemings, which has in recent decades become more accepted by both popular and academic audiences, has almost seamlessly fit into the model of earlier romantic connections of Jefferson's and has breathed new life into old efforts to humanize the cerebral, inaccessible, private world of one of our most important Founders.

Hemings: A Romance Befitting a Great Man

The story that Jefferson fathered children with Hemings, which emerged in his lifetime, did not fade away, and among a new generation it later served a different purpose from that of the original Federalist political enemies of Jefferson. By the 1830s, it was being used by abolitionists. William Lloyd Garrison's *Liberator* published a column on the alleged sale of Jefferson's daughter in New Orleans, underscoring that no one was safe from the evils of that market. Attesting to the widespread knowledge of the Jefferson-Hemings relationship, the author never feels the need to provide any background information or to assert that the mother of Jefferson's daughter was an enslaved woman. The notice quotes an American veteran: "'I never thought,' said he, 'when I was periling my life in the bloody struggle of the revolution, that I was fighting for the last resort of slavery. . . . [I]f I had, I could not have fought at all.'"[92] The core of this story, the sale of Jefferson's daughter at New Orleans, also serves to frame a poem, "Jefferson's Daughter," that was published in a British periodical in 1839. Versions of it were reprinted in the *Liberator* in 1848.[93] Fugitive slave and abolitionist writer William Wells Brown also includes it in his collection of antislavery poetry published that same year. It would later serve as the basis of his 1853 novel that was published in London and entitled *Clotel; or, The President's Daughter: A Narrative of Slave Life in the United States.*[94] In the early 1860s, Brown serialized the story in the African American newspaper the *Weekly Anglo-African*.

During Reconstruction, several accounts of Monticello slaves appeared in print. In 1873, the *Pike County Republican*, a local Ohio newspaper with a limited circulation, published a brief essay entitled "Life among the Lowly, No. 1." The account was Madison Hemings's recollections of his family history as the son of Jefferson and Sally Hemings. He describes both his mother and his grandmother as having been taken as a "concubine" by their owners, John Wayles (Martha Jefferson's father) and Thomas Jefferson, respectively. The account describes that Hemings became pregnant while she was in Paris and that shortly after returning "she gave birth to a child, of whom Thomas Jefferson was the father." Although that child "lived but a short time," Hemings "gave birth to four others," including Madison, "and Jefferson was the father of all of them."[95] It would be more than a century before the account would be taken seriously by a broad audience.

The reaction of many Americans was to ignore the issue entirely. For his three-volume account published in the 1850s, Randall interviewed Jefferson's family and chose to leave aside old scandals, including Hemings. He "boasted privately to Sparks" that he had learned from the family that Jefferson's nephew Peter Carr was the father of Hemings's children.[96] Randall does refer to Callender, calling him a "blackguard" but little else. In the preface, he explains that he would not just repeat charges from partisan newspapers because to do so would just give them more voice. Some Victorian biographers, such as Morse, allude to the controversy, but none airs the specific charges or takes the story at face value. Morse refers to it as "the pitiful story of Callender's malicious defamation" without mentioning Hemings by name. And Morse defensively does not explicitly address the story: "His many tales were scandalous and revolting to the last degree. Naturally, these slanders will not bear repetition here; for they were worse than mere charges of simple amours."[97]

As scholars have shown, by most Americans the Hemings story remained either ignored or coolly noted.[98] There has been great resistance to the story of Jefferson's fathering children with Hemings—far greater than any resistance to the characterizations of his other romantic relationships (all of which are equally lacking in strong documentary evidence). Oftentimes the story would simply be alluded to with no explicit mention of Hemings at all. His being emotionally withdrawn, one turn-of-the-twentieth-century biographer explains, came only "after he had been through the fiery ordeal of politics, had been beat upon as fierce a storm of abuse and slander as ever assailed a statesmen so essentially pure, so absolutely patriotic, so consistently unselfish and benevolent."[99] A chapter entitled "Moral and Religious Views" notes the Callender newspaper charges but describes Callender as personally and politically begrudged and dismisses Madison Hemings's claim that he was Jefferson's son. The author quips, "In early days, and up to a recent period, nearly every mulatto by the name of Jefferson in Albemarle County, and they were numerous, claimed descent from the Sage of Monticello, which gratified their pride but seriously damaged his reputation."[100]

For the author, the justification of his dismissal was not based on Jefferson's character but rather alleged documentary evidence that Jefferson had at one point produced a birth record that showed that Madison Hemings could not be his son and implied that the overseer was the father by his confession to a clergyman. One early-twentieth-century biographer who writes that the individual who broke the story, Callender, engaged in a "campaign of calumny" places this information in a footnote: "A low class Richmond paper, edited by Callender, throve for a time on the circumstantial lies which he circulated against Jefferson's private life and character"—again, not mentioning Hemings by name.[101]

By mid-century, the story of Jefferson's enslaved children was being used by both friend and foe of integration. Some did not deny the story but rather used it as an object lesson in the dangers of "racial mixing." Others used the story as a reminder of a long history of exploitation at the hands of white slave-owners.[102] In the 1950s, the Hemings story gained traction during the African American civil rights movement, appearing in *Ebony* magazine in 1954.[103] The article, entitled "Thomas Jefferson's Negro Grandchildren," depicts Jefferson as the father of all the slaves whom he had freed in his will, including five who were the children of "several comely slave concubines who were great favorites at his Monticello house."[104]

But many others, however, explicitly reference the relationship only to dismiss it. Typical of those who reject the veracity of the scandal is a heavy finger pointing directly at the "unscrupulous hack" Callender, who in 1802 published the first words in print about Jefferson and Hemings in the *Richmond Recorder*: "Federalist newspapers all over the country gleefully circulated the libel, and the legend was born. It has been resurfacing ever since."[105] Similarly, a mid-twentieth-century biographer explains, "Among other accusations Callender declared that Jefferson, when appointed minister to France, had taken to Paris with him in 1784 a black woman named Sarah or Sally, and that her son, Tom, bore 'a striking though sable resemblance' to the President." The author explains in a footnote that "Sarah or Sally" "was a bright mulatto girl whose father, according to Monticello gossip, was an unknown white man. She escorted Maria Jefferson to Paris."[106] The 1964 book on the "romantic side" of the Founding Fathers includes an extensive discussion of the Walker scandal and the Cosway affair. Yet in discussing Callender, the author includes only one sentence on Hemings. After describing Callender as a "notorious scandalmonger," he adds, "He added a variation concerning Jefferson's conduct with one of his attractive slave women."[107] Another biographer in typical fashion describes Callender as an "unattractive human" and explains that "most of the scandalous stories about Jefferson that have circulated through the years go back to this wretched journalist, and almost without exception they were false. The story of a slave mistress is the most notorious, and it is wholly without foundation in fact."[108] In another example, "to drag the President in his own mire, Callender added industrious circulation of all the malicious stories about Jefferson's personal life that he could pick up or invent, including the vilest of all the canards—one about intimate relations with a female slave."[109]

In addition to singling out the political motives of Callender, a second prong of the defense hinges on Jefferson's character: "In light of overwhelming evidence that Jefferson was a loving and solicitous father, the claim that he seduced a sixteen-year-old slave girl and traveled in the intimate company of his two young daughters with her in an advanced state of pregnancy cannot be believed."[110] Similarly, one 1970s biographer writes, "If this account can be believed, Jefferson emerges as the seducer of a young, innocent, attractive colored girl, hardly out of puberty, who yearned only to be free and to remain in a country where she would not be despised as a 'Negress' and humiliated as a slave." This account captures the typical view in a comprehensive manner:

> For Jefferson to have conducted a clandestine love affair with a slave woman and to have raised his children as slaves is completely at variance with his character, insofar as it can be determined by his acts and words, the strict moral code by which he professed to live and which he constantly enjoined upon others, especially young men and women, and his conception of women and their place in society. He was not a womanizer; in his relations with the opposite sex he was temperate to the point of continence. On the occasion when he was tempted to transgress the bounds of discretion and propriety, he curbed his sexual desire—with the result that the love affair did not go beyond a romantic friendship. After the death of his wife, his "affairs of the heart" did not usually involve more than his affections.

Individuals who avoid or deny the Hemings relationship also emphasize the love between Cosway and Jefferson while he was in Paris. This account manages to accomplish both goals with one line: "The woman with whom Jefferson conducted his most intimate romantic liaison in Paris met, in most respects, the exacting standards he always maintained in affairs of the heart."[111]

For many biographers who reject the relationship yet acknowledge that a relative of Jefferson was the culprit, the allegation indicates a distinct lack of proper masculine authority so expected in a Founding Father like Jefferson.

At best, one who notes that Jefferson was likely not engaged in the relationship points out, "If Jefferson can convincingly be absolved of the charge of being the father of five mulatto children, the fact remains that at Monticello he presided over a scene of miscegenation."[112]

Some biographers revert to the earlier depiction of Jefferson as able to control his sexual passions—essentially, the view of him as chaste widower. As John C. Miller writes (in an exhaustive list), "Almost certainly, after his wife's death, he sublimated the sexual drive in such activities as music—'the favorite passion of my soul'; architecture—building Monticello took over thirty years; gardening and farming; exercise (he spent one to three hours a day on horseback); reading science, and philosophy; his love for his daughters and grandchildren and delight in the company of his friends."[113]

In the late twentieth century, as popular depictions of Hemings and Jefferson as lovers gained mainstream traction, Jefferson image makers would become more vehement in their denial of the possibility of a Hemings-Jefferson relationship. This 1970s account explains, "It was impossible for Jefferson to carry on a romance or even a friendship without constant letter-writing." The author continues, "Jefferson's real love-letters were written to his daughters and to his wife, Martha, not to Sally Hemings or to any other woman." And, he reiterates, "The ten years of unalloyed happiness with Martha had made it impossible for him really to love another woman."[114]

Over the course of several decades at the end of the twentieth century, popular and academic blockbusters would reintroduce the American public to the Hemings-Jefferson relationship. The most influential popular depictions of Jefferson as Hemings's lover begin in 1975 with Professor Fawn Brodie's best-selling psychological biography, re-released in 2010 with an introduction by Professor Annette Gordon-Reed. That same year, *Ebony* carried a feature on Jefferson that depicts him as a man of contradictions who "fell in love with" Hemings. The article also asserts that Jefferson "had other concubines" and includes a photo of a Chicago woman who descended from one of those relationships.[115] This was followed quickly by a best-selling novel, *Sally Hemings*.[116] The academy was slower than the public to warm to the story. Historian Jordan's 1968 *White over Black: American Attitudes toward the Negro, 1550–1812* is one of the first to take the possible relationship seriously. The book won a National Book Award in 1969 and was widely sold as a Penguin Books paperback.[117] But the academic ice on the issue of paternity would not truly begin to melt until Gordon-Reed's careful examination of the persistent academic resistance, which she shows has largely relied on assumptions about Jefferson's character and has tossed historical inquiry aside in deference to his stature as a Founding Father.

What has also propelled the story forward is the depiction of romantic love between the two. In the absence of documentation, chroniclers have differed on how to characterize the relationship. The earliest nineteenth-century accounts meant to damage the reputation of Jefferson portray this affair as tending toward rape of an enslaved child, a description that works in the hands of both Jefferson's political enemies and later abolitionists who focused on the horrors of enslavement. Yet beginning in the 1970s, those seeking to make the Hemings story accepted by mainstream audiences broke with this interpretation to argue that a genuine bond of affection existed between the two. This portrayal also holds appeal for recognizing the agency of Hemings in the affair rather than depicting her as a helpless victim of Jefferson's lust.[118] Brodie, for example, writes, "If the story of the Sally Hemings liaison be true, as I believe it is, it represents not scandalous debauchery with an innocent slave victim, as the Federalists and later the abolitionists insisted, but rather a serious passion that brought Jefferson and the slave woman much private happiness over a period lasting thirty-eight years."[119]

Taking his cues from Brodie's book, which argues that *love* bonded Jefferson and Hemings, one 1970s biography by a professor of literature asserts that the relationship was "a most touching and tender association." The "gentleman" and the "lovely girl" who "fell in love" in France, he explains, "lived together, in the face of all social prohibitions in their time and place, for nearly four decades, in common law marriage." Depicting them as trailblazers, he concludes, "The difficulties of such a life, though great, were endured with each other's support, even in slavery-ridden Virginia. It was after all, their secret pursuit of happiness."[120] This depiction of Jefferson and Hemings as lovers across a forbidden color line is generally the one currently employed in popular memory, making its way from biography to cinema. In such films as *Jefferson in Paris* (1995), for example, Hemings lives with Jefferson, romantically sneaking in and out of his bedroom so as to avoid the condemnation of their less enlightened family and friends.

In contrast to the decades of resistance in both popular and academic writings, it has become more commonplace for this story to be mentioned as established fact—and for both the rich and complex Jefferson personal life and legacy and the Hemings family story to be reduced to the Jefferson-Hemings relationship, which has captivated public imagination. Thus, Gordon-Reed's *The Hemingses of Monticello* has received popular and academic praise, garnering a National Book Award and a Pulitzer Prize. The *Washington Post* named it one of the top ten nonfiction books of 2008, and although its major accomplishment is the brilliant piecing together of the history of the Hemings family, the blurb describing the recommended title zeroes in on only Hemings and Jefferson, noting that Gordon-Reed "convincingly argues that Thomas Jefferson cohabited for more than 30 years with an African-American woman with whom he conceived seven children."[121] Public response to the book reveals that long before its publication, the Jefferson-Hemings relationship was increasingly accepted. When Gordon-Reed was on the popular political call-in show *Washington Journal* on C-SPAN, for example, she received no calls to challenge the basics of the story. Indeed, on a program that is known for argument, including racial controversy, this segment was noteworthy for its absence. Doubt about the Hemings story has been largely overcome, with many Americans having accepted the new Jefferson in place of the old. In his review of *The Hemingses of Monticello*, Morgan writes, "Sally Hemings bore Jefferson six children. That is established as fact, though it has been the subject of hot dispute."[122]

How did the story go from being almost entirely rejected to being generally accepted by mainstream audiences? In part, the increased attention to Jefferson's romances and the developing characterization of him as a passionate man laid the groundwork for several other factors. First, the relatively recent scholarship on the history of sexuality in early America established for the academy what had been an open secret—the historical prevalence of both interracial relations, and specifically master-servant and master-slave sexual relations.[123] Thus, although in Virginia sexual contact between master and slave would not have been as openly discussed as in the lower South and in the West Indies, it was nonetheless not an uncommon facet of that slave society. Sexual contact ran the gamut, ranging from brutal violent rape to tender displays of affection. An intimacy of some sort between slave-owner Jefferson and his slave Hemings therefore fits a classic feature of early American life. Second, the 1873 newspaper account attributed to Sally Hemings's son Madison began to be taken more seriously by scholars who felt it had been unreasonably dismissed as untrustworthy by generations of earlier scholars more interested in "protecting" Jefferson's image than in establishing the truth of the relationship. Finally, the DNA testing in 1998 that established that *a* Jefferson had fathered at least one of Hemings's children—and, almost more importantly, that a Carr (Jefferson's nephew) had not fathered at least one of the children—persuaded many to accept the romantic versions fully. The Carr brothers had long been held up as one of the most likely fathers by those who argued against the possibility of Jefferson as Hemings's lover.

Media reporting on DNA testing to determine the paternity of Hemings's own children helped almost as much as the testing itself, given that many media outlets, including the original account, exaggerated the findings. The story broke in *Nature* magazine with the headline "Jefferson Fathered Slave's

Last Child." It did not matter that the test did not conclusively prove this fact. In effect, the headline both captures and propels the image of Jefferson as positively linked to Hemings. Popular biographer Ellis writes that the DNA finding "constituted conclusive evidence that Jefferson fathered at least one of Sally's children." For Ellis, the DNA test "in conjunction with the preexistent circumstantial evidence" makes it "highly probable that a long-term sexual relationship existed between them." Despite the weakness of the evidence for either interpretation, Ellis declares, "Now we also know that he fathered several children by one of those slaves while claiming to regard racial amalgamation as a horrific prospect and a central reason why slavery itself could not be easily ended."[124] Some alleged that the timing of the DNA story and scholarly reports on it were motivated by Bill Clinton's impeachment trial. Radical conservatives went as far as to accuse historians of distorting history so as to provide cover for the president by providing a historical example of a similarly brilliant, if flawed, leader.[125] As biographer Joseph Ellis, who was one target of the criticism, notes, this was accomplished "presumably by demonstrating that illicit liaisons with younger women had a distinguished presidential pedigree."[126]

For popular audiences, the story has been made plausible and appealing over the course of several decades at the end of the twentieth century, because in film and in print, these tellings of the Jefferson-Hemings relationship emphasize love and compatibility—indeed, romance. This detail makes the story palatable. One need not lose an American hero to gain a sense of finally seeing the "truth" in early American history. Americans could have their cake and eat it, too. In 2000, in the wake of the media coverage of the DNA testing, *Sally Hemings* (based on the novel) aired on CBS. Shown on the night before Valentine's Day, the film emphasizes romance across the color line. The film's DVD cover touts "the true story of the controversial *romance* between President Thomas Jefferson and Sally Hemings" (italics mine). Academic historians, of course, generally take a more nuanced and historical approach to understanding their relationship. Professor Virginia Scharff's book on the women whom Jefferson loved uses both a historical approach and an expansive interpretation of the concept of love to include Hemings. Love in Jefferson's time, she explains, "did not imply equal power or responsibility between people." Employing an abstract definition of love, she also assert, "Love is never, ever simple. Love can be exploitative and terribly cruel," noting that Jefferson was thirty years older than Hemings and stating that "his conduct toward her was predatory and exploitative." The space that this approach opens is, of course, a dangerous one that flirts with favoring Jefferson by portraying his emotional orientation as one of "love" toward Hemings.[127]

Today, few Americans realize how relatively thin the documentary evidentiary base is for any stories about Jefferson's affective life with Hemings.[128] No letters survive between the two, she is rarely mentioned in his papers, and the most detailed source comes from her son, who published a very brief account in an Ohio newspaper in 1873—long after the dust had settled. That account tersely mentions that in Paris she became Jefferson's "concubine," yet the brevity of detail has not prevented popular depiction in film and print of how their relationship unfolded. Yet as one scholar reminds us, even on the time spent in Paris, "the evidence is meager. Apart from nine notations in Jefferson's *Memorandum Book* recording purchases of clothing, her servant's pay, and a fee for smallpox vaccination, Sally Hemings is completely absent from the Paris record."[129] Indeed, we do not even know for certain where she lived while in Paris or what she did. This absence of mention of Hemings is used as evidence that she meant a great deal to him. Historian Joyce Appleby astutely notes, "The record is silent about the form the Hemings-Jefferson relationship might have taken, leaving commentators a clean canvas upon which to paint a loving intimacy or a cruel exercise of white male power."[130]

In recent popular depictions, the absence of hard evidence of the nature of the relationship has been compensated for by claiming that documents have been destroyed as part of a cover-up. The 2004 film *Sally Hemings*, for example, imagines Jefferson's distraught daughter, Maria (Polly), burning letters exchanged between Hemings and Jefferson, saying, "You will be silenced." And the film includes scenes with love letters being written to Hemings. Moreover, throughout the film, Hemings gives voice-over narration as if taken from letters and diaries. The novel, which the film is based on, includes several passages that claim documentary evidence exists or existed to support them. The preface to *Sally Hemings* includes this suggestive passage from none other than John Adams: "Records are destroyed. Histories are annihilated, or interpolated, or prohibited." The author's note at the start of the book goes one step further: "There are documents included in this novel which are not only authentic, they are central to the story of Sally Hemings and Thomas Jefferson." Whatever those documents may be, they could not have been, as is revealed in the novel, a diary kept by Hemings while in Paris, nor could they have been the letters that in one scene Jefferson commands Hemings to burn. We have no evidence that any letters or diaries ever existed and were destroyed.[131]

Some depictions emphasize the imagined agency of Hemings. The film *Sally Hemings* imagines that *she* seduces Jefferson by taking the initiative to break sexual tension between the two by undressing herself in front of him when he comes to her room one evening with unclear intentions. The next morning, when he attempts to apologize for what has happened, she again takes the initiative, kissing Jefferson passionately on the mouth. As a biographer explains, seeing Jefferson and Hemings as two people "[who] fell in love" "helps make Jefferson once again human—to be the warm, sensitive, intelligent person he was capable of being—and it acknowledges Sally Hemings' humanity far more fully than any other theory ever advanced."[132]

Another aspect that has made the story more plausible for Americans has been the emphasis on Hemings's beauty. Following traditional standards of beauty and companionate compatibility, scholars have sought to portray the two as suitable for one another. Hitchens correctly notes that "all reports" "speak of her as strikingly attractive."[133] Thus, the film *Sally Hemings* presents numerous scenes that emphasize how Jefferson sees her as an equal of sorts. But referring to Hemings as Jefferson's virtual "wife" or describing the relationship between John Wayles and Elizabeth Hemings as "long-lasting and filled with affection" is misleading for contemporary readers. Even the best eighteenth-century union viewed men and women as unequal, let alone the union of master and slave.[134] Yet in the film, Hemings is portrayed as living in the house with him in Paris, the power and control of the Hemings family at Monticello is depicted, Jefferson sees her as "a good mind worth instructing," and in dialogues he tells her, "You look exactly like my wife" and "The resemblance is uncanny." Such accounts emphasize innocence, and the two fall helplessly in love. With spotty records of what Hemings actually looked like and no evidence that Jefferson spoke any of these words, filmmakers and writers have taken liberties to emphasize compatibility along lines that speak to contemporary Americans. In general, the love bond between Jefferson and Hemings has supplanted the very earliest nineteenth-century newspaper accounts that virtually charge Jefferson with the child rape of his adolescent slave.

Historian Clarence E. Walker's recent book *Mongrel Nation* captures the important connections between the establishment of Jefferson as sexual and the acceptance of the Hemings relationship. Here we see the unintended effect of decades of crafting a romantic persona for Jefferson: "Central to the denial of the Jefferson-Hemings affair has been an effort to deflect attention from the likelihood that Jefferson was highly sexed." But, as Walker points out, biographers have established that "he tried to seduce another man's wife," "had a brief affair with a married woman in Paris," and may have "'rogered' his wife to death," given that some suggest she died from giving birth to six children in ten years. As he sums it up, "To describe Jefferson as a man of restrained sexuality seems to suggest that once he was widowed at the age of forty-one, he lost his sex drive and became passionless."[135]

Jeffersonian Legacy Intact

Historian Gordon-Reed predicts that Jefferson's legacy might weather the storm "given the enormous head start that Jefferson has had in the public's affection" and that, if Jefferson's conduct in the relationship were to be portrayed in a relatively positive manner, Jefferson and Hemings could, however "false" the image might be, emerge as "multicultural heroes."[136]

For Jefferson image makers, portraying the intensity and perfection of personal connections to women allows them to emphasize one aspect of Jefferson's personal life that twentieth-century chroniclers would eventually see as decidedly lacking: Of all the Founders, Jefferson was perhaps the *least* romantically oriented. Chroniclers who wish to develop his private life can do so by writing about his feelings and interactions with a variety of women, including an early courtship with Burwell, and his relationship with his wife, Martha—but also relationships with married women, Walker and Cosway, and eventually even his slave, Hemings.

Although Jefferson's transition from chaste widower to Hemings's lover took generations and is not free from resistance, his legacy has largely emerged intact. The DNA evidence persuaded many turn-of-the-twenty-first-century Americans that Jefferson had fathered Hemings's children, but it did not change their overall view of Jefferson. Noted biographer Ellis, for example, simply issued a revised edition of his best-selling biography, inserting a mere handful of changes outlined in his preface: "I have made four significant changes: first, added the story of the Foster study to my account of Jefferson's contemporary relevance (Prologue, 24–26); second, revised my account of the scandal when it first emerged on the national scene in 1802 (chapter 4, 258–61); third, added a paragraph on the Jefferson-Hemings relationship at the very end of Jefferson's life (chapter 5, 347); fourth, inserted a discussion of the Foster study into my account of the history of the controversy (Appendix, 366–67)." Summing up the lack of change to his account, "I have changed my mind on the Sally Question, but not on Jefferson. He emerges in this revised edition as more of an American sphinx than ever before, more complicated and inscrutable, more comfortable in his contradictions."[137]

The comments of some authors indicate that not all, of course, embrace the new Jefferson without criticism. According to one, "On the issue of Sally Hemings, Jefferson turns out to have been a serious hypocrite."[138] Another account of slavery and Jefferson sums up problems with the late-twentieth-century Jeffersonian image: "I do *not* mean for it to join an unfortunate recent trend toward Jefferson-bashing. I disagree with those who would diminish his great achievement, the Declaration of Independence. Or those who call him more a friend to despotism than to freedom. Or those who would reduce his whole life to one affair with a slave."[139] Yet the loudest cries about Jefferson's being reduced to a hypocrite come from only those who deny the relationship and his paternity (two different subjects). Those who oppose the interpretations of the relationship set up the sharpest figuring of "guilt" and "innocence," of his name being "dragged through the mud" or "vindicated." Those who write about the relationship tend to describe it in the context of the late-eighteenth-century world of enslavement in America.

The notion that Jefferson and Hemings engaged in a loving relationship has given birth to a new Jefferson—Jefferson the trailblazer and victim of his own period, certainly not a hypocrite or sexual predator. Writer William Bottorff's biography, for example, emphasizes the love and "tender association" between Jefferson and Hemings and its endurance in a place and time hostile to it. He repeats this theme, explaining that Jefferson's daughter served as first lady during his presidency while parenthetically noting "(Sally Hemings, of course, could not serve publicly in any such capacities.)." And in another example, he writes, "The most judicious interpretation of known facts and testimony establishes the probability that Sally Hemings and Thomas Jefferson were deeply in love and that they had to love clandestinely because of just the kind of prejudice that Jefferson himself often expressed. . . . Theirs was a common law marriage, and they were loyal to one another."[140] Bottorff's depiction typifies the writings of many of those biographers today who accept Jefferson's paternity of Hemings's children. Many focus on the assertion that the relationship was decades long (built on the assumption of monogamy between Jefferson and Hemings) to argue that the participants must have felt "at least some mutual affection."[141] No writers are arguing for the possible scenario wherein the relationship could have included decades of emotional difficulty or even of exploitation or coercion. As Ellis explains it, Jefferson "had lived a biracial private life. In that sense he was our long-lost multicultural hero."[142]

Today's Jefferson as "multicultural hero" takes one exceptional model and replaces it with another. Unlike the concerns of some mid- and late-twentieth-century biographers, their worst fears have not been realized—the nation has not turned on Jefferson, abandoned revering his greatness, dismantled Monticello, or erased his visage from the nickel. Indeed, the statements end up sounding like fearmongering for those who want to consider the possibility of a Hemings-Jefferson relationship. Recall that many have denied the Hemings relationship out of fear of repercussions: "To give credence to the Sally Hemings story is, in effect, to question the authenticity of Jefferson's faith in freedom, the rights of man, and the innate controlling faculty of reason and the sense of right and wrong," writes one.[143]

This view of Jefferson as "multicultural hero"—which accepts his biological paternity of Hemings's children (with no evidence of the nature of the relationship) and leaps right over the question of abuse or exploitation—has found remarkable widespread acceptance both among popular and academic audiences. One recent academic work on Jefferson sums up how Jefferson's legacy has endured: "Only recently, however, in the wake of DNA evidence establishing the strong likelihood of his long-term sexual relationship with his slave Sally Hemings, have they begun to put private and public Jeffersons back together again, bringing the planter-statesman back down to earth and resituating him in his mountaintop home, in the midst of his white and black families."[144]

Jefferson, in public imagination, goes from chaste widower to someone far more complicated sexually, a man who spoke against miscegenation yet who loved and fathered children with his slave. Public memory of Jefferson has created for him sexual selves that have been easy to embrace and in which Americans could see themselves. For early-nineteenth-century Americans, the chaste widower who focused on his farming was appealing. For later generations, his love interests in Burwell, Walker, and Cosway would be fanned into small flames to compensate for his apparent lack of virile heterosexuality. As interest in the personal life of Jefferson has taken on new resonance, his sexual self has become the very site of debates about the promise of America—was it a dream founded on lies and hypocrisy, or was it something more real, more achievable, if only we could recognize its true roots and its complicated nature? The scandal or corruption was not just connected to Jefferson the man, some have argued. It bled into the political realm and affected the foundational ideas of the nation. Jefferson, of course, never publicly addressed the rumors of his sexual connection to Hemings.

Thinking of Jefferson as the father of his slave's children and as a Founder with both his black and white families on Monticello has been recently more easily accepted for many Americans. As the Walker and Cosway scandals appealed to mid-twentieth-century audiences, the Hemings story has for some enhanced rather than hurt Jefferson's position as a Founding Father. Indeed, it seems that Americans today can much more easily embrace a Founder with a secret sex life—and an active sex life—than one who espoused and lived racist beliefs and who remained sexless and chaste for most of his life. The Hemings story, reworked for decades, has emerged as one more romance. But in this version, Jefferson becomes not only more human and virile but also a champion of racial equality—a model American, yet again.

3

JOHN ADAMS

THE 2008 HBO MINISERIES *John Adams* won more Emmy, Screen Actors Guild, and Golden Globe Awards than any other miniseries in history.[1] The film—which is based on David McCullough's blockbuster Pulitzer Prize–winning biography and stars Paul Giamatti and Laura Linney—depicts the marriage of John (Figure 3.1) and Abigail Adams as one of the great romances of the era, referring to their attraction as being "like steel to a magnet."[2] Abigail is the utterly devoted wife during their long separations. One scene in particular catches the attention of many viewers: *TV Guide* calls it one of the top seven "ickiest sex scenes" ever and quips, "Their reunion after an eight-year separation quickly turned into a sloppy, Colonial-style gruntfest."[3] Bloggers also have had a field day with it. Clearly, as much as memorializers have tried to sexify Adams, most Americans hold fast to the image of him as a prickly prude.

Short, balding, and known as "his rotundity," the Adams captured in popular imagery does not personify modern physical ideals of manliness. Perhaps this is why he has not garnered the attention of those who promote

Figure 3.1 (*above*). Portrait of Adams. (*A Painting of President John Adams [1735–1826], 2nd President of the United States.* Asher B. Durand. Naval Historical Center, Washington, D.C.)

the physical image of many of the Founders. No commonly used coins or bills place his visage in American hands on a daily basis. No major monuments or memorials, impressive statues, or popular portraits come to mind when most Americans think of the man.

But the view of Adams as especially moralistic, once properly tempered by reassuring stories of romantic heterosexual orientation and healthy libido, serves well to connect Americans to the mythic moral purity of the Founding Fathers. Indeed, the moral presentation of the HBO movie is not lost on many reviewers. One praises the movie as a refreshing break from contemporary sex scandals. In an article entitled "No Sex Scandals Taint Power Couple of HBO's 'John Adams,'" the writer describes the miniseries as largely "the chronicle of a solid political marriage" and exclaims, "What a relief! Thank you, John and Abigail Adams and HBO, for providing TV viewers with a portrait of a real union that's not defined by cheating and remorse." Published on the heels of New York Governor Eliot Spitzer's resignation following a sex scandal involving prostitutes, the author makes explicit the comparison of the greatest generation to today's politicians by lamenting, "Adultery, it seems, is a requisite for political marriage these days."[4]

Adams memorialized stands in contrast to the other Founders in this book. Unlike Washington, Adams fathered a large family, including sons—one of whom would go on to become president of the United States himself. Unlike Benjamin Franklin and Gouverneur Morris, Adams did not fit well with European society—especially for moral reasons. He did not suffer from any whisper scandal, as did Thomas Jefferson. And, unlike Alexander Hamilton, he avoided any public sex scandals—and remained a steadfast model of monogamy despite years apart from his wife. Today, more than any other Founder, Adams's popular characterization is forever linked to his marriage. This popular image of Adams as part of a pairing is perhaps the reason no singular statue dominates the tourist landscape in Washington, D.C.—and perhaps the reason that the memorial now being proposed is likely to incorporate his wife, his famous son and his son's wife, and other notable Adams family members.[5]

When we look at how previous generations of Americans thought about Adams's intimate life, we see that we have long been content to accept Adams's own assertions that he was above moral reproach. But this characteristic monogamy and self-control is itself a sexualized manliness and fits well with traditional ideals. By the early twentieth century, stories about an early heartbreak emerged to emphasize his normative urges. And by the advent of women's history in the 1960s, a more explicit discussion of Adams's intimate life occurred. Historians interested in the life and experiences of

Abigail Adams began to write profusely on the correspondence carried on between the husband and wife during their long periods of separation. From this was born the image of John and Abigail as the "power couple" of the American Revolution and John as the husband and father ideal.[6]

Lifetime

Adams was born in 1735 to a Braintree, Massachusetts, farmer. He graduated from Harvard in 1755. After having briefly considered the ministry, he taught for a few years and soon decided to pursue law, becoming a lawyer in 1758 at the young age of twenty-three. Just shy of thirty years old, he married Abigail Smith. Together they had five children, three boys and two girls. Adams was a leader of the patriot movement in Massachusetts. He served as the Massachusetts delegate to the First and Second Continental Congresses. During the Revolution and for several years after, he served as a diplomat in Europe, eventually becoming the new nation's first vice president and second president. In one of U.S. history's greatest coincidences, Adams died on July 4, 1826—the fiftieth anniversary of the Declaration of Independence—only hours after Jefferson also had passed.[7]

Adams would be pleased with how Americans have cast his moral core. After all, if any Founder were proudly wagging his finger in disapproval at the men discussed in this book, it would be Adams. As an eighteenth-century Massachusetts denizen, Adams self-consciously performed the role of Puritan descendant. To paraphrase H. L. Mencken's famous stereotype, Puritanism was marked by the "haunting fear that someone somewhere might be having fun." Modern Americans roll their eyes at the Puritan prohibitions on theater and Christmas celebrations, the death penalty statutes for adultery, the compulsory church-attendance laws, and the religious fervor that gave rise to the Salem-witchcraft episode.

Americans have long embraced this view of the Puritans as sex-phobic, but historians of sexuality have shown it to be superficial. On the one hand, historians point to the stringent laws, brutal condemnation from the pulpit, and harsh punishments meted out for anyone engaging in sex outside marriage. Yet they remind us that this does not mean that Puritans were entirely opposed to sexual expression. Puritans and their descendants celebrated the sexual union of husband and wife. Sexual intimacy was seen as an expression of the household, a romantic, familiar, intimate, and loving bond that husband and wife shared in their hierarchical relationship.[8]

A fourth-generation resident of Massachusetts, Adams was a typical product of eighteenth-century New England culture. He was exposed to broader Atlantic influences, moral codes, and ways of structuring sexual lives and identities. He lived in a region with a high rate of premarital sex, an appetite for erotic English literature, and an exposure to people who traveled the Atlantic and knew firsthand of its more liberal sexual subcultures. Like many eighteenth-century New Englanders, he generally disapproved of sex outside marriage and fashioned his identity in opposition to nontraditional sexuality, including the appearance of excess and immodesty.

As a young man, Adams cultivated a personal self that took part in the emerging world of eighteenth-century sexuality with its move away from strict Puritan morality. Yet at the same time, he lauded himself for being a man who stood above that developing culture, and he modeled himself as wise, courageous, and moral.[9] This posturing would become his trademark. Perhaps most famously, he adopted the position of moral observer while a statesman in Europe.

Of course, Adams was not the only American who claimed to be surprised by European culture. John Jay, like Adams, was also disapproving of other Founders. Yet, like Adams, Jay was also able to couch his critiques in the socially acceptable witty banter of the day. He once wrote to Franklin, "There is no man of your age in Europe so much a favorite with the ladies."[10] Shortly after Morris suffered a debilitating accident, he wrote to him, "Mrs. Plater, after having much use of your legs, has occasioned your losing one of them."[11] Such double meanings were intended to be both witty and gently chastising—and they reveal a personal certainty not "shocked" by sexual liberties.

Adams was not quite as adept at this type of banter, although he was not above trying. On his second night in Paris, Adams found himself in a dinner-party conversation that would come to typify his assessment of European manners and morals. According to Adams's posthumously published autobiography, at dinner a married woman ("One of the most elegant Ladies at Table") asked playfully, "Mr. Adams, by your Name I conclude you are descended from the first Man and Woman, and probably in your family may be preserved the tradition which may resolve a difficulty which I could never explain. I never could understand how the first Couple found out the Art of lying together?" We can only surmise the look on Adams's face, but he claims to have "blushed." He writes, "To me, whose Acquaintance with Women had been confined to America, where the manners of the Ladies were universally characterised at that time by Modesty, Delicacy and Dignity, this question was surprizing and shocking." But despite what he calls shock, he demonstrated skill and sociability. With, as he put it, a facial expression of "Ironical Gravity," he replied, "Madame My Family resembles the first

Couple both in the name and in their frailties so much that I have no doubt
We are descended from that in Paradise. But the Subject was perfectly understood by Us, whether by tradition I could not tell: I rather thought it was by
Instinct, for there was a Physical quality in Us resembling the Power of Elec-
tricity or of the Magnet, by which when a Pair approached within a striking
distance they flew together like the Needle to the Pole or like two Objects in
electric Experiments." She responded to this answer with an emphasis on the
sexual pleasure of erotics: "Well I know not how it was, but this I know it is
a very happy Shock." Adams, however, writes that he had the savvy to bite
his tongue and refrain from adding that this pleasure would have come "in
a lawfull Way" (within marriage) for fear that she and everyone else would
think he was a man of "Pedantry and Bigottry." Adams boasted that he had
done his best to engage and yet stand above for all to see.[12]

Paris would present Adams with not only actions by Europeans that
were beyond his moral code but also behaviors by his fellow political leaders
of the new nation that he, like Jay, would critique. And using tact similar to
that of Jay, he playfully mentions Franklin's behavior in a letter to Abigail:
"My venerable Colleague enjoys a Priviledge here, that is much to be envyd.
Being seventy Years of Age, the Ladies not only allow him to embrace them
as often as he pleases, but they are perpetually embracing him.—I told him
Yesterday, I would write this to America."[13] Yet his criticisms could also be
deeply serious. Adams found Franklin to be quite ineffective, overly social,
and irksome in moral stature. Here the politics and the personal were both
woefully lacking and linked for Adams. Corresponding with a Mr. Mar-
bois the following year, he writes, "No, said Mr. M., Mr. F. adores only
great Nature, which has interested a great many People of both Sexes in
his favour.—Yes, said I, laughing, all the Atheists, Deists and Libertines, as
well as the Philosophers and Ladies are in his Train—another Voltaire and
Hume.—Yes said Mr. M., he is celebrated as the great Philosopher and the
great Legislator of America.—He is said I a great Philosopher, but as a Legislator of America he has done very little."[14] Adams also became well-known
for his moral criticism of his political enemy Hamilton. In January 1797,
he writes to Abigail from Philadelphia, "Hamilton I know to be a proud
Spirited, conceited, aspiring Mortal always pretending to Morality, with as
debauched Morals as old Franklin who is more his Model than any one I
know."[15] At one point, Adams famously referred to Hamilton as a "bastard
brat," drawing attention to his birth out of wedlock.[16]

Throughout his life, Adams would shake his head with disapproval and
then pat himself on the back for doing so. Fashioning his sexual identity as
the descendant of Puritans, biographers have largely portrayed him as he

saw himself—a moral Founder. As this chapter shows, this view of Adams couples well with the contemporary view of him as an ideal husband to Abigail, and it also dispels virtually any question of nonmonogamy during their long years apart.

Early Memory of Adams

His very earliest chroniclers echo his own view of himself as a model of moral manhood. Thus, in her 1805 history of the American Revolution, Mercy Otis Warren remarks, "Mr. Adams, in private life, supported an unimpeachable character."[17] This depiction continues unabated through the century. Although not a work of popular biography, in the 1850s Adams's grandson published a multivolume collection of his papers, including his unpublished autobiography, his diaries, and portions of a biography written by his son John Quincy in the 1830s.[18] For his biographers, Adams's own moral compass demonstrated itself at a young age. His grandson's publication includes many such passages. While a young man, he records in his diary his judgment of others. "Let others waste the bloom of Life," he writes, "at the Card or biliard Table, among rakes and fools, and when their minds are sufficiently fretted with losses, and inflamed by Wine, ramble through the Streets, assaulting innocent People, breaking Windows or debauching young Girls." Adams developed an identity that took no pleasure in such immoral pastimes—yet took pleasure in their absence. He boasts, "I envy not their exalted happiness."[19] As a young man, according to Adams, he wrestled with youthful urges and established a moral code that would guide his life. Adams pointed out that he was not without passions to control. He complains to his diary in 1759, "My Thoughts are roving from Girls to friends."[20] In his autobiography, he indicates his belief in the significance of sexuality by remarking, "Here it may be proper to recollect something which makes an Article of great importance in the Life of every Man." "I was of an amorous disposition and very early from ten or eleven Years of Age, was very fond of the Society of females," he writes. "I had my favorites among the young Women and spent many of my Evenings in their Company."[21] His diary entries and autobiography attest to his attempts to control his desires and stay focused on virtuous and productive tasks. Publication of his papers has helped biographers and popular memory of the man follow the image that he cultivated of himself, one that he describes as developing early in his life.

His son's publication includes Adams's barbs aimed at other Founders and European culture in general. Some of Adams's comments suggest a calculated distancing from Franklin and others who passed less judgment in the social world of Parisian diplomats. After hearing about two entangled adulterous couples, he comments, "When I afterwards learned both from Dr. Franklin and his Grandson, and from many other Persons, that this Woman was the Amie of Mr. Brillion and that Madam Brillion consoled herself by the Amitie of Mr. Le Vailliant, I was astonished that these People could live together in such apparent Friendship and indeed without cutting each others throats." The polyamorous relationship was apparently comfortable for them and known by Franklin and others. Yet Adams liked to see himself as unaware (despite being well-read and circulating among elite colonials and Europeans). "But I did not know the World," he writes. "I soon saw and heard so much of these Things in other Families and among allmost all the great People of the Kingdom that I found it was a thing of course. It was universally understood and Nobody lost any reputation by it." But Adams also argues that any outward acceptance was artificial, "a mere conformity to the fashion." And he counters the notion that participants were content. "Internally," he believes, "there was so far from being any real friendship or conjugal Affection that their minds and hearts were full of jealousy, Envy, revenge and rancour. In short that it was deadly poison to all the calm felicity of Life. There were none of the delightful Enjoyments of conscious Innocence and mutual Confidence." Although aware of nontraditional practices, Adams always has the last condemnatory word in a manner that positions himself as a moral authority. "It was," he declares, "mere brutal pleasure."[22]

So it was that the nineteenth century remembered Adams in the manner that he himself established. Much the way Warren writes at the start of the century, John T. Morse in 1884 writes that Adams was "like the better men of the day" in New England; unlike those who wrestled with "hard drinking" and "carnal sins" in the face of strict Puritan teachings, Adams succeeded at being "rigid in every point of morals."[23] Similarly, Mellen Chamberlain, a judge, librarian, and member of the Massachusetts Historical Society, memorializes the "provincial" Adams in the fashion that Adams had established in his lifetime. For Chamberlain, Adams had "established in his character, and exhibited by his life and action, the best influences of the Reformation."[24] Summing up the man, he echoes Warren, stating that his "life, public and private, was without blemish."[25]

As was not unusual in the period, little is said about the Adamses' marriage in nineteenth-century accounts. Adams's grandson's collection includes a typical early-nineteenth-century assessment of a Founder's marriage, in that it notes the date and the lineage of the families united by the marriage. According to his grandson, the match was "congenial to his character" in part because of the education of Abigail.[26] But the volumes published by his grandson leave out virtually all the letters he penned to Abigail during their courtship. Charles Francis Adams was evidently "unwilling to break entirely through the crust of Victorian propriety."[27] Mimicking their achievement of the nineteenth-century domestic ideal, in 1884 Morse tersely but positively notes that theirs was a "singularly happy union."

An Amorous Puritan Emerges

Many twentieth-century biographers continue to repeat Adams's own assertions about his disposition as written in his self-reflective, posthumously published autobiography. But increasingly they highlight passages published by his grandson that speak to the concerns of the "first sexual revolution" and that demonstrate he was a normal red-blooded American man, with appropriate levels of sexual interest in women.[28] Thus, a 1926 account by popular writer Meade Minnegerode repeats his description of himself as "'of an amorous disposition,' and 'fond of the society of females.'"[29] This assertion safely establishes him as normative and well-suited to the early-twentieth-century understanding of heterosexual urges and desires as natural and appropriate. In keeping with the morality of the day, the author also relies on Adams's own claims to moral virtue, noting that despite these carnal desires, his "youthful flames were all modest and virtuous girls, and always maintained their character through life."[30]

Virtually all early-twentieth-century accounts similarly repeat his own assertions about his moral uprightness and likewise underscore that he was of an "amorous" nature that he "controlled" until he was married to Abigail. Taking pains to highlight Adams's normative desires, in 1928 Samuel McCoy—a Pulitzer Prize–winning journalist and novelist who also published under the name Ellery Queen, Jr.—published his biography just a few years after Minnegerode's, rescuing from Adams's diary the passages that speak to his having remained a virgin. He also includes Adams's writings about sexual immoralities that he witnessed in his own New England community. Moreover, McCoy quotes a passage in which Adams writes that "*every* excess—of passion, prejudice, appetite; of love, fear, jealousy'" and others "'may in some sense be called a disease of the mind.'"[31] For McCoy, this attitude is "modern to the last degree" and "removes Adams from the ranks of those who have died with their century and makes him alive today." Using Adams's language again to characterize his morality, he concludes that Adams was without his wife for years while he was in France and England: "Constantly, nightly, during all these years of separation from her he meets the brilliant, beautiful, sophisticated women of the two capitals, Paris and London; but as he says sturdily, at the age of seventy-six, 'Among all the errors' . . . 'I cannot recollect a single insinuation against me of any amorous intrigue'" [as] . . . a "'bachelor or a married man.'"[32]

By mid-century, the centrality of youthful loves to the depiction of proper manhood had given rise to the new inclusion of an early love noted in his personal writings but often overlooked by earlier writers. In the final decades of the twentieth century, biographers routinely mention Adams's relationship with one Hannah Quincy. In 1969, one such account by journalist and biographer Alfred Steinberg notes that the girl fell in love with Adams, who did not share her interest in marriage, given that "he had no money, nor was he yet established in law."[33] But little else would change in the mid–twentieth century, especially with regard to the portrayal of Adams's sexuality. Writes one, "John had a particular fondness for girls and they, in turn, responded to him."[34] In 1979, biographers were still relying almost exclusively on Adams for their assessment of his sexual compass. Thus, writes one, he had an "early fondness for girls," underscoring his normativity in the absence of scandals.[35] And, as would become stock, a 1979 academic biography points out that while in Paris, Adams expressed an "uneasiness about their religion and morals."[36]

By the end of the twentieth century, Adams's old reputation as a moral man was serving him well but within a very new cultural context. In 1992, historian John Ferling again finds in Adams a man of extraordinary background but suitably ordinary qualities. Writing at the rise of multiculturalism, Adams, a Federalist, elite and stuffy, with a reputation for being priggish, was certainly one of those "dead white males" that so many complained were being pushed aside as the nation focused on the histories of "underrepresented groups." Yet, Ferling has no trouble reaching a broad audience for his Founder.

His characterization of Adams's morality is similar to that of previous generations and is yoked to Adams's body. In contrast to the virile physical portrayals touted for George Washington, Adams's desexualized physique reinforces his image as a man about whom there could be no sexual scandal. The image adorning the frontispiece of Ferling's book is one of Adams nearing fifty years old. And Adams, Ferling tells us, was a man who at thirty was "pudgy and jowly," a man who "looked soft and flabby." This particular body type could be easily associated with Adams the moral man. Readers are also reminded of his reputation for being "priggish" and very much unlike the charming Washington, Hamilton, Morris, or Franklin. Adams, Ferling points out, "had no idea how to conduct a conversation with a female." Turning Adams's critique of French morals into a positive attribute, Ferling writes that for many of his contemporaries, Adams was a man who failed as a diplomat because he could not "talk small talk or flirt with the ladies."[37]

It might strike some as odd that a person who begins as a nineteenth-century model of moral manhood could appeal to modern readers. Yet it is precisely this kind of man who may well serve as the antidote to an increasingly alarming number of contemporary politicians and public figures who seem sexually unhinged. The long line of political sex scandals that would most recently emerge at the turn of the new millennium includes Gary Hart's withdrawal from the 1988 presidential race when pictures surfaced of him and a girlfriend on his boat, the aptly named *Monkey Business*. Adams, readers are reminded, was a man with utter control over his sexual desires, which he had mastered at a young age. His one serious crush, on Quincy, had never blossomed. Ferling is quick to point out that he, indeed, felt all the appropriate and healthy attractions, "love" and desire for her "beauty" and "coquettish ways." Indeed, she "captivated Adams." But he was a young man of "constraint in sexual matters," and he was determined to develop his law practice. And then before he knew it, the story goes, she had become engaged to another man, breaking his very normative and healthy heart.[38]

The depiction works well for Adams's image in that it firmly establishes him as having all the appropriate desires of a young man. It depicts him in a way that is accessible to readers and sympathetic in his heartbreak but above moral reproach in the clear absence of any innuendo that the relationship was ever consummated. Adams remained for Ferling, as he had for many other chroniclers, a chaste man. Ferling even points out that although Adams might well have had plenty of opportunity for sexual dalliances with available women while in Europe, he remained faithful to Abigail. This behavior came naturally for him, although such "month after month of living alone would have tested the mettle of even the most disciplined man."[39]

As noted at the start of this chapter, in 2001, McCullough published his blockbuster Pulitzer Prize–winning biography, which went on to be developed into an HBO miniseries that won Emmys and numerous other accolades. McCullough, like so many before him, relies on Adams's declaration of being "amorous" and states about him that "the appeal of young women was exceedingly strong," that he was naturally "lively" and "amiable," and that he enjoyed "flirting" with girls. As for the connection to Quincy, McCullough describes it as fully engaging and claims that Adams was "devoting every possible hour to her" before the relationship abruptly fizzled after they were interrupted when he was about to "propose" to her.[40]

As biographers have long enjoyed pointing out, Paris provided Adams with much to shake his head over. Indeed, one biographer, borrowing from Warren's own observation, explains that Adams was an ineffective European diplomat because he wouldn't "flirt with the ladies."[41] In one letter to Abigail, he assesses European morals in his typical fashion: "Luxury, dissipation, and Effeminacy, are pretty nearly at the same degree of Excess here, and in every other Part of Europe."[42] Even after nearly ten years in Europe, he would comment in his diary while he was in London, "The Temples to Bacchus and Venus, are quite unnecessary as Mankind have no need of artificial Incitements, to such Amusements."[43] Typical of most biographers, his self-fashioning has been taken at face value. Popular writer Judith St. George, for example, explains, "John especially objected to Franklin's constant partying, his open flirtations with women."[44]

Charles Tansill in the 1960s does not include a chapter on Adams in his work about the Founding Fathers, presumably finding him too lacking for Tansill's method of focusing on sexuality to "humanize" his subjects. But in the new millennium, Adams's image was too starched and Puritanical for many modern audiences. Adams's early romance with Quincy was highlighted and framed as evidence of his capacity to love *and* of his view that such desires were in conflict with his drive and determination in political and legal affairs. In the new millennium, several authors would attempt to make more of Adams's romantic life than before, hoping to fan the embers of any stories they could pinpoint.

Historian John Patrick Diggins's 2003 biography, published as part of the *American Presidents* series edited by Arthur M. Schlesinger, Jr., portrays Adams as raging with heteronormative desires. Describing the "Wild and Giddy Days" of his youth, Diggins takes pains to wrench Adams from his Puritanical portrayals and highlight his "wit and charm" that he used with the "belles." Setting up a juxtaposition of public and private male selves, Diggins writes, "Long before he was a practicing attorney, Adams felt himself drawn to the female sex." Adams was "warned" of the dangers of premarital sex by his friends, but "even so, Adams spent hours 'gallanting the girls.'" Quincy, in this version of his youth, becomes but one of many unnamed loves he may have had. She "captivated" him as she did many young men (who, we are told, could not help "swarming around her like moths to a flame"). And she is not described as a massive failed relationship on his part but as someone who left him "lovesick." Although years passed before he would marry Abigail, the quick succession of the telling here makes it seem only a short while before he would do so.[45] Diggins reasserts the contrast between the youthful heteronormative and appealing Adams and his stuffy, offensively prudish Puritanical reputation to set the scene for Adams in Paris. As this chapter demonstrates, calling him the "Puritan Diplomat in Paris" shows how Adams's moral compass and above-reproach conduct set him apart from those colleagues of his who had love and romance on their minds while in Paris: Morris, Jefferson, and Franklin.[46]

In 2005, John Grant, like so many writers before him, lets Adams's passage about his youthful interest in sex and self-restraint stand for itself with no commentary afterward and only this setup: Calling the autobiography a "truth-telling" account, he observes that there is an "extraordinary passage in the early pages about sex." He also argues that Quincy "may have been" an early "distraction" for him but firmly establishes that Adams liked women and they liked him, even if he was a "hard and unsentimental judge of the opposite sex." Grant notes that Adams may actually have been tempted by sex in Paris rather than repulsed by it. He claims that "we have it on his own authority that John Adams was a hot-blooded youth, and his amorous fires were only partially banked in middle age, or so Abigail's letters suggest."[47]

In 2009, Fleming attempts to create love interests for Adams in the manner of the other great Founders. Calling him "an amorous Puritan," Fleming emphasizes Adams's personal writings in which he self-consciously chastises himself for having a wandering eye and wandering thoughts of amusements, including socializing with girls. While Adams's focus is on showing that he has mastered his carnal self, Fleming uses the passages to highlight that Adams did, indeed, have a carnal self, a side of Adams perhaps lost for many who celebrate him as without "blemish." For Fleming, the youthful Adams was, indeed, inherently sexual: "Growing up on a farm, he had no need for sex education." And Fleming observes that Adams had many "'favorites' throughout his Harvard years." Fleming links him specifically to Quincy, whom he describes as a "beautiful" young woman with whom Adams "found it extremely difficult to discuss love and marriage" (her favorite topics, according to Fleming) "without asking her to be his wife." Fleming asks Americans to imagine Adams and Quincy "almost certainly" "strolling" in "a lover's lane not far from her house."[48]

If we compare two moments from Adams's diary with Fleming's interpretations, we can begin to see how the relationship with Quincy developed from something left out of many earlier accounts to a love and loss of high order. Fleming describes a scene where Adams and Quincy were alone: "John leaned toward Hannah, breathing her delicate perfume, lost in the liquid depths of her tantalizing eyes. The words of love and commitment were on his lips," but they were interrupted by Hannah's cousin and her fiancé.

And the relationship sputtered and died, with Hannah becoming engaged to another young suitor the following month. The actual diary passage is much less romantic, including no references to perfume or "liquid depths." It reads:

> Accidents, as we call them, govern a great Part of the World, especially Marriages. Sewal and Esther broke in upon H. and me and interrupted a Conversation that would have terminated in a Courtship, which would in spight of the Dr. have terminated in a Marriage, which Marriage might have depressed me to absolute Poverty and obscurity, to the End of my Life. But the Accident seperated us, and gave room for Lincolns addresses, which have delivered me from very dangerous shackles, and left me at Liberty, if I will but mind my studies, of making a Character and a fortune.[49]

According to Fleming, the experience was "heartbreak" for Adams, and it pushed him to focus more intently on building his law practice.[50] Again, this interpretation is one that favors the heart and tends to make Adams more accessible to modern readers. The original passage on which Fleming bases his interpretation is one that describes a man whom many today would find more difficult to understand. It reads:

> Now let me collect my Thoughts, which have been long scattered, among Girls, father, Mother, Grandmother, Brothers, Matrimony, Husling, Chatt, Provisions, Cloathing, fewel, servants for a family, and apply them, with steady Resolution and an aspiring Spirit, to the Prosecution of my studies. Now Let me form the great Habits [illegible] of Thinking, Writing, Speaking. Let my whole Courtship be applyed to win the Applause and Admiration of Gridley, Prat, Otis, Thatcher &c. Let [illegible] Love and Vanity [illegible] be extinguished and the great [illegible] Passions of Ambition, love Patriotism, [illegible] break out and burn. Let little objects be neglected and forgot, and great ones engross, arouse and exalt my soul.[51]

The eighteenth-century man, complete with his considerations of marriage and career as distinct from love and romance, is one perhaps too alien for contemporary readers to embrace. Fleming, like many biographers before him, looks to sex and romance to give his readers an avenue to Adams that is familiar and also appealing.

Romeo for Juliet

Although biographers have long pointed to the bond of husband and wife, only with the advent of early women's history did the Adamses rise to the ranks of *the* couple of the Revolution.[52] It was not until the bicentennial that popular audiences had some access to the letters of a personal nature that John and Abigail exchanged. Their courtship letters are, indeed, quite playful, as we might expect given eighteenth-century conventions, and many of his letters contain expressions of romantic desire. "The Conclusion of your Letter makes my Heart throb, more than a Cannonade would," declares one.[53] Like most of the Founders, Adams maintains a certain romantic touch in his letters throughout their marriage.

The depiction of the couple as unusually matched, of course, presents an overly simplistic view of the "happy couple," one that is seized on by popular mythmakers who seek to portray the Founders in a positive light and as exceptional individuals both publicly and privately. His self-consciously fashioned identity as a morally upright sexual man ensures the assumption of monogamy during his long absence; the estrangement of husband and wife then becomes one of romantic longing rather than questionable pairing or an absence of love and desire. In an early-twentieth-century account, his courtship is romantic, described in an innocent way as "making love."[54] Despite the fact that Minnegerode's 1926 account is a mini-biography of Abigail herself, their marriage is described as being marked by long separations and Abigail's lively correspondence with others is obscured, making her seem wholly dependent on John. In her letters, she is said to have "poured out her heart to him" and to have told him "many tender, foolish things."[55]

The romantic gauze that later-twentieth-century writers wrap around John and Abigail is largely woven from the threads of what to biographers appears to be Abigail's endless pining. Her letters are often expressive, romantic, and loving.[56] In 1777, signing one such letter to John, she writes, "Good Night Friend of my Heart, companion of my youth—Husband and Lover—Angles watch thy Repose."[57] But he was throughout their marriage, as Abigail writes, her "long absent Husband."[58]

Abigail was sending sad, lonely letters to John as early as 1767. As time went on, letters came less and less frequently from John. "Dearest Friend," begins one letter from Abigail, "Five Weeks have past and not one line have I received."[59] We do know that as time went by, she became frustrated by and resigned to her separation from John. In some letters, she seems to be coaxing and cajoling him to behave better toward her. To this type of expression, he nearly always responds with a combination of reassurance and defensiveness: "In one or two of your Letters you remind me to think of you as I ought. Be assured there is not an Hour in the Day, in which I do not think of you as I ought, that is with every Sentiment of Tenderness, Esteem, and Admiration."[60]

Adams's absences at times seemed unwarranted. While the Second Continental Congress was in recess during August 1775, Adams headed to Massachusetts, but instead of going home he went straight to Watertown for the sessions of the General Court. During this period, John and Abigail visited on weekends—an eighteenth-century commuter couple. And after returning to Philadelphia, John did not write home for three weeks. During that time, Abigail's mother, John's brother, and his son all took ill. In John's response to the news from Abigail that her mother has died, he expresses heartfelt sympathy, a somewhat defensive explanation for not being there for her, and uncertainty about what to do—to stay or to return to his family: "You may easily conceive the State of Mind, in which I am at present.—Uncertain and apprehensive, at first I suddenly thought of setting off, immediately, for Braintree, and I have not yet determined otherwise. Yet the State of public Affairs is so critical, that I am half afraid to leave my Station, Altho my Presence here is of no great Consequence."[61] We can only wonder whether such words were comforting or distressing to Abigail. Her letters are full of references to events and moments that John has missed and should have been present for; perhaps her letters intend to tug on his heartstrings at the same time that they confirms her faith in him as the "tenderest of Husbands."[62] This was a marriage of almost constant separation—by John's decision.

John and Abigail's extended time apart generated a body of letters replete with both complaints and expressions of love. Their separations resulted in a marriage experienced largely in letters—a written record that has enabled generations of Americans to ponder their marriage and their private lives apart from each other. In 1779, John again engages Abigail's complaint: "You complain that I dont write often enough, and that when I do, my Letters are too short. If I were to tell you all the Tenderness of my Heart, I should do nothing but write to you. I beg of you not to be uneasy. I write you as often and as much as I ought. If I had an Heart at Ease and Leisure enough, I could write you, several sheets a day, of the Curiosities of this Country. But it is as much impossible for me to think of such subjects as to work Miracles."[63]

By the last third of the twentieth century, the image of Adams's intimate world would begin to truly come alive. As historian Edith B. Gelles points out, Abigail had a full life in John's absence, with intense emotional bonds with her children and sister.[64] And she carried on lively correspondence with many others. Gelles sketches out the changing portrayals of Abigail. In the nineteenth century, she was the idealized woman; in the twentieth century, she was a "romantic silhouette of a woman consecrated in dutiful service to her great husband," and she became a feminist figure in the later twentieth century; "Political Abigail" also came about at this time, which merged the protomodern feminist with the dutiful wife. "The Adams marriage has become legendary in American history," she writes. "Just the mention of 'Abigail and John' calls forth an image of an ideal marriage, one founded upon love, loyalty, friendship, and courage." They had an "ideal correspondence if not an ideal marriage." Given her "visibility," their marriage has come to represent "companionate marriage." As Gelles's work allows us to see, what is often overlooked in the depiction of Abigail as living a life of "constant loneliness" and pining is the very full life that she led in her own right—during his absences. She was not only running the family household, managing the finances, and raising the children but also corresponding with many other individuals, including Warren and one James Lovell. In a romantic, flirtatious manner, Lovell calls her "Lovely Portia." For Gelles, Lovell was an "emotional affair" and a "virtuous affair." Abigail relied chiefly on her sisters for emotional support and described her daughter as her "closest companion."[65]

In the last third of the twentieth century, popular memory of the American Revolution cast John and Abigail as not only the first "power couple" of the United States but also a romantic pairing of the highest order. Fulfilling the American dream of happy family and romantic pairing, in such tellings John is more than a patriot and Founding Father—he is the founder of the husband ideal. "John Adams was in love," according to one biographer. The author notes that "he had been in love before" and that "he was of so amorous a bent" that he would write in his autobiography that no one needed to worry that he had sired another family. But the marriage is a remarkable one, according to this author, in part because Abigail was "delightfully feminine, [John] robustly masculine."[66] Their "love did not wither during these absences but progressed to new heights," with each "continually declar[ing] unabated love between the partners, despite all hardship and separation."[67]

In 1979, Robert A. East describes theirs as "surely one of the most glorious marriages ever made." Calling them "ideally suited" and their union "a real love affair," this biographer notes that some have even claimed that "his marriage saved his sanity because he had been exhibiting paranoid (i.e., suspicious) behavior; but whether that was sexual in origin is anybody's guess." Their marriage, and Abigail's position in it, is readily romanticized in simple terms, downplaying the complexities of distance and time apart, of other significant bonds developed, of feelings of betrayal, and of opportunities for nonmonogamous expression that might have gone unrecorded. Portraying her as his perfect "helpmeet," East describes them both in remarkably easy terms—he "a farmer" and she a "dairymaid"—and notes that he "thought of himself primarily as a farmer, and of Abigail as a farmer's wife."[68]

The depiction of a chaste, moral man with no skeletons in his closet could serve as a healthy counterbalance to the sordid tales of Jefferson and others. But it could also veer too far off course, making Adams inaccessible to modern readers, save one detail: his supposedly well-documented marriage. By the 1990s, accounts begin to present two versions of the marriage. In 1992, for popular biographer Ferling, the match was, indeed, one of extraordinary love, as has been depicted in previous decades. Their happiness as newlyweds is warmly described, their letters are mined for expressions of deep sentiment, and their reunions after long absences are portrayed as electric. But Ferling is also quick to emphasize that Abigail's longings were not simply romantic and touching but also sources of deep dissatisfaction in the relationship. Indeed, in Ferling's account, Adams eventually becomes truly comfortable with "full intimacy" with his wife too late in the relationship, as Abigail has already "changed" from the years apart. This failing, Ferling points out, was part of a "transformation that is not uncommon among men in their later adult years," an explanatory phrase that would have connected Adams to readers in that very demographic.[69]

In recent years, the more "realistic" depiction of their marriage as troubled but strong continues to grow. Appealing to a culture of marriage advice that emphasizes the "hard work" of modern, more equitable partnerships, the Adamses emerge as a secondary type of ideal American marriage, the one of "real" life. In 2002, journalist Richard Brookhiser also tempers the view of Abigail and John as in love. "Theirs was a marriage of true minds— smart, clever, censorious, and passionate," he concedes. But Brookhiser does not romanticize their time apart, noting that "Abigail found herself less and less remembered."[70] In a clear break from a romantic view of their marriage, another author notes the separation and difficulties of the marriage and does not frame it as picture perfect. At one point, he suggests that if John had not been absent, they would have "stopped talking to each other"—"the only thing worse than the letters she didn't get were the few that reached her." Moreover, he notes that the "flirtatious and affectionate correspondence" between Abigail and Lovell met her "emotional needs" in a way that John could not due to his absence and his inability to write in such a manner.[71]

But despite the efforts of some recent biographers to depict their prolonged and painful separations more realistically, for the most part the romanticized characterization remains cemented in public memory. Whatever their difficulties, the view of John and Abigail as not simply romantic but *uniquely* romantic has captured the imagination of biographers and the American public. This presumption plays on the contemporary view of early American sexuality as devoid of passion and thus marriages as stuffy and Puritanical.

Abigail's pining itself is romanticized in popular depictions of the couple. Indeed, the statues erected in 2001 in Adams's birth place, Quincy, Massachusetts, place John across the street from Abigail and their son, with Abigail looking lovingly across the street at him.

The discussion of the rockiness of their marriage, therefore, has done little to tarnish Adams's reputation as a moral man (virtually no writers speculate that either may have had an affair) and has had no effect on the romance industry that has sprung up around them. In recent years, the relationship of John and Abigail has been cast as one of the "great love stories" of the American Revolution, inspiring popular historians to refer to them as the "Romeo and Juliet of the American Revolution."[72] Such titles as 2001's *John and Abigail Adams: An American Love Story* highlight the relationship and imply that it was somehow unusual. In 2003, Diggins's biography depicts the couple as extraordinary. Indeed, he argues, "The forty-five-year marriage between John and Abigail Adams constitutes one of the great romances in the history of the American presidency." Calling it a "rapture of fused souls," his book describes their marriage as one that was able to weather the long absences, in part because of their true love for one another (illustrated by passages from letters that express fondness rather than bitterness at absence). This interpretation is enhanced by Abigail's dedication and the fact that she "accepted the conventional code of female behavior," which led her to be devoted to managing home and farm. Her letters, it assures readers, are "whimsical rather than whining."[73]

The extraordinarily large number of their letters that survives today—in contrast to the lost or destroyed correspondence of many famous early American couples—has prompted historian Page Smith to call it "one of the greatest epistolary dialogues between husband and wife in all history."[74] In many ways the surviving database is more unusual than the relationship that it captures. When viewed from a historian's perspective, "the historical record of their family life is at best sketchy," yet most Americans use the letters exchanged during their separations to describe their relationship when together. Indeed, Americans "imagine" the couple "walking hand in hand" with the "children skipping alongside them," at one "blissful reunion."[75] Casting their relationship as a great love, the interactive website for the popular 2005 series *American Experience* presents five letters to attest to this love.[76] These include, rather unremarkably, (1) a courtship letter in which John asks for kisses, (2) a letter from Abigail in which she attests to missing him greatly in his absence,[77] (3) a letter from John to Abigail during her pregnancy,[78] (4) a letter from Abigail expressing her loneliness,[79] and (5) a letter from John asking Abigail to come to New York as soon as possible.[80] Exaggeration is typical of popular interpretations of their relationship, but the substance of their letters is not very different from that of correspondences between other eighteenth-century couples, whether courting or long married. We know, for instance, that such letters were exchanged between Hamilton and his wife as well as between other Founders and their lovers and wives. Romantic letters about each other portray the members of these couples as in love and romantic—similar to the Adamses.[81]

The depiction of a "singularly happy union" is noted as early as 1884 and is in full swing today. A recent review of the 2007 edition of John and Abigail letters, *My Dearest Friend*, captures this romantic emphasis. In a collection of letters notable for including not only their courtship and war years but also his presidency and retirement, the reviewer nonetheless chooses to focus the beginning of the review on what has become familiar to many, the romantic bond of husband and wife: "He was her 'Lysander,' after the Spartan hero," the review begins. "She was his 'Diana,' after the Roman goddess of the moon. She called him 'My Dearest Friend.' He called her 'Miss Adorable' and his 'Heroine,' who sustained "with so much Fortitude, the Shocks and Terrors of the Times." "They were" the reviewer writes, "uncommonly well-matched partners who shared a passionate dedication to the Revolutionary cause, as well as a love of books and history, a playful sense of humor, a voluble literary gift and deep and abiding affection for each other." The blog promoting the book rhetorically asks, "*The* Romance of the 18th Century?" (italics mine).[82]

Currently in stage plays and popular biographies and websites, the depiction of John and Abigail as the "Romeo and Juliet" of the American Revolution endures.[83] For Adams, this portrayal has meant being heralded as the uniquely ideal husband—half of a rare and extraordinary couple. Indeed, they have been called "America's greatest love story."[84] Best-selling, Pulitzer Prize–winning writer Joseph Ellis declares them the "premiere husband-and-wife team in all American history." This was a couple who, while Adams was in Europe, "learned to love each other at an even deeper level than before and locked that love in place, and nothing they experienced for the rest of their lives ever threatened their mutual trust."[85]

Adams's self-congratulating prudery was part of his masculine identity as much as Washington's virile masculinity. This reminds us of the multiple models of sexual masculinity in eighteenth-century America and the variety of ways that sex could inform manliness in the Founding era. Tracing the stories that Americans have told and retold about Adams—stories that emphasize his sexual morality, his romantic marriage, and his early heartbreak—lays bare a long history of cultural importance, with significant bearing on assessments of character and personhood that Americans have attached to the sexual and romantic desires and behaviors of the Founders.

4

BENJAMIN FRANKLIN

ENJAMIN FRANKLIN (Figure 4.1) is the Founder who has come to be most associated with Americanness. He has been the subject of biographies bearing such titles as *Benjamin Franklin: An American Life* and *The First American: The Life and Times of Benjamin Franklin*. Even scholars wrestling with the constructedness of this image must contend with the notion that he is viewed as *genuinely* American and has been for more than a century. Thus, historian Gordon S. Wood, who argues that Franklin was in many ways our most European Founding Father, entitled his biography *The Americanization of Benjamin Franklin*.[1] Franklin, one recent author argues, had great "influence on the American character," including "virtues and traits that he, more than anyone, helped to imprint onto our national fabric."[2]

The notion of Franklin as not just American but a *modern* American is fueled in part by the embrace of his allegedly liberal approach to sexuality. In the words of one of his recent biographers, journalist and writer Walter Isaacson, "Benjamin Franklin is the founding father who winks at us. . . . [T]hat ambitious urban entrepreneur, seems made of flesh rather than of

Figure 4.1 (*above*). Portrait of Franklin. (*Portrait of Benjamin Franklin.* Engraving by H. B. Hall, 1868. Courtesy of the Library of Congress, Washington, D.C., LC-USZ62-25564.)

marble, addressable by nickname, and he turns to us from history's stage with eyes that twinkle from behind those newfangled spectacles. He speaks to us, through his letters and hoaxes and autobiography, not with orotund rhetoric but with a chattiness and clever irony that is very contemporary, sometimes unnervingly so. We see his reflection in our own time."³ Today's depiction of him as essentially one of *us*, a modern, not one of *them*, a colonial, draws partly on how he approached his most intimate relationships.

Even though Thomas Fleming describes him as a man with an "ungovernable sex drive" and as a "septuagenarian" "with sexual appetites of gargantuan proportions," today Franklin is virtually never the womanizer, rake, seducer, or sexual harasser.⁴ Instead, public memory recalls him as a harmless, elderly, "ladies' man," "flirtatious," and humorous. There is no one answer as to why his sexuality appears benign in contemporary public memory. Some aspects of his behavior speak in his favor. He did not abandon the son he fathered before his marriage but instead took him in and raised him. Biographies universally characterize his marriage as monogamous, and he never had a reputation for adultery à la Alexander Hamilton. His reputation for being a ladies' man emerged largely from Parisian salon culture and not from the nineteenth-century fears of urban seduction and abandonment of young women. Biographers routinely emphasize that women fell for him, conveying the sense of him as charming rather than predatory. Finally, it matters most that Franklin was the old man of the Revolution, in his seventies when the other Founders were in their twenties and thirties. In his most commonly circulated images, he is frozen in time at a point in his life past his prime—balding, overweight, older, his sexuality nonthreatening and endearing. He is more like Santa Claus than a seducer.

There is still great public interest in his intimate life. As biographer Paul Zall puts it, "If Washington was the father of his countrymen, Franklin was their foxy grandpa."⁵ It has become something of a national inside joke, an open secret enjoyed. Franklin historian Claude-Anne Lopez notes that as she gave lectures across the country, she was "asked repeatedly how many affairs Franklin had" and "how many illegitimate children."⁶ Similarly, the first executive director for the Benjamin Franklin National Memorial in Philadelphia, at the turn of the twenty-first century, notes that the "most commonly asked question by letter or phone and in conversations with thousands of people . . . had something to do with Franklin and women. Have you ever figured out who was the mother of Franklin's illegitimate son, William? How many illegitimate children did he have? How could he have sex with all of those women in France when he was already seventy years old at the time he arrived there?"⁷

As this chapter shows, Franklin's general eighteenth-century openness about the body and sexuality for centuries has divided many Americans, making them either uncomfortable with his views or thrilled by his apparent modernity. For some, Franklin's sexually explicit writings have served to bolster the image of Franklin as modern, forward-thinking, and uniquely American. Yet for others, the ambiguity of his personal writings, the depiction of him as aged and not youthful, and the nature of his transgressions have allowed for a willful disengagement with the sordid specifics of his personal life.

In His Lifetime

Franklin is the best-known Founder never to have served as president. He was born in 1706 in Boston and died in Philadelphia in 1790. He began his career as a writer and publisher, and in his own lifetime, he became oft-quoted for his aphorisms, which still populate the lexicon today. But he eventually garnered even greater fame as an inventor and American statesman. As Americans for generations have learned, among his most famous inventions are the lightening rod, bifocals, and the Franklin stove. During the American Revolution, as a diplomat, he secured the vitally important support of the French, which ultimately enabled American victory in the War for Independence.

It has never been a secret that Franklin transgressed norms of masculine sexuality in a host of ways, including fathering a child out of wedlock, writing ribald prose, and, according to many, in his widowhood having sexual relationships with women. And as we have seen in previous chapters, such details of intimate life have long figured in the public assessment of political figures. His public demonstration of his ease with amorousness made him the topic of talk in his lifetime and controversial in memory.

Franklin contributed to the genre of ribald essays that proliferated in early American print culture. Franklin's essay "Advice on the Choice of a Mistress," for example, published in Philadelphia in 1745, typifies his titillating oeuvre. Written as an epistle to a friend, the essay on the surface argues that young men should marry. But if they do not, he quips, they should choose old women over young women as lovers. In typical Franklin fashion, he lists eight points explaining why. Beyond the first two points, which extol older women as more "knowledgeable" and more "amiable" than younger women, his advice becomes racier. Points three and four note that older women risk no "hazard of children" and are better at keeping an affair secret, thereby protecting a man's reputation. Point five playfully anticipates the reader's association of youth with sexual pleasure, asserting provocatively that "regarding only what is below the girdle, it is impossible of two women to know an old from a young one." Moreover, "as in the dark all cats are gray, the pleasure of corporal enjoyment with an old woman is at least equal, and frequently superior, every knack being by practice capable of improvement." The sixth point notes that one risked the "ruin" of a "virgin" with young women. Number seven, the "compunction is less." Number eight, the punch line, as it were, states that old women make preferable lovers because "they are so grateful!" "Choice of a Mistress" and similar writings exhibit Franklin's interest as a printer in capitalizing on the public's appetite for sexually charged material. Franklin's early writing, "Speech of Polly Baker," a satire written in the voice of a young woman on trial for having her fifth child out of wedlock, was written earlier but published in American newspapers in 1747; it too has been used to demonstrate his humor and his open sexuality. Other essays, such as "Hooped Petticoats and the Folly of Fashion," glibly cover topics that would later distress Victorians more than they did Franklin's colonial readership.[8]

Unlike Hamilton, who publicly confessed to his adultery, Franklin's public declarations do not necessarily reflect on his comportment, nor do they always carry an explicitly immoral message by standards of the day. As satire, their multiple meanings and interpretations leave his legacy open to a variety of viewpoints regarding sexual morality. Indeed, most of his writing in this vein, although it significantly gives voice to radical sexual erotics, more often than not also makes the point of monogamy, marriage, and moderation so typical of the dominant norms of the day. Thus, some Americans could read the "Speech of Polly Baker," for example, as a critique of Puritanical laws and a celebration of extramarital sexual expression, but others could see it as poking fun at such immoralities.

His most famous writings reveal that eighteenth-century readers embraced Franklin in part because at the surface (and perhaps at the core as well), his message emphasizes mainstream early American sexual cultures— marriage, monogamy, and moderation. In his *Autobiography*, for example, Franklin notes that not marrying his lifetime companion, Deborah Read, was one of his life's "great errata." When we consider Franklin's writings in conjunction with his life collectively, they suggest a much more normative sexuality than they seem to suggest individually. Modern readers would be wrong to assume that they and Franklin alone can recognize the more radical, sexual meaning of his writing. Early Americans would also have simultaneously appreciated the humor and frankness while embracing marriage. Franklin published numerous tracts that demonize the bachelor and draw attention to the deviant sexuality of the single life. Franklin singles out bachelors in not only his writings but also his will. Regarding funds that he leaves to the city of Boston, he specifically denies financial benefit for them.

As the writer of such pieces and a public figure, Franklin could not escape the scrutiny of his sexual conduct. His political opponents first used allegations of sexual transgressions in an attempt to discredit him in local contests. Historian Wood describes the scandals that were part of the Pennsylvania elections in October 1764: "Franklin was accused of a host of sins," including "lechery" and "abandoning the mother of his bastard son."[9] In the 1764 election for Pennsylvania Assembly, Franklin's personal integrity was skewered in the press. Pamphlets charge him with, among other things, fathering his son William by a "kitchen wench." Another exclaims, "Franklin, though plagued with fumbling age, Needs nothing to excite him, But is too ready to engage, When younger arms invite him."[10]

Even after that election, given Franklin's fame, the stories continued in America and abroad. In the 1770s, London newspapers carried scurrilous stories about Franklin, most speculating on the identity of his son's mother. The June 1, 1779, *London Morning Post*, for example, alleges that William's mother was an "oyster wench" and accuses Franklin of abandoning her to "die of disease and hunger in the streets."[11] At the height of the Revolution, Franklin's sexual reputation not only could impugn his manhood but could also be enlisted to denigrate American national identity.

At this point in his life, Franklin was a well-known diplomat in Paris, having sailed there at the age of seventy. He settled outside Paris in the suburb of Passy, where he surrounded himself with "fellow commissioners, deputies, spies, intellectuals, courtiers, and flirtatious female admirers."[12] Franklin's landlord was Jacques-Donatien Leray de Chaumont, a wealthy merchant who was sympathetic to the American cause. Franklin's presence in Paris salon culture became legendary—or infamous. Franklin liked to play the role of norm-breaker. He shocked his compatriots and enjoyed positioning himself in contrast to their supposed narrow-mindedness. One such notable example is Franklin's association with the Chevalier D'Eon, a controversial figure in late-eighteenth-century England and France who confounded a fascinated public that debated whether D'Eon were a man or a woman.[13] A French diplomat, D'Eon had lived first as a man but later lived as a woman.

Most often Franklin's conduct with salon women captured the imagination of his friends and critics. Franklin's own colleagues comment on his conduct in France, some ambiguously. John Jay writes to Franklin in 1780, "I believe there is no man of your age in Europe so much a favourite with the ladies."[14] Less ambiguously, as we have seen, neither John nor Abigail Adams could find positive things to say about Franklin and his interactions with women in Paris. Abigail sharply criticized the women whom he associated with for being, as one scholar explains, too full of "warmth and naturalness."[15]

Early Memory of a Controversial Founder

Schoolbooks in the nineteenth century created a hero from Franklin but only by narrowly focusing on his economic life. "Next to Washington," argues scholar Ruth Miller Elson, "the greatest individual depicted" in schoolbooks was Franklin. The two "appear in these books more than anyone else." Elson argues that his fame was not for his connection to the European world or his "cosmopolitanism" but rather for serving as the model for the "self-made man."[16] Biographical stories that focus on the self-made man were enormously popular in the middle decades of the nineteenth century. Franklin's *Autobiography*, first published in English in 1793, was a foundational text for this genre, capturing his rise from humble beginnings to international fame and extraordinary wealth.[17] If told in the right manner, his life story, with its message of the financial rewards for developing the self, perfectly illustrates the American Dream.

Franklin's *Autobiography* famously includes a passage in which he describes taking a wheelbarrow through the streets to deliver his paper to his publishing house. Franklin did this work himself, though he could afford to hire someone to handle the manual labor. As he explains to the reader of his account, "In order to secure my Credit and Character as a Tradesman, I took care not only to be in *Reality* Industrious and frugal, but to avoid all *Appearances* of the Contrary . . . to show that I was not above my Business, I sometimes brought home the Paper I purchas'd at the Stores, thro' the Streets on a Wheelbarrow."[18] Although the *Autobiography* has been used to argue that Franklin created his own image for his readers (and the public), all of his writings collectively produce the Franklin who was once rejected and now is adored. Even his seemingly private letters, which appear to shed light on a personal hidden-from-the-public aspect of his life, should be viewed as public and part of his self-promoted Franklin image. We know of his affairs because he wanted us to know. His sexuality was part of his identity and part of his story of success that he wanted to share. Indeed, all the Founders self-styled their sexual selves for us with their keen sense of history, some to a greater degree than others.

Franklin's death in 1790 did not bring about an apotheosis of reputation, as was the case for other Founders. It is hard for us to imagine today—given contemporary adulation for Franklin—but his memory generated some ambivalence. In his own lifetime, Franklin was adored in Europe, but Americans were less enthused, despite his fame and respect. When he died, for example, the U.S. Senate would not endorse the House's resolution in honor of Franklin.[19] For some, the scandals that swirled around Franklin in his own lifetime became justification for characterizing him as a man of relaxed morals and thus worthy of censure by Victorian Americans.[20]

In his *Autobiography*, Franklin first details (albeit tersely) aspects of his life that for many Victorians would be troubling. First published in France in 1791, it was then published in England and America beginning in the early nineteenth century and continues to be widely republished and read to this day.

Describing his life from birth through middle age, the account includes several single-sentence declarations regarding personal relationships. Nearly every aspect of his life that gives his earliest biographers pause comes from his own hand. Franklin portrays himself as a man who feels little embarrassment about what some would find to be immoral. For example, Franklin explains that as a young man, he found himself wanting to leave the troubled apprenticeship he held under his brother. He eventually ran away to Boston, lying to secure a place on the ship. Franklin reveals the false story, at once confessing and engaging in a type of boasting. It is difficult to imagine George Washington, Thomas Jefferson, or Adams allowing a friend to convince a ship's captain that he had "gotten a 'naughty girl' pregnant and had, therefore, to slip away."[21] In his *Autobiography*, Franklin does not hide the fact that he and his wife, Deborah, were unable to legally marry, although, as we have seen, at least as early as the 1764 Pennsylvania election, it was an open secret that his son William was born out of wedlock.

Immediately after his death, a 1790 London publication entitled *Memoirs of the Late Dr. Franklin* includes the following introduction and discussion of "infidelities," especially those that took place when he lived in Paris as an American diplomat: "In private life this philosopher was not exempted from the little imperfections and weaknesses of human nature: irregular in his addresses to the Cyprian goddess, the legal partner of his bed complained of infidelities. It is well known, he had mistresses plenty; and there are several living testimonies of his licentious amours."[22] The account circulated at a time when there was serious concern about the unfolding of the French Revolution and a developing anti-French ethos.[23] The association of immorality with Parisian culture then would bolster that sentiment and could equally target Franklin's own character. In 1791, one of the nation's first magazines, *American Museum*, published in Philadelphia, Franklin's hometown, includes a jocular tale about Franklin and his relationships with French women, pokes fun at his age, and raises the specter of sexual intimacy outside wedlock.

Through the nineteenth century, Franklin's reputation was, therefore, not without controversy, as his personal life placed him at odds with nineteenth-century moral teachings.[24] At the end of the nineteenth century, when Massachusetts Senator George F. Hoar was given a list of names for the National Hall of Fame, he crossed out Franklin's name, explaining, "Dr. Franklin's conduct of life was that of a man on a low plane. He was without idealism, without lofty principle, and one side of his character gross and immoral. . . . [His letter] on the question of keeping a mistress, which, making allowance for the manners of the time, and all allowance for the fact that he might have been partly in jest, is an abominable and wicked letter; and all his relation to women, and to the family life were of that character."[25] As Franklin scholar Larry Tise argues, "Franklin[,] for his deeds in life and for the despicable words . . . [that] emanated from his pen, was a morally condemned man."[26]

Some criticized Franklin specifically for being a womanizer. In 1869 and through the 1870s, the famed suffragist and women's rights activist Elizabeth Cady Stanton gave speeches that included sharp derision toward Franklin, especially as a reaction to any developing adoration of him as an icon of American manhood, because she saw in Franklin's story a hero at "the expense of women's marital freedom." In her speech "Home Life," she mentions that Franklin abandoned his wife in Philadelphia, had illegitimate children, disowned one of his sons, and had questionable morals in general. "The less said of Franklin's private character," she says, "the better."[27]

Recognizing the animosity directed at Franklin's sexual morality, many biographers take a tack that Franklin does not: They attempt to sanitize his life. Of Franklin's essays and aphorisms that were deemed unsuitable for Victorian audiences, early biographers often omit the more salacious ones in favor of others that espouse nineteenth-century middle-class virtues.

The essay "Choice of a Mistress," which escaped censorship in the colonial publishing world, took friendly fire in nineteenth-century America. William Temple Franklin inherited his famous grandfather's papers, and in 1817–1818 he published *Memoirs of the Life and Writings of Benjamin Franklin*. The essay "Choice of a Mistress," as he explains, "cannot be published under the rules of modern taste, and, in fact, Franklin himself speaks of it as having 'too much *grossierete*' to be borne by polite letters. I shall, however, give as much of the letter on the choice of a mistress as is proper to publish": He cuts out the fifth, sixth, and eighth reasons entirely.[28] Even at the end of the century, the intact piece was still being left out of accounts. According to Franklin scholar Tise, Secretary of State Thomas F. Bayard, who eventually archived the essay, would not allow it to be included in any publications between 1885–1889 "because of what he considered its indecency."[29]

Some of these accounts, then, render Franklin a model American man, according to the period's prevailing views. Parson Weems, for example, believes that Franklin's writings are sufficiently virtuous to serve the purposes of his early-nineteenth-century morality. In his early biography of Franklin, Weems includes some of Franklin's writing about sex and marriage, such as "On Early Marriages." "Young bachelors," writes Weems, "would do well to read it once a month."[30]

But by the end of the century, as sex became increasingly seen as a marker of liberal character in contrast to Victorian hypocrisies, biographers would more often highlight the aspects of his *Autobiography* that previous writers would avoid. In 1897, Benjamin Morse published *Benjamin Franklin*, which takes its cues from his *Autobiography* and outlines the marriage to Deborah Read, stating that Franklin "hardly knew what he was wedding, a maid, a widow, or another man's wife."[31]

Neither Franklin nor his son ever revealed the identity of the woman who conceived William, and it has remained a centuries-long mystery. One late-nineteenth-century author quips, "An early contribution of his own to the domestic *ménage* was his illegitimate son, William, born soon after his wedding, of a mother of whom no record or tradition remains. It was an unconventional wedding gift to bring home to a bride."[32] In 1887, one biographer writes that Franklin became "the father of an illegitimate son. The name of the mother most happily is not known; but as the law of bastardy was then rigidly enforced against the woman and not against the man, she was, in all likelihood, one of that throng who received their lashes in the marketplace and filled the records of council with prayers for the remission of fines."[33]

In the late nineteenth century, biographers also reference the autobiography entry where Franklin mentions making sexual advances toward the girlfriend of his friend Ralph. "Worst of all," writes John Stevens Cabot Abbott, "we regret to say that he commenced treating her with such familiarity, that she, still faithful to Ralph, repulsed him indignantly." Abbott in a footnote also includes the exact passage and wording from Franklin and notes how Franklin felt about this: "Franklin does not conceal these *foibles*, as he regarded them, these *sins* as Christianity pronounces them. He declares this simply to have been another of the great errors of his youth."[34] In a chapter entitled "Mental and Moral Conflicts," Abbott also draws on Franklin's own words to describe his "intrigues with low women." Biographers would have had an easier time glossing over this detail if Franklin had not written of it: "With his remarkable honesty of mind, in strains which we are constrained, though with regret to record, he writes." Abbott also references passages from Parton's biography, quoting him as referring to "his illegitimate son William Franklin, who became Governor of New Jersey. If laws were as easily executed as enacted, Benjamin Franklin would have received, upon this occasion, twenty-one lashings at the public whipping-post of Philadelphia."[35]

Abbott also notes the complications surrounding the marital status of Franklin's wife, Read: "And at length he proposed that, regardless of all the risks, they should be married. It seems that he had announced to her very distinctly that he had a living child, and very honorably he had decided that that child of dishonor was to be taken home and trained as his own." And he continues, unromantically, "These were sad nuptials. The world-weary wife knew not but that she had another husband still living, and a stigma, indelible, rested upon Franklin." But he also refers to a marriage that never took place: "The marriage took place on the first of September, 1730. . . . The child was taken home and reared with all possible tenderness and care."[36] Not all biographers were as explicit in their references to Franklin's own admissions. Frank Strong in 1898 includes no mention of the famous "intrigues with low women" passage, instead only euphemistically noting that he had led a somewhat "dissipated" life while in London.[37] Strong also mentions the date of his marriage and says little to nothing about women in France.

Some nineteenth-century accounts also repeat from Franklin's account the lie that secured his passage on a boat out of Boston. Thus, one account reads, "Collins made an agreement for him with the captain of a sloop, bound for New York, to take him on board, saying that he was a young man of his acquaintance who had got into trouble with a girl of bad reputation, and who her parents insisted should marry her; in consequence of which, he could neither make his appearance in public, nor come down to his vessel except privately."[38]

Franklin as a Sexual Modern

In part because he championed what would become viewed as the American Dream, Franklin is also the Founding Father who enjoys the longest association with American modernity. Historian Frederick Jackson Turner in 1887 calls him the "first great American."[39] One year later, novelist William Dean

Howells refers to him as "the most modern, the most American, of his con-temporaries."[40] In the early twentieth century, Phillips Russell published his biography of Franklin, subtitled *The First Civilized American*.[41]

By the turn of the twentieth century, the emphasis on Franklin as a modern American relied on not only his economic self but also the depiction of his intimate life. Russell captures the idea of Franklin as a middle-class American ahead of his time in a Puritanical past. According to Russell, he was the first "civilized" American because "at an American period eminent for narrowness, superstition, and bleak beliefs he was mirthful, generous, open-minded, learned, tolerant, and humor-loving." His "most marked char-acteristic" was "gusto for living."[42] Franklin has also held great appeal for his down-to-earth sensibility and middle-class ease of manner. One modern biographer emphasizes that Franklin's life could "show us how many-sided our human nature is." Explains one such account, "if we imagine a circum-ference which shall express humanity, we can place within it no one man who will reach out to approach it and to touch it at so many points as will Franklin."[43]

Many turn-of-the-century writers like to position themselves as modern in sharp contrast to their Victorian ancestors. As one explains, "his humble origin, his slow rise, his indelicate jokes, and his illegitimate children,—there were not a few people who cherished a most relentless antipathy towards him which neither his philanthropy nor his philosophic and scientific mind could soften." Franklin's negative reputation was beginning to shift at the time of that writing, and the author takes the opportunity to trace the neg-ative sentiments. Thus, he continues, "This bitter feeling against the 'old rogue,' as they called him, still survives among some of the descendants of the people of his time, and fifty or sixty years ago there were virtuous old ladies living in Philadelphia who would flame into indignation at the men-tion of his name."[44]

Although biographers differ in their approaches to his nonmarital sexu-ality, virtually all of them agree on discussion of his relationship with his wife, Read, which is always noted, even through the nineteenth and early twentieth centuries. Biographers generally approach Franklin's marriage to Read as illustrative of his broader character trait of pragmatism. For some authors, this meant providing an outlet for his sexual desires—and coupling that with his need for a helpmeet. In a chapter on Franklin's marriage in Carl Van Doren's early-twentieth-century definitive biography, he describes Franklin as "strongly built, rounded like a swimmer or a wrestler . . . [and] restless with vitality." "As in London," he continues, "the chief impulse he could or did not regulate was sexual. . . . He went to women hungrily, secretly, and briefly." Marriage to Read, he concludes, brought sensible relief to Franklin: "The most unreasonable of Franklin's impulses had now been quieted by this most reasonable of marriages. And he was free to turn his whole mind and will to work."[45]

But beyond the topic of his wife, approaches to Franklin's life differ. In the early twentieth century, many accounts gloss over details that are present in some nineteenth-century accounts. Journalist and writer Paul Elmer More in 1900, for example, makes no mention of the story of the lie Franklin told to be allowed on board a boat that was sailing to Boston. Similarly, author E. Lawrence Dudley in 1915 includes no mention of the story.[46] One year later, Frank Woodworth Pine's account also omits the story, and Pine does not include it in his edition of Franklin's autobiography—in effect, erasing it from Franklin lore.[47]

More also presents Franklin's famous list of thirteen virtues to guide one's life, which include frugality, industry, moderation, and the like. He deletes Franklin's description of virtue twelve, Chastity: "Rarely use venery but for health or offspring, never to dulness, weakness, or the injury of your own or another's peace or reputation"; More abbreviates the entry to "Chastity," followed by ellipses.[48]

In contrast to such reticence, other contemporary writers celebrate Franklin's sexuality as a signature aspect of his modernity. One early-twentieth-century biography of Franklin not only remarks favorably on Franklin's friendship with D'Eon but even goes so far as to include a portrait of D'Eon with the caption "in the woman's clothes he chose to wear during the latter part of his life." The author of this biography also includes a copy of a letter from D'Eon "with signature in the feminine." "D'Eon was living in exile in London while Franklin was there," he explains, "and there is evidence that they became friends."[49] Published at a time described as "sex o'clock" in America by a contemporary magazine, the association of Franklin with a figure like D'Eon put him at the vanguard of a new sexual culture.[50]

Many early-twentieth-century Americans viewed his writings as humorous and progressive, in direct contrast to the perceived repression and censorship of previous generations. One early-twentieth-century biographer includes an odd selection of suggestive Poor Richard's aphorisms largely without comment: "A ship under sail and a big-bellied woman, are the handsomest two things that can be seen common." "After three days men grow weary of a wench, a guest, and weather rainy." "You cannot pluck roses without danger of thorns, nor enjoy a fair wife without danger of horns." "Neither a fortress nor a m——d will hold out long after they begin to parley."[51] Such earthy sayings underscore Franklin's roots and serve to make him appealing to early-twentieth-century Americans self-consciously breaking free of Victorian propriety.

In addition to giving rise to a consistent memorial voice that extols Franklin's sexuality, the twentieth century's public memory of Franklin differs from the Victorian era's because of an important change in how historians have approached him. The advent of women's history and the significant work done on his papers from his time in France open up an examination of the portion of Franklin's life that his *Autobiography* does not cover. The autobiography so dominates the depictions of him in nineteenth-century America that these later accounts seem revelatory. Thus, a remarkable transformation occurred in the mid–twentieth century with regard to how Franklin's personal life would be discussed.

According to Tise, until the early twentieth century, "public discussion of his views on women and involvements with them was pretty much put aside." For fifty years before this, "historians almost uniformly considered it improper and ungentlemanly to talk about Franklin's dealings with women."[52] Women's history has aided the development of Franklin's new legacy, especially given the depth of scholarship on Franklin's time in the salon culture of Paris. Historian Lopez's work, for example, reveals the significance of the relationships that Franklin had with women and the important context for appreciating the role of women and the nature of heterosocial interaction in salon culture.

Even depictions of Franklin's marriage take on a new gloss in this new context that celebrated his flirtatious and amorous persona. Attempting to make the marriage seem more sexual and romantic, Charles Tansill writes about Franklin's choice of wife: "She had a good figure, however, and in Ben's visual arithmetic this added up to a nice sum. But his response to her physical charms had to be restrained," for at first he did not have enough money to secure her hand in marriage. Very shortly thereafter, he explains, Franklin "began seriously to court Deborah, who now was looking boldly at Ben over the high rampart of her ample bosom."[53] Franklin was the perfect subject for Tansill's project. His self-professed reason for focusing on the "secret loves" of the Founders, as we have seen in previous chapters, is to use sex and romance to "humanize" them. Franklin's personal reputation, never a stuffy one, needed little of this help but does blossom from Tansill's depictions of his disposition.

In some accounts, women are fashioned as a diversion from the *real* work at hand. For example, one argues that the tensions between his neighbor Madame Brillon and Franklin were a kind of ritual: "His quarrels with her were never serious; they were part of the game they were playing, a mannered, eighteenth-century-style love minuet. He enjoyed and valued her friendship, which helped him relieve the pressures of his nerve-straining negotiations with Vergennes."[54] But most often the view of Franklin as enlightened in his view of women, even a near feminist, only deepens through the twentieth century and fits well with the idea of him as a modern American, ahead of his eighteenth-century counterparts. According to one early-twentieth-century biographer, at the age of sixteen, Franklin was already showing himself to be a "free thinker," "foe of religious intolerance," "potential rebel against powers arbitrarily exercised, and a defender of women's rights."[55] Historian Lopez states, "Women, young and old, loved him because he took a keen interest in them, not merely as objects of desire, but as people with a different outlook, with their own contribution to make."[56] Franklin, writes one twentieth-century chronicler, "loved the ladies, flirted outrageously, [and] talked and wrote at length about love affairs." Yet, "he genuinely liked women, well beyond sexual attraction."[57] Another late-twentieth-century account similarly notes, "Almost inevitably French ladies took an important part in making this circle work. They probably realized that Franklin liked them as people—and appreciated them because they were women."[58]

Part of the misplaced emphasis on Franklin's relationships with women, especially while he was in France, stems from a sexist perception that devalues the role of women in early modern society. As Lopez argues, this view is typical of "our modern culture, which pays so much attention to sex and so little to women."[59] And she continues, "The myth that Franklin in Paris behaved like an old lecher having a jolly time is still with us. The truth is far less titillating. He was, simply, the greatest ambassador that America ever sent to France."[60]

Some academic scholars are right to point out that his relationships with women in Paris went well beyond social calls. Reducing women to romantic objects, and refusing to view them as correspondents, has warped our view. His letters to Madame Brillon, for example, are partly "grammar lessons," written to practice his French and returned to him with corrections in red ink. They would "play an important role in his mission, for women were skillful courtiers and their salons were excellent lobbies for foreign and secret agents."[61] His landlord, Chaumont, for another example, viewing Franklin's salon comportment in a favorable light, was able to secure valuable items for the cause of the American Revolution, including fifteen thousand uniforms. Famously, King Louis XVI told Franklin as they finalized France's support for American Independence, "I am very satisfied with your conduct since you arrived in my kingdom."[62]

By the 1960s, Franklin's reputation as a ladies' man was fully embraced. As Tansill puts it in 1964, "Ben obviously warmed more beds . . . than most people realized."[63] Part of the contemporary curiosity feeds off willful confusion—was he sexually "modern" or all talk and no action? The ambiguity of the nature of his relationships with women allows him to favorably straddle the Culture Wars. For those who wish to see him as sexually liberated, there's a Franklin, a man who is at ease with human sexuality, especially in contrast to the commonly held view of the stuffy Founding Father. In this public memory, Franklin emerges as compatible with the post–Sexual Revolution values of modern America. It has been said, for example, that Franklin "wrote his own code of morals." Many Americans today view Franklin as a trailblazer and self-made man, even in the areas of sex and romance. "The Puritan way of life," that same mid-century writer explains, "had little attraction for him. He had few inhibitions to check his warm impulses, and seldom did the fearsome shadow of sin put fear into his heart."[64]

Franklin's ribald writings on the surface present an ease with sexuality that frightened nineteenth-century Americans yet pleased those of the later twentieth and twenty-first centuries. Indeed, Franklin's reputation as a romantic man has usefully kept him relevant. As Fleming notes, Franklin had flirtatious relationships on this side of the Atlantic long before Paris, and such stories show that "romantic love" "was (and is) ancient and forever modern."[65]

Today, Americans consider the controversial essay "Choice of a Mistress" to be virtually "modern" and one that reveals Franklin to be a man of our period and not his own. On the "Choice of a Mistress," professor of political science Jerry Weinberger remarks that "the last reason is the one most remembered by posterity. Ask any ten people . . . [and] most will say: 'Oh yes, the one where old ladies are said to be so grateful.'" He goes on to say that he has conducted this "questioning experiment (in the locker room of my athletic club). It's no wonder it remains the most familiar line: It is funny and charming in its appeal to common decency—gratitude, after all, is a virtue associated with love and beneficence and akin to justice but without the compulsion or harshness of justice. The line is tender and it picks up other sweet things said about old women earlier on." Thus, today we can see that Franklin's lines resonate with male heterosexuality (note the "locker room" and "athletic club" locations). But Weinberger also frames it as short of typical locker-room objectification. "When, for a further experiment, I asked a professional woman in her early sixties," the author explains, "she said it was racy, to be sure, but really sweet and kindhearted."[66] Here again, we see the view of him as a friend to and not user of women—an idealized modern heterosexual male.

And controversial aspects of Franklin's *Autobiography* have similarly been offered in a positive and more sexually explicit light. Consider, for example, the translation of a contemporary edition that seeks to remove any ambiguity from the meaning of one passage where Franklin describes "intrigues with low women." The full passage from Franklin's *Autobiography* reads, "In the mean time, that hard-to-be-govern'd Passion of Youth, hurried me frequently into Intrigues with such low Women as fell in my Way, which were attended with some Expence & Inconvenience, besides a continual Risque to my Health by a Distemper which of all Things I dreaded, tho' by great good Luck I escaped it."[67] A 2005 edition of his *Autobiography*, subtitled *Franklin's Autobiography Adapted for Modern Times*, includes an updated translation of the famous passage: "In the mean time, my passions drove me to frequent relations with prostitutes and other low women. Admittedly, such behavior was both expensive and a risk to health and reputation. I'm grateful that I never caught any diseases."[68] In contrast to previous generations who tended to whitewash such topics, the editor of this translation ensures that the eighteenth-century prose would not obstruct readers from understanding Franklin. With a more contemporary wording, Americans today are able to see Franklin as someone they can relate to—in this regard, if not in others.

Today, the depiction of Franklin's marriage is highlighted more than ever before. One biographer today wanting to portray Franklin as ever-pragmatic (and yet oh-so-appealingly sexual) notes that "Franklin had a sexual appetite that he knew required discipline. So he set out to find himself a mate, preferably one with a dowry attached."[69]

Historian Wood explains their common-law marriage not as a product of immorality (as some Victorians saw it) but in terms of the legal setting: "Since Pennsylvania law did not allow divorce for desertion, Franklin and Deborah in 1730 decided to avoid legal difficulties by simply setting up housekeeping as husband and wife." And Wood also rightly explains that common-law marriage was "much more prevalent" in the eighteenth century "than today": "Known already was his child from an unknown woman who he brought to live with him and Deborah shortly after their marriage. They would raise him as their son. As you might imagine, Victorian biographers struggled with all of these revelations."[70]

Given the importance of marriage, perhaps most importantly for Franklin's portrayal as nonthreatening, is his biographer's consistent depiction of him as loyal to his wife. For all his failings, public memory contends, he was no adulterer like Hamilton. Academic and popular depictions of his marriage as stable have continued to the present day, where he is described as an "averagely good family man."[71] One recent account points out that "there is no hint anywhere in his correspondence that he was unfaithful to her."[72] Decades earlier, another similarly explains, "There are no letters, diaries, or memoirs that ever mention a specific liaison after Franklin's marriage to Deborah Read."[73] With similar certainty, a college newspaper interview with Franklin scholar Leo Lemay covering "myths and facts" explains, "Franklin was a notorious womanizer. False. Although Franklin was an inveterate flirt, and he sired an illegitimate child before his 1730 wedding to Deborah Reed [*sic*] Rogers, there is no evidence that he had any affairs during his marriage."[74]

Franklin and French Beauties

As for Franklin's reputation while a widower in France, today Franklin appears to be the harmless older man and not the threatening sexual deviant. The "French beauties," one mid-twentieth-century biographer explains (gleefully), whom "he visited most" while living in and outside Paris were Madame Brillon and Madame Helvétius. Given the letters that were exchanged and the surrounding company who observed Franklin in the salon culture of Paris, the relationships are well-documented and commented on by virtually all his biographers. As with his writings, through the twentieth century, the relationships have become increasingly embraced and enjoyed as evidence of Franklin's joie de vivre, his ease with women and sexuality, in sharp contrast to the oppressive Puritans of stereotypical early America.

Thirty-three-year-old Madame Brillon was his neighbor in Passy. In the hands of many biographers, romantic mist encircles the depiction of Franklin and Madame Brillon. Consider the following passage from an article in a special 2003 issue of *Time* magazine, entitled "Why He Was a Babe Magnet":

> Music is her Cupid's arrow. The lovely and talented Anne-Louise d'Hardancourt Brillon de Jouy plays the harpsichord and piano like an angel. Eager to meet her new neighbor in the fashionable Paris suburb of Passy, the celebrated envoy from America, she inquires about his musical tastes and woos him with a recital of Scottish songs. She follows with invitations to tea, chess games and tête-à-têtes in which she pours out her troubled soul to him. The delighted Franklin, now in his 70s, soon presses her for more tangible evidence of her affection. She plays coy, however, and steers the relationship with "Cher Papa" (her endearing term for him that soon catches on widely) into a safer daughter-father pattern, over his useless protests.[75]

Lopez explains the relationship with Brillon as including 103 letters from her and 29 letters from him, "at least as many letters as for all the other

French ladies taken together."[76] According to another author, "her attitude toward Franklin was purely maternal." "Despite his age," however, "he grew naughty and made advances." His letters to her are flirtatious and even carry a "definite hint of sex," but she always turned him down—and also would not stop her well-known habit of sitting on his lap.[77] One of his letters to Madam Brillon, which is often quoted, reads, "When I was a young man and enjoyed more favours from the sex than at present, I never had the gout. If the ladies at Passy had more of that Christian charity which I have so often recommended to you, in vain, I would not have the gout now."[78] As far as the relationship with Brillon went, historian Robert Middlekauff remarks, "How an aging man, now seventy-one, played the part of gallant without appearing and feeling foolish is not clear, but Franklin evidently managed. Madame Brillon played, not the temptress, but the faithful wife and mother. . . . It was her talent and charm that held Franklin's attention after Madame Brillon made him realize that she would not fulfill his sexual demands."[79] Brillon's husband did "not mind the attention Franklin paid to his wife."[80] In one letter, he writes playfully, "I am certain you have been kissing my wife"—yet he also adds, "My dear Doctor, let me kiss you back in return."[81]

An exchange between Madame Brillon and Franklin often commented on includes Franklin's referring to the Commandments that he has broken by coveting her. She replies by referring to the seven deadly sins—lust going unnamed but clearly being emphasized—and he responds with creative additions to the Commandments, bringing them up to twelve. The two he added? "Increase, multiply and fill the earth; the twelfth (a commandment I enjoin you to obey): love one another." "She . . . openly professed her love for Franklin, leaving out the physical aspect he kept seeking from her."[82]

If Franklin's role as "Cher Papa" with Madame Brillon provided ample evidence of his playful nature, most biographers agree that his relationship with Madame Helvétius was much more serious. Madame Helvétius, a wealthy sixty-year-old widow, also lived near Franklin. In the words of Isaacson, "by September 1779, he was ardently proposing marriage."[83] Here, too, *Time*'s special issue wraps a romantic gauze around the subjects and is also worth quoting at length:

> The Franklin libido really stirs when he encounters the brilliant and beautiful Anne-Catherine de Ligniville d'Autricourt, a descendant of Austrian nobility known by her married name, Madame Helvé-tius. Outgoing, exuberant and earthy, she uses her late husband's fortune to operate a bohemian, animal-filled estate on the fringes of the Bois de Boulogne, where she reigns over a salon of Enlighten-

ment philosophes. To Franklin, this is an intellectual heaven. Franklin proposes marriage to Madame Helvétius but frames the offer so coyly that it can be seen either as serious or as a joke, a canny way of saving face for both parties. He tells her that her late husband and his late Deborah have tied the knot in heaven, so it would be fitting revenge if she accepted him on earth. Ah, *mon cher ami*, she tells him in effect, it cannot be. When he finally decides to return home to America, her friends chide her for not accepting his proposal and keeping the adored Franklin in France.[84]

As for Helvétius, "she was the queen of them all, the only one to whom he wrote more often than she answered, who did not call him papa, but, as an equal, *mon cher ami*, the one woman with whom he did not want to have merely a flirtation, a passing adventure: he wanted her for a wife."[85] Another account remarks that she "won his heart" and that he proposed "seriously" and that after being turned down was "disappointed; he had wanted her badly and would have remained in France for the rest of his days had she married him."[86]

Although Franklin has often been portrayed as flirtatious and even a romantic, he has rarely today been maligned as a womanizer or as hypocritical in his romantic practices. Historian Ruth Bloch rightly reminds us that Franklin's writings reveal "deeply conflicting conceptions of women" that alternate between portraying women as "wasteful" and "praising" them as "productive assistants." Overall, much of his writing is infused with typical eighteenth-century "misogynist" strains that "depict women as sexually demanding, haughty, and contentious."[87] Nonetheless, there is no shortage of biographers who portray his views about women as enlightened (and ahead of their time), not exploitative. However, this is an old view. As Carla Mulford argues, by the early nineteenth century, for some, Franklin could be seen as "virtuous *because* he admired women. . . . Franklin's sexual attractions became the stuff of an affectionate and masculinized sense of national identity. . . . To the popular imagination, Franklin, male-dominant heterosexuality, and virtue would be registered and linked in a way that has come down to us even in today's culture."[88]

Take, for example, Edwin S. Gaustad's biography, which includes an image and caption that are regularly used. The caption reads, "Franklin entertained—and was entertained by—the ladies of Paris during his years there. His letters to particular women were flirtatious, amusing, and filled with memories of the many happy evenings spent in their company." Downplaying the critical role that such women and their salons played in this political world, Gaustad explains that the "ladies" were a component of "high society" who stood in addition to, rather than as part of, other elements: "The ladies loved him, and he returned their sentiments." Although he notes that Brillon's salon, for example, included Paris's "cultural and artistic leaders," the obvious connection to politics is overlooked. As for Helvétius, "grateful that she had given him so many of her days, Franklin thought it only fitting that he offer her some of his nights. That offer, so far as the historical record reveals, was never accepted."[89]

The 2003 *Time* magazine coverage of the "Adventures of Ben Franklin" uses sex to sell the issue, but it includes an essay that explains the important roles that women played in French society and thus the American Revolution via Franklin. Although it emphasizes his sex appeal in the title "Why He Was a Babe Magnet," in the blurb it asserts that masculine sex appeal need not be about physical appeal, and it argues that by listening to women and taking them seriously, "even when he was old and rotund, Ben had sex appeal. He knew the way to a woman's heart was through her head." The article at one level reduces Franklin's relationships to women as a lesson for the war of the sexes.

But such depictions of socializing with women as a political and diplomatic activity do not appeal as much as less complex accounts that present women as sex objects—nor do they highlight Franklin's all-American heterosexual *desires*. Indeed, to underscore the political utility of flirtation would run the risk of portraying him as a deceiver and user of women rather than a red-blooded man with appropriate romantic interests.

The controversy over his written record will be familiar to readers of this book, with the central question being whether he did consummate his relationships while in France. Summing up his relationships, Middlekauff tentatively writes, "There was sexual attraction in several of these friendships, and perhaps at times there was sexual fulfillment." Many, for example, try to correct the view of Franklin as overly sexual. Thus, Middlekauff concedes that people who consider Franklin's ill health and advanced age could probably conclude that Franklin was "all talk and no action" but that "thinking of Franklin as a lover is not an absurdity." Nonetheless, he continues, "the great love of his life was not a woman. He loved his work more, and his science, and his country. . . . They were the great loves that stirred him most deeply." Finally, he concludes that "most of the gossip about Franklin's sexual exploits in Paris can be safely discounted."[90] Isaacson more narrowly explains, "Franklin's relationship with Madame Brillon, like so many of his others with distinguished ladies, was complex and never fully consummated."[91] Finally, Lopez maintains her conclusion that most of his relationships with Parisian women were "never consummated. In fact, Franklin was a master of what the French call *amitié amoureuse*, whose English translation, amorous friendship, gives only a hint of its true meaning: a delicious form of intimacy, expressed in exchanges of teasing kisses, tender embraces, intimate conversations and rhapsodic love letters, but not necessarily sexual congress."[92] That Americans want to know the intimate details of Franklin's sexual life with certainty highlights the importance of sex in our national identity.

Franklin's transformation from ribald author worthy of Victorian censorship to "foxy grandpa" illustrates the dramatic changes that have occurred in the way that the private lives of the Founders have been depicted. As we have seen in previous chapters, sex has long figured in the public assessment of the political Founders of the nation. In the twentieth century, the stereotyped view of Puritanical early America bolstered the depiction of Franklin as unusually liberated and at ease with human sexual desire. So, too, did the negative reaction of Victorian and early-twentieth-century writers to his more ribald writings, as it reinforced the assumption that he was espousing a radical message—one that late-twentieth-century Americans would appreciate as ahead of its time.

Historian Wood has rightly noted that it is puzzling that we view Franklin as the ultimate or "first American," as he spent nearly a quarter century of his life in Europe and embraced a European lifestyle more so than any other of the Founders. It is equally surprising that we should find him to be the quintessential middle-class sexually liberated forerunner that so many think he was. We recognize that, although elite, he fooled us with his fur cap and performed the middle-class American, but he also fooled us into thinking he was somehow not fettered by the sexual morality of his day. Perhaps that is why he is today viewed as a harmless, endearing "foxy grandpa."

5

ALEXANDER HAMILTON

IN A TWIST OF LOGIC, Alexander Hamilton (Figure 5.1) has been remembered as an "outsider" among insiders in the pantheon of Founders. In 2007, the well-regarded *American Experience* series produced an award-winning documentary entitled *Alexander Hamilton*. Based on the book by journalist and popular biographer Ronald Chernow, it crystalizes the view of Hamilton that had emerged in the new millennium.[1] In the film, a narrator explains that "Alexander Hamilton was unique among the Founding Fathers" and links this quality to his birth status: "He was an outsider—born in 1755, not in the American colonies but on Nevis, a tiny tropical island in the Caribbean. He came into this world at the very bottom of the social order. He was a bastard—illegitimate, because his mother, as a divorced woman, was not legally married to his father. As a bastard, Hamilton was prohibited from attending a Christian school, and had no rights of inheritance."[2] Echoing a core theme of his book, Chernow explained to the audience, "I think that the illegitimacy had the most profound effect,

Figure 5.1 (*above*). Portrait of Hamilton. (*Portrait of Alexander Hamilton*. John Trumbull. Oil on canvas, 1806.)

psychologically, on Hamilton. It was considered the most dishonored state, and I think that it produced in Hamilton a lifelong obsession with honor."[3]

Although his reputation soared in the late nineteenth century, today Alexander Hamilton does not hold the same larger-than-life standing as other Founders. Some might recall him as the man who was shot and killed in a duel with then–Vice President Aaron Burr. But most Americans unknowingly encounter him only through the ten dollar bill and would struggle to tell you anything about his accomplishments. No grand memorials cement his presence in the American imagination.

As this chapter shows, Hamilton's bastard status might be well-known by those familiar with John Adams's famous slur, but he has also been labeled, at various times, a homosexual, an adulterer, and a lothario. Unlike Thomas Jefferson's biographers, who seek to bolster his manhood by making mountains out of every romantic molehill that they can find, those who memorialize Hamilton downplay his nonmarital romances. Why? He publicly acknowledged an extramarital affair. In his own lifetime, his political enemies tried to tar him with the brush of his birth status and the even more serious public scandal that emerged when he confessed to the affair. His biographers, however, have long employed various explanations to counterbalance both components of his life, portraying him as a man of impeccable public integrity and personal masculine honor.

In His Lifetime

As his biographers point out, Hamilton's contributions to the country undoubtedly make him one of the most important of the political leaders of the Revolution and early Republic. Hamilton was a military hero of the American Revolution. He was a delegate to the Constitutional Convention and one of the primary authors of the influential *Federalist Papers* that proved to be so instrumental in the ratification of the U.S. Constitution. Under George Washington, Hamilton served as the first secretary of the Treasury. Hamilton helped found the U.S. Mint and the first national bank. Given his strong views on the importance of a powerful centralized government and a strong nationalized economic system and his vision of the United States as a major world economic and military power, Hamilton has been called the Founder who made possible the "American century." Franklin may be called the first modern American but it is Hamilton, as a recent exhibit at the New York Historical Society noted, who is "the man who made modern America."[4]

Hamilton's remarkable public achievements are all the more impressive given his humble origins. Hamilton was born in 1755 or 1757 on the island of Nevis in the British West Indies. At the time of his birth, Hamilton's father, James, and mother, Rachel Lavien, were not married, because James could not release himself from his previous marriage. When Alexander was ten, his father abandoned the family. When he was thirteen, his mother died, leaving him an orphan. After serving as a clerk, Hamilton went to the mainland colonies, eventually studying law at King's College (now Columbia) in New York City. In 1775, he joined the militia, ultimately rising to the rank of captain and high-level aide-de-camp to Washington. In 1780, he married Elizabeth Schuyler, a wealthy woman from a powerful New York family. Together they had eight children. After a much publicized extramarital affair, Hamilton's public reputation suffered, although he continued to be politically active. In 1804, he was killed in a duel with Vice President Burr, and amid great national mourning, he was laid to rest.

Hamilton differs from other Founders in that he publicly acknowledged his sexual transgression. His case is unlike that of Washington or Jefferson, both of whom left very little documentation, giving writers more room for imagination with their personal lives. Washington's emphasis on his stepchildren and kin enhanced his image as the family man, and Jefferson's refusal to remarry abetted those who would portray him as the chaste widower—but Hamilton in his own lifetime acknowledged his birth status and confessed his extramarital affair.

In 1791, Hamilton conducted an eight-month affair with a married woman, Maria Reynolds. The affair began when Reynolds showed up one day asking for Hamilton at his house. As a fellow New Yorker, her story went, she had sought him out for assistance—she needed money because her abusive husband had recently abandoned her in Philadelphia with nothing for her support. Hamilton requested that he be permitted to bring her some money at her house that evening. Once the affair began, he received letters from both Reynolds and her husband explaining that he was aware of the affair and required $1,000 to forget Hamilton's transgression. But this was not the end. A month later, this time allegedly with Mr. Reynolds's permission, the affair resumed. In 1792, several men approached James Monroe with the information that Hamilton had used public moneys for personal gain. When Monroe and two other congressmen confronted Hamilton at his office, he asked them to meet with him and the comptroller at his home that evening. At that meeting, he explained that he had never used public money illegally and had found himself instead in the position of paying off a blackmailer to conceal his extramarital affair with the man's wife. Monroe and the committee viewed the matter as private and considered the matter closed. But some years later, one of them spoke with reporter James Callender, and mention of it appeared in print when Callender published the allegation in his *History of the United States for 1796*.[5]

In 1797, Hamilton tried to clear his name by publishing *Observations on Certain Documents . . . In Which the Charge of Speculation Against Alexander Hamilton, Late Secretary of the Treasury, is Fully Refuted. Written by Himself.* The lengthy pamphlet details the affair and explains that he had been ensnared and blackmailed by Reynolds and her husband. He denies misusing public funds and admits that his "real crime is an amorous connection" with Reynolds. Hamilton writes that he was something of a victim of her scheming with her husband—"brought on . . . by a combination between the husband and wife with the design to extort money from me."[6] "Mrs Reynolds," he charges, "employed every effort to keep up my attention and visits." The public financial allegations were never proven to be true, and Hamilton was very forthcoming with both his public and private records in an effort to clear his name.

Modern Americans surprised to learn of Hamilton's affair may be reacting to national rhetoric that memorializes the Founding Fathers as men of unusual virtue and morality—paragons in public and private affairs. In part, this view relies on stereotyped notions of early America as a place of monogamy and morality and associations that link sexual expression and nontraditional modes of sexuality with modernity. Conservative commentators also stoke this idealized image by calling on Americans to remember and return to the morality of the Founding generation.

Hamilton's affair might seem striking and jarring to us now, but it should not be seen as radical or extraordinary for early America. Although adultery had long been illegal in early America—perhaps most dramatically outlawed under penalty of death by Puritans when they established the colony of Massachusetts—adultery also constituted the primary reason for justifying the dissolution of marriage in many regions. By the 1790s, especially in such places as New York and Philadelphia, the dominant ideal of monogamy was just that—an ideal. In the words of one historian, a sexual "revolution" of sorts had occurred in social mores and behaviors by the end of the eighteenth century.[7]

Hamilton's own actions (and the reactions of those around him) reveal something of the standards of the day—he chose to discuss the affair, in print, publicly, and in the greatest of documented detail to *save* his public honor. He was not divorced. His wife did not denounce him. Washington publicly supported him, as did others. He went on to hold high office after the scandal, becoming commander of the army—perhaps the highest office of his career. Recall too that when the affair first came to light, he confessed it to a congressional committee that was investigating the payments Hamilton made to his lover's husband to keep silent—and none of the men saw fit to make the situation public. They considered it a private matter.

Contemporary Americans may also be surprised to learn that Hamilton's affair became so publicly known. Scholars interpret the public nature of the affair as a product of the political times. As Jacob Katz Cogan argues, the scandal came to light at a period when politics were being rewritten. The "colonial edifice of political and social deference" had collapsed, and in the Revolutionary and early Republic eras, politics and political relationships shifted from a sense of prioritization of "social status" to one based on "virtue" and "individual character."[8] The affair is often used to illustrate party conflicts in the contentious 1790s and the emerging divisions between the Federalist and Republican political parties.[9]

In his lifetime, his opposition made use of cultural tropes that depicted him as a violator of the masculine ethos of marriage (via his adultery) and protection of wife and family (through his public revelation of the affair). They also compounded this with a particular emphasis on the status of his lover. The earliest depictions of the affair, which appeared almost immediately after publication of the pamphlet, portray Hamilton as immoral and Maria as a "forlorn middle-class woman."[10] Although the infidelity remains unchanged in various tellings, by deploying certain class and gender stereotypes and by positioning Hamilton as something of a victim—not only of his own weakness but also of the schemes of another—writers could change the shape of Hamilton's affair. Thus, when some of his detractors learned that Maria was not middle-class or reputable, they changed their tune. In 1802, one writer explains, "I have represented that woman as an amiable and virtuous wife, seduced from the affections of her husband by artifice and intrigue." But upon learning that she was "destitute of every regard for virtue or honor" and like women who "lay their snares to entrap the feeling heart and benevolent mind," he decides to publicly vindicate Hamilton as victim not perpetrator.[11] Some political enemies in his lifetime and after his death sought to unman him, but, despite their best efforts, he was memorialized as one of the most virtuous of the Founders.

Tension over Romantic Connections

Unlike Washington's and Jefferson's biographers, most of Hamilton's chroniclers make little of his possible early romantic connections—indeed, his past served no purpose for those biographers seeking to characterize his extramarital affair as a "lapse" and not a typical action. By removing these aspects of his biography, most accounts are more easily able to portray the adulterous affair as a one-time event, an aberration for a man meriting the label of Founding Father through his unblemished character.

Yet we glean from a few other accounts that Hamilton may have also deserved a reputation as a lothario. "Charges of the same kind," Hamilton's grandson explains, "spattered many of the leading men of the times."[12] Writing in the 1930s, as Hamilton's reputation began to sharply decline, one biographer mobilizes what for many would seem to be damning evidence of a highly sexualized individual. Perhaps responding to the public reassessment of Hamilton as not being a man of the people—a problematic view as the Great Depression took hold—Johan Smertenko declares, "Hamilton from his college days bore the reputation of a ladies' man." The author finds Hamilton to have had many affairs—indeed, with "a score of nameless women." And he continues, "His erotic adventures were as necessary to him as his political activity. Psychically both served the same purpose; both were assertions of the legitimacy of his position in the world despite the illegitimacy of his birth." Finally, the author argues that Hamilton had an affair with his sister-in-law Angelica Church and concludes that the relationship was consummated.[13] To further underscore Hamilton's broad sexuality, the author includes one of the racier letters that Hamilton sent to his friend John Laurens to request assistance in finding a wife, in which Hamilton writes, "'You will be pleased to recollect in your negotiations that I have no invincible antipathy to the *maidenly beauties*, and that I am willing to take the *trouble* of them on myself.'" He also notes the suggestive tone Hamilton takes when asking Laurens to talk him up to women: "'To excite their emulations it will be necessary for you to give an account of the lover—his *size*, make, qualities of mind and *body*, achievements, expectations, fortune, etc. In drawing my picture you will no doubt be civil to your friend, mind you do justice to the length of my nose, and don't forget that I——.'"[14] Hamilton's abrupt ending is itself titillating and evocative.

Smertenko's account is unusual for a Hamilton biography, but academic scholars and biographers of other Founders have from time to time repeated the assertion that Hamilton was known for his sexual "adventurism." Martha Washington, it is sometimes noted in such portrayals, named her tomcat, Hamilton, after him.[15] Other biographers similarly offer clues to a Hamilton who is almost unrecognizable from his general portrayal in public memory, which emphasizes that he was a man of human failings but also one of great moral integrity. Some of these indicators come through in biographies of Jefferson, who is often positioned in opposition to Hamilton.

Jefferson biographer and historian Fawn Brodie, for example, declares that women "saw in Hamilton the potentially seductive lover," adding that "he had the reputation of being a rake" who "openly paraded affection for his wife's exquisite sister, Angelica Church."[16] Similarly, one other biographer tells us he was charming and attractive to women and during the Revolution was often visited in the camps.[17] The connection to his sister-in-law, Church, for select few writers, qualifies as an "affair" itself. A mid-century biography by John C. Miller, for example, refers to the love shared between them as intense and lasting for decades—although he concludes that it was probably not consummated.[18]

But for most Hamilton memorializers, the adulterous affair looms so large that they often choose to overlook or downplay other relationships. The contrast with depictions of other Founders is most notable when one thinks back to the Washington and Jefferson biographies, so many of which expand discussions of early "loves" and devote entire chapters to individual romances. Virtually no twentieth-century biographers include separate chapters on Hamilton's alleged romances with women while in the Revolutionary War. None includes separate chapters on a loving relationship with Laurens. And none includes separate chapters on the alleged affair that some authors contend he had with his sister-in-law. Thus, they are able to portray Hamilton as virtuous and married—with one exception—rather than viewing the affair as typical of his romantic self. Indeed, the dominant view of Hamilton, firmly established by his memorializers, is that (as Smertenko put it) he was "not a successful philanderer."[19] Explains another biographer, "That Hamilton was a novice at marital infidelity is painfully obvious in the clumsiness with which he handled the affair."[20] And even the affair with Reynolds is virtually never told as a story of love or romance—it is always couched as the "Reynolds Affair," a political scandal.

Bastard Founder

Initially, polite biographers try to omit the detail of his birth out of wedlock (something occasionally referred to in his own lifetime). One early biography authored by his son John C. Hamilton portrays Hamilton as decidedly *not* born to unwed parents. Hamilton, he writes, was the "offspring of a second marriage," his mother having "obtained a divorce" before she "married the father" "and had by him several sons, of whom Alexander was the youngest."[21] Typical of nineteenth-century biographers, he leads readers to believe that Hamilton was in fact born to married parents. In 1840, engineer by training Henry Brevoort Renwick—like Hamilton, a New Yorker—and his father, James Renwick, a popular writer for such publications as *American Quarterly Review* and *New York Review* and a chemist by training, published their biography of Hamilton. They similarly note the background of Hamilton's parents and call him the "youngest child of this marriage."[22] Likewise, Lewis Henry Boutell in 1890 describes Hamilton's mother and father without noting his illegitimate birth.[23] Writing in 1890, William Graham Sumner, an economist and sociologist, notes Morris's declaration, but rather than endorse the characterization, he chooses to say, "Little is known about the birth and parentage of Alexander Hamilton."[24] In 1898, Massachusetts Senator Henry Cabot Lodge writes, "On the eleventh day of January in the year 1757, the wife of a Scotch merchant in the island of Nevis gave birth to a son, who received the name of Alexander Hamilton."[25]

In the twentieth century, Hamilton's bastard status received much attention from friend and foe alike. The advent of psychology infused biographical interpretations of childhood and youth in new ways. Hamilton's birth status could be used to demonstrate either blameless victimhood (a powerful theme in Hamilton's biographies) or deep-seated corruption and immorality (a note his detractors love to sound).

Charles Conant, a turn-of-the-century journalist and author whose work focuses on banking and finance, comes close to noting Hamilton's bastard status: "A mystery hangs over his birth and parentage, which repeated inquiries have failed to clear away . . . but the fact that all these relatives remained so much in the background gave some color to the slanders of his enemies concerning his birth."[26] In 1910, in *The Intimate Life of Alexander Hamilton*, Hamilton's grandson Allan McLane Hamilton begins defensively, responding to what he calls "unnecessary speculation" regarding Hamilton's "antecedents" that began with Gouverneur Morris and others. Mustering family letters and records as hard evidence in the face of gossip, Allan Hamilton presents the longer genealogy of his ancestors. "The general ignorance that exists regarding Hamilton's origin and intimate life has prompted me to publish fully all I know about him," he explains. "There was no doubt of the sincerity and depth of their love for each other," he writes, dispelling the negative image of the "bastard" child as the product of sordid, unbridled lust.[27] Hamilton, like other twentieth-century chroniclers, points out that in his funeral eulogy, Morris did not see the need to sugarcoat this aspect of Hamilton's extraordinary life and wrestled with how to address what he considered to be on people's minds. He includes Morris's statement: "'The first point of his biography is that he was a stranger of illegitimate birth; some plan must be contrived to pass over this handsomely.'"[28] This tactic of not harping on these damaging aspects of his personal life served biographers well when Hamilton's legacy enjoyed popularity. In addition to explaining the reason for his bastard status, biographers would rail against those who made use of it to suggest something about his character. Hamilton's grandson does not use the potentially derogatory term in his account, and he takes pains to fully describe the legal bind that Hamilton's mother found herself in—asserting that the marriage was not simply unhappy but abusive. Hamilton's mother and father, according to the account, took a "bold step" and in doing so followed custom whereby marriage rites were often "informal" and also played on "local sympathy," given that her first husband was a "course man of repulsive personality." Another early-twentieth-century writer simply explains, "His father was a Scotch merchant and his mother was of Huguenot descent."[29]

But by the 1920s and 1930s, most biographers point out that those who knew Hamilton's parents understood why they could not marry and were sympathetic to her decision to leave her first husband. In his 1932 account, writer Smertenko defensively observes that "enemies of Hamilton stopped at no exaggeration. Callender, their foulest mouthpiece, called Alexander, 'the son of the camp-girl'; and vindictive John Adams could not resist repeating his favorite scurrility, 'the bastard brat of a Scotch pedlar,' in a letter to Jefferson written nine years after Hamilton's death."[30] The following year, Ralph Edward Bailey's biography similarly contains a defensive explanation for his "bastard" status: "James Hamilton and Rachael Lavine loved each other and wished to be married. Insuperable hindrances, however, precluded their becoming husband and wife." Hamilton's mother, he writes, had been "utterly unhappy" in her first marriage, but the laws did not allow for free divorce: "The lovers, thus prevented from the desired conventionality of a wedding, agreed in the establishment of a home without marriage."[31]

In the second quarter of the twentieth century, the influence of theorists who regarded early childhood development as psychologically central to adult characteristics is readily apparent in such accounts as Smertenko's. In the preface to his study, which makes use of "psychological interpretation," Smertenko explains to readers that Hamilton was a man of "flashes of genius as well as the lapses of frailty." Increasingly in the twentieth century, memorializers depict Hamilton's birth status as perhaps the most significant element in his life—a life, they argue, that he believed placed him at a disadvantage to others and generated an outsider status that drove him to succeed. Thus, Smertenko argues that Hamilton's birth out of wedlock was, indeed, significant: "His illegitimacy was both the secret problem of his life and the subconscious motive of his activity, even including the erotic episodes." He continues, "The decision of his biographers to dismiss the question of his parentage as trivial and irrelevant to the saga of his heroic deed is palpably disingenuous." Indeed, Smertenko's account sees the parentage issue as central to understanding Hamilton: "Hamilton was a warrior, statesman, lover, orator, and author, but first and foremost he was the illegitimate son of an unknown father seeking a place in the genealogical tables both of the past and of the future."[32] The explanatory power of his birth status would endure through the twentieth century. For example, one mid-century writer sees his status as an outsider unconnected to the powerful families of New York as directly influencing his approach to marriage and leaving "little likelihood that he would throw himself away on a tavern keeper's daughter."[33] A 1970s biography opens with the assertion that "much of Hamilton's makeup derived from his parents and his childhood."[34] One late-twentieth-century account argues that even the famous duel stemmed from Hamilton's bastard status by postulating that he envied Burr's family background, thereby creating a "fatal friendship."[35]

More recent writers have dismissed Hamilton's extramarital affair as the product of his troubled childhood—in particular his bastard status— thereby absolving him of any responsibility. Combining this view with the view of him as virile, Chernow writes, "The problem was that no single woman could seem to satisfy all the needs of this complex man with his checkered childhood." Similarly, he explains, "It was as if, after inhabiting a world of high culture for many years, Hamilton had regressed back to the sensual, dissolute world of his childhood." As an outsider, Chernow's Hamilton is driven, and the affair is almost inevitable: "Like many people driven by their careers, he did not allow himself sufficient time for escape and relaxation."[36] This view positions Hamilton as blameless, not one who might be worthy of scorn.

Marriage and Affair

For biographers, Hamilton's very public adulterous affair, which threatened to ruin both his life and his legacy, has presented a double challenge: (1) how to characterize an extramarital affair when a Founding Father is supposed to be a moral and virtuous role model for Americans and (2) how to handle the fact that the affair became public by Hamilton's own detailed confession— that he, himself, had so publicly humiliated his wife and family.

Generally the very earliest accounts, for the sake of decorum and in deference to his memory, make little of the indelicate personal matter. To some extent, the popularity of Hamilton's legacy at this point in time discouraged extensive explanation of the affair. Some writers, such as his son, say very little about the Reynolds affair. When Henry and James Renwick mention it in their 1840 biography, they do not mention Reynolds by name and cast the event as a political scandal that places Hamilton in a favorable and understandable light: "Hamilton valued his character as a public servant beyond his domestic peace; and, rather than leave any imputation on his official purity, exposed frailties which he was not suspected of. The temporary aberration of passion which was thus laid open may lower the opinion which we might otherwise entertain of the absolute spotlessness of his moral character, but his avowal serves to enhance our estimate of his delicate sense of official purity."[37]

In the wake of the Civil War, Hamilton's views on strong central government again added another aspect to an already-developing positive national memory of him. As political theorist Stephen Knott explains, the contrast set up between the Republican Jefferson and the Federalist Hamilton dominates nineteenth- and twentieth-century depictions of the men.[38] Pro-Hamilton accounts, of course, depict their subject in a positive light. For a typical negative portrayal of the Reynolds affair, we must turn to a biography not of Hamilton but of Jefferson. Thus, James Parton's 1874 biography of Jefferson includes a chapter entitled "Hamilton's Amour with Mrs. Reynolds" on the Hamilton-Reynolds affair, deeming it a personal failing. As if tearing the cloak off the successful treasurer and exposing the true scoundrel beneath, the author concludes, "The sinner in the case was not the Honorable Secretary of the Treasury, but only a weak, vain, and limited human being, named Alexander Hamilton."[39]

Parton penned these revelations about the adulterous Founder at about the same time as the scandalous news of Henry Ward Beecher's adultery riveted public attention. Beecher, a minister and author who had achieved fame as a political and moral force in the nation, became infamous for a years-long affair with his wife's friend, Elizabeth Tilton. When word of this liaison got to free-love advocate Victoria Woodhull, whom Beecher had publicly excoriated as an immoral woman, she vowed to expose him. In 1872, she printed "The Beecher-Tilton Scandal Case" in her paper, *Woodhull and Claflin's Weekly*. The story of his hypocrisy became a sensation, and within days, 150,000 copies had been printed and sold. When Mr. Tilton was excommunicated from the church because of the scandal, he sued Beecher, and the adulterous affair continued to make national headlines, despite bringing no conviction. Parton writes, therefore, in a climate of scandal that immediately associated adultery with political and moral outrage.[40] When Parton draws on the original gendered depiction of Hamilton as a man who erred doubly—not only by violating his marital vows but also by making the transgression public—he also may have been weighing in on the Woodhull controversy: "It is a highly interesting fact," he sarcastically begins, "that, A.D. 1797, one of the foremost men of the United States, a person who valued himself upon his moral principle, and was accepted by a powerful party at his own valuation in that particular, should have felt it to be a far baser thing to cheat men of their money than to despoil women of their honor. In this pamphlet he puts his honorable wife to an open shame, and published to the world the frailty of the woman who had gratified him."[41]

While his nineteenth-century detractors rail against him as a "weak" man who "could be false to women," Hamilton's memorializers place the blame elsewhere.[42] Writing in 1877, just two years after the famous trial, George Shea concedes that "Hamilton's name is not free from reproach for libidinousness." But, echoing what Hamilton himself had established as his characteristic defense, they point out that Hamilton was virtually victimized "by an artful and illiterate adventuress called Maria Reynolds, the reputed wife of a depraved and mercenary man." And in contrast to his detractors, for his memorializers the confession is the defining moment of the affair. Highlighting it, they believe, enables them to dress Hamilton, in true Founding Father fashion, as extraordinary in private life and public accomplishments. Thus, Shea continues, "He himself, curiously and characteristically, confessed it publicly. . . . He admitted this frailty: but so as to enable him to defend his honor." His "candor, the absence of feigned regret . . . commended him to the sympathy even of his political opponents, and gained a popular absolution not readily given in this country to like offenses."[43]

Biographers also defend Hamilton by noting the social and political climate of early America. In 1882, John T. Morse notes, "Very few of those great men whose public virtues adorned the earlier period of our national existence numbered a strict chastity among their private excellences. And some of the most revered among them fell into opposite extremes." He continues, "The fault which he committed was no uncommon one; that he was no worse than his contemporaries." Indeed, in the short list of famous political leaders of the American Revolution, virtually all the men with the exception of Adams had been publicly linked to rumors of extramarital affairs. And for Morse, only Hamilton suffered so exquisitely: "But they were never brought up for public castigation; it was only Hamilton who had the misfortune to live in a glass house into every cranny of which the full noon-tide sunshine seemed to be ever pouring." For Morse, Hamilton was "so unfortunate" as "to be *led* into an intrigue" (italics mine).[44]

Such tactics, marshaled in his defense, would become standard in Ham-

ilton biographies. At the end of the nineteenth century, Republican Senator Lodge musters all of them, placing blame on Democrat Monroe for the
scandal and deflecting blame from Hamilton by railing against those who
would sully his name: "The miserable Reynolds affair has cast a shadow
upon the honor of James Monroe, and its wretched details have found a
place in one of the biographies of Jefferson." Moreover he seeks to use the
scandal to shore up Hamilton's image as a man of integrity: "No one can
desire to rake over the ashes of this miserable scandal, but in its effect it
showed the courage of Hamilton in a most striking manner." Lodge, similarly, emphasizes the status of Reynolds, calling her "a worthless woman."
And he frames the publication of Hamilton's confession as evidence of his
Founding Father status: "The manliness of the act, the self-inflicted punish-
ment, and the high sense of public honor thus exhibited, silenced even his
opponents; but the confession was one which must have wrung Hamilton to
the quick, and it shows an amount of nerve and determination for which our
history can furnish no parallel."[45]

Ultimately, those who explain (and explain away) his affair focus on a
variety of components that would resonate with Americans and place Hamilton in a more favorable light—essentially as a victim. Some use the story
to emphasize his humanity, and some mobilize the language of gender—
either tarring Reynolds with a misogynist brush or framing his confession
as manly. Still others highlight the strength of his marital bond. That Hamilton died young in a duel shores up their view of him as being of strong
character and masculine honor.

Twentieth-century biographers writing of the affair tend to hew to the
concept of "lapse" or a "folly."[46] They, in effect, position the sexual transgression outside Hamilton, in opposition to who he really was.

Refusing to allow the adultery to define their subject, memorializers
and biographers emphasize that his marriage was a generally happy one.
For Smertenko, it is imperative that his readers understand that "regarded
through the eyes of his family, he appears the ideal husband and father:
affectionate, comradely, sympathetic, and considerate."[47] Love letters in
courtship and through the marriage are marshaled to attest to the Hamiltons' bond. Writes one biographer, the Hamiltons, "father and mother, with
three sons and a daughter, had been happy together in the ways of affection
and under the best of fortune."[48] Extant letters from Hamilton greatly aid
biographers in characterizing the relationship as a strong one. During his
courtship, Hamilton writes to Elizabeth's sister and "confesse[s] the influence" that Elizabeth has "gained over" him. He describes her as a woman
who has "all the beauties and graces of her sex without any of those amiable

defects." Shortly after, he writes to Elizabeth (whom he calls Betsey), "My Betseys soul speaks in every line and bids me the happiest of mortals." In another letter he declares, "I love you more and more every hour. The sweet softness and delicacy of your mind and manners, the elevation of your senti-ments." Later during the war, he writes, "I have told you and I told you truly that I love you too much. You engross my thoughts too entirely to allow me to think anything else. You not only employ my mind all day, but you intrude on my sleep. I meet you in every dream and when I wake I cannot close my eyes again for ruminating on your sweetness."[49] Many such let-ters come from their courtship; Elizabeth notably destroyed much of their correspondence from their marriage. For many authors, the affair could be downplayed in contrast to the strength of Hamilton's marriage. The Reyn-olds affair does not warrant a separate discussion for Bailey, for example. He weaves it through a chronological discussion of Hamilton's life so that it comes and goes amid other events occurring at the same time. Socialist poli-tician and economics professor Broadus Mitchell also gives little attention to the affair, burying it in the middle of a paragraph on Hamilton's political difficulties at the time: "Another distraction had no excuse except the frailty of the human frame. . . . He had abundant reason to repent his brief infatua-tion—in disgust, depletion of pocket, fear of exposure, and tax on his atten-tion."[50] And, operating as a counterweight to the scandal, an appendix to the book includes many love letters to his wife.

In those few accounts that do find discord between Hamilton and his wife as a possible explanation, the emphasis is generally on his potent sexual-ity. This view has roots in accounts from the early twentieth century. One early-twentieth-century biography argues that he did not get enough sex with his wife—a woman the author calls "under-sexed"—and explains, "And so Hamilton sought lighter love elsewhere."[51] In his 1960s book on the intimate lives of the Founders, Charles Tansill similarly floats this explanation: "At home his large family was proof that he did not neglect the demands of an affectionate wife. His affair with Mrs. Reynolds showed clearly that he had an excess of virility that could only delight women with strong passions."[52]

Most accounts, however, focus on their loving bond and highlight Eliza-beth's devotion to him. By emphasizing that his wife stood by him through-out the ordeal, biographers encourage Americans to do the same. After all, if there was a wronged party here, it was his wife. Hamilton's grandson empha-sizes that Elizabeth remained devoted to the memory of her husband and illustrates this fact by the grudge she held toward Monroe, whom she held directly responsible for leaking the story to the press: "Mrs. Hamilton could never forget the behavior of Monroe when he, with Muhlenberg and Venables, accused Hamilton of financial irregularities at the time of the Reynolds incident." And he describes a moment when she was elderly and Monroe visited her home. She "did not ask him to sit down." He told her that as they were both elderly and time softened hardened hearts, he sought conciliation. But she replied that "no lapse of time, no nearness to the grave, makes any difference." Upon hearing this, Monroe "turned, took up his hat and left the room."[53] Decades later, another account explains that Elizabeth simply "did not waver in her loyalty to her husband."[54] One mid-twentieth-century biographer likewise emphatically asserts, "However shocked Elizabeth may have been by these sordid disclosures, there is no evidence whatsoever that the ugly episode affected their marriage."[55] Yet another similarly repeats that Elizabeth did not mention wanting a divorce and stayed loyal, singling out Monroe as the cause of her anger.[56]

Many other accounts directly and extensively discuss the affair and defend Hamilton from nearly every aspect of it, including by singling out the Reynolds as especially blameworthy. One 1902 account, purported to be a slightly romanticized biography, defensively describes the Reynolds affair as follows: "I shall not enter into the details of the Reynolds affair," the author explains. "No intrigue was ever less interesting." But as in most accounts, it is the elephant in the room and needs to be addressed. So the author continues, "Nor should I make even a passing allusion to it, were it not for its political ultimates." Describing Mr. and Mrs. Reynolds as a "couple of blackmailers" and the affair as "a trap" they "laid," the author is quick to note that Hamilton's actions made him no different from "the wisest of men" who had all "done before and since, when the woman has been sufficiently attractive at the right moment." Taking a tactic from the earliest of his defenders, this early-twentieth-century account depicts Mrs. Reynolds as "common and sordid" and "designing and seductive."[57]

Typical in this line of thinking is the depiction of Reynolds as beneath Hamilton. Thus, several years later, his grandson writes, "The wonder is, how a man of Hamilton's refinement and critical sense should ever have been led into an amour with a course and illiterate woman, apparently of a very low class, and this is quite inconceivable to most people." And physical attraction is not used as an explanation: "There certainly could not have been anything but rather indifferent physical attractions." (After all, her letters contain "moments of vulgarity and bad spellings.") And Allan Hamilton, much like his fellow early-twentieth-century biographers, explains the affair in a tragic manner, as something typical of other men: "Such an entanglement can only be understood by those who are familiar with the sporadic lapses upon the part of other great men who have been tempted to give way to some such impulse, and for a time degrade themselves, often to their lasting ruin."[58]

Contrasted with Hamilton's allegedly manly conduct is the behavior of those political enemies, such as Jefferson and Monroe, who sought to destroy him. Eugene E. Prussing notes in 1925, "A base attempt was made to besmirch the character of Alexander Hamilton as a public man." Calling Jefferson "directly responsible," he praises the confession as indicative of the strength of Hamilton's character.[59] For some biographers, the villain in the story, however it might reflect on his personality, is certainly not Hamilton but Monroe and others who used the story for political gain. After Bailey describes in his 1930s biography how Hamilton published information on the affair to clear his name in the financial scandal, he writes, "It must have been impossible for the public to read the pamphlet without realizing that Monroe was the man whom its complete and scandalous truth most destructively condemned."[60]

Most accounts, however, emphasize Reynolds's status as particularly unworthy of Hamilton's attentions. One author establishes the novelty of this situation by contrasting it with that of Hamilton's colleagues: "The women who had fascinated Washington, Franklin, Jefferson, and Gouverneur Morris had possessed both beauty and brains, and in France Morris's mistress was a person of culture who became a famous novelist." Those defending Hamilton's character rely on age-old depictions of lower-status seductresses to portray the elite Hamilton as a victim. Tansill's depiction of Reynolds follows the model of her as lowly: "The woman who attracted Hamilton's attention in 1791 had no claim to culture, and her letters to him reveal her to have been a person of neither education nor refinement. Maria Reynolds was a brazen hussy with a strong penchant for sex who seemed to set Hamilton's nerves on urge." The author continues, "Her sultry beauty, combined with sexual charm he had seldom encountered, seems to have made his warm Caribbean blood come to a sudden boil." Finally, this account emphasizes her as a seductress: "It was plain that she had laid a trap which was as old as Eve and had used a bait which has been attractive to men since Adam showed that free will is often on the side of sin."[61]

Airing Dirty Laundry

The affair was one thing in assessments of Hamilton's true character, but the public confession was quite another. In Western society, the "confession," especially of sexual transgression, has long held great cultural significance as the revelation of the soul.[62] That Hamilton, unlike Jefferson, who remained silent on the charges hurled at him, publicly revealed the details of his extra-marital affair seemed to elevate the event as one that captured his essence. To counter this powerful message, biographers and memorializers attempt to extend their justifications and explanations beyond simply an analysis of *why* he had the affair—they also attempt to frame for audiences how best to understand his actions afterward, including his published confession.

Many frame the act as brave and manly. Explains one early-twentieth-century writer, Hamilton's political enemies foolishly thought he "would never . . . be man enough . . . to admit his connection with Mrs. Reynolds."[63] In 1920, Henry Jones Ford notes that the confession was quite distinct from the affair and highlights how it reveals Hamilton to be a man of honor. Regarding his "personal integrity," he was "as sensitive as a good woman is to her reputation for chastity."[64] "The manliness with which he had faced every accusation affected even inveterate enemies," he explains.[65] This approach would continue through the century. Thus, one mid-twentieth-century chronicler praises him, noting that he "wrote and issued a pamphlet in which he disclosed the entire story, proving conclusively to every prejudiced man that he had not been guilty of using his public office for private gain. It required a great deal of courage to do so and many Republicans jeered at his embarrassment."[66] Another captures the view of Hamilton's greatness as visible in his public confession: "His integrity as a public man was at stake; his private life must be sacrificed. It was an amazing performance. Never in American history has a public man shown greater candor."[67]

Many accounts also position the public confession as another layer of victimization, thereby making Hamilton into a sympathetic adulterer. One mid-century biographer portrays the affair as essentially a one-time transgression—and one that had been "paid" for: "Gallantry might pass the bounds of flirtation or discretion. In one case it did, and Hamilton paid dearly for his indiscretions."[68]

The Reynolds affair itself is readily dismissed by characterizing it as an aberration, a "lapse," by those biographers who emphasize that it did not jeopardize the bond of husband and wife. Thus, the popular documentary *Alexander Hamilton* (2007) describes their marriage as weathering the public scandal and remaining an "extremely close and affectionate marriage."[69] In this portrayal, Hamilton and his wife are able to maintain their Founding marriage as a model for strength and enduring love. Chernow writes, "It is easy to snicker at such deceit and conclude that Hamilton faked all emotion for his wife, but this would belie the otherwise exemplary nature of their marriage. Mrs. Hamilton never expressed anything less than a worshipful attitude toward her husband. His love for her, in turn, was deep and constant if highly imperfect."[70] In addition to the weight that her alleged forgiveness carries, one other individual's support for Hamilton is mustered and is as persuasive for Americans. As the documentary explains, "But, after this whole thing somewhat subsided, what did Hamilton receive in the mail but a very beautiful silver bowl from Washington. Washington was no longer president now. He was telling Hamilton—you're still my man."[71] Readers are encouraged not to turn away from Hamilton in light of the fact that neither his wife nor the father of the nation did so.

Biographers seeking to complicate culpability for the extramarital affair have no shortage of explanations to draw on. For some, blame lay partly on the shoulders of Hamilton's wife. Chernow explains that Elizabeth's being away provided him with an opportunity that could not be resisted: "It was a dangerous moment for Eliza to abandon Hamilton." And he notes her inability to satisfy him, explaining Hamilton's womanizing as a product of being married to an always-pregnant wife.[72] For others, Hamilton continues to be portrayed as something of a naïve, honorable man caught up in a dirty political world. "He and his family had to endure the torment of having this affair made public, years after its termination," Joseph A. Murray quips.[73] The documentary *Alexander Hamilton* similarly highlights the politics involved: "It is a classic smear campaign," the narrator explains. "While his political enemies know very well that Hamilton was only paying blackmail money to Maria Reynolds' husband, they use the letters to claim that Hamilton was speculating with money from the Treasury."[74] With Hamilton ever the victim, thus, Hamilton's enemies take delight in what seems to be his innocence. "Jefferson and Madison couldn't believe their eyes. It was the most . . . one of the most self-destructive things they ever saw anybody do, and they just rubbed their hands. They really, more or less, realized Hamilton was finished; he never could be president now."[75] Finally, in addition to being a victim of the political world, he is also portrayed as the Reynoldses' prey. Murray explains, "He engaged in an extra-marital affair with a woman who, in collusion with her husband, had set out to destroy him politically."[76] Writing at the turn of the century, conservative journalist Richard Brookhiser says, "Mrs. Reynolds was a whore, her husband was a pimp and both were blackmailers; Hamilton was a john and a gull."[77]

However naïve Hamilton might come across in accounts that position him as a victim of politics, he is still able to appear virtuous by his behavior in handling the events that unfolded. Writer Murray, for example, praises Hamilton's conduct: "When confronted with a public accusation of this indiscretion he did not attempt to deny it or cover it up, but acknowledged his wrongdoing; he also exposed the political calumny of his opponents who had engineered the scandal."[78] The documentary *Alexander Hamilton* similarly portrays Hamilton as rising to an honorable challenge. The script reads as follows:

ALEXANDER HAMILTON (as portrayed by actor): I trust I shall always be able to bear newspaper scurrility when they accuse me of errors of judgment. But when they so unfairly attack my integrity, I cannot control my indignation.[79]

Biographers mobilize the language of frailty, making Hamilton seem vulnerable and sympathetic, despite his deceitful actions. In such accounts, the affair confirms that he was an ordinary American. This view could serve as the ultimate excuse—after all, it virtually naturalized his actions. In his preface, Murray writes that "Hamilton was subject to the frailties of his humanity and paid a severe price for his human weaknesses."[80]

As we have noted, in the Victorian era, biographers are writing about the Reynolds affair as the scandal of the Beecher-Tilton affair plays out around them. At the turn of the new millennium, Hamilton biographers are writing as another very public and politicized extramarital transgression claims public attention. In the wake of Bill Clinton's impeachment hearing, Hamilton biographies continue to sound a positive note, particularly when referring to his public confession. Perhaps gesturing to public memory of Clinton's initial public denial, Chernow explains, "When confronted with a public accusation of this indiscretion he did not attempt to deny it or to cover it up, but acknowledged his wrongdoing."[81] With strong resonances of popular analysis of the Clinton scandal surrounding his affair with Monica Lewinsky, Fleming portrays Hamilton's adultery as the product of an ego that soared when he was at the height of his political power and accomplishments. "Sexuality," Fleming explains, "became intermingled with his political triumphs and his growing fame—a phenomenon that would be repeated by more than one American politician in future decades."[82] Willard Sterne Randall sounds this relatively unsympathetic note a few years earlier when he also characterizes the affair as the product of an overweening political ego and the particulars of Hamilton's parentage, which propelled him to sexual connections with working-class women.[83]

A Gay Founding Father

In the final quarter of the twentieth century, among a relatively small circle of Americans, Hamilton has come out of the closet. The basis for the characterization of Hamilton as gay or bisexual is not that he had few heterosexual connections to his name, but rather extant letters penned by Hamilton to Laurens. In his short lifetime, Hamilton wrote romantic letters to men as well as women, and his declaration of "love" for Laurens has been recognized by some scholars as evidence of an intense emotional bond that the two men shared. Laurens and Hamilton served in the military together as part of a close inner circle of staff and supporters who made up Washington's military "family." Laurens, a South Carolinian of roughly the same age as Hamilton, also had the same military experience and status. He was a military hero who died in battle late in the Revolutionary War. The letters that Hamilton wrote to Laurens when they were separated from time to time during the war express a depth of emotionality like that appearing in Hamilton's letters to his wife.

How best to interpret the relationship shared by Hamilton and Laurens? Many wonder whether such declarations of love indicate that a physical intimacy was also shared. Others point out that we should not assume that physical intimacy did not occur—that to do so places an unfair burden on LGBTQ people, who most certainly would not have left an obvious record for fear of legal or moral persecution. The declarations most clearly point to an intense romantic bond that may or may not have been physical. Beyond that, little can be discerned. Caleb Crain's essay on the homoerotic friendship of two Philadelphia men in the 1790s contextualizes it by referencing the letters between Hamilton and Laurens. As Crain explains, it was not "unheard of for gentlemen to exchange the word *love*." Crain finds that the "affection seems genuine" but that the "tone is somewhat arch"—indeed, following conventions of the day. Historian Richard Godbeer similarly notes that the letters between the two (and among Washington and his aides) contain expressions of love and affection, yes, but that it would be "anachronistic" to read phrases, even such as Hamilton's complaint that correspondence is "the only kind of intercourse" he and Laurens can enjoy while separated, as "necessarily implying sexual intimacy." The term "intercourse," after all, means "spending time."[84]

The letters are certainly not censored in earlier accounts. At the end of the nineteenth century, for example, Sumner notes that Hamilton includes in his letters some writings that "profess very warm affection for Laurens." He characterizes the relationship as a friendship: "His most intimate friend at this period was John Laurens."[85] Similarly, in the early twentieth century, when his reputation was strongest, his grandson does not shy away from noting the bond between Hamilton and Laurens: "There is a note of romance in their friendship, quite unusual even in those days." He also explains that the Marquis de Lafayette, also part of Washington's military family, was "on the closest terms with Hamilton." Allan Hamilton's biography also includes a letter from Hamilton to Laurens. Prefacing it with "probably none of his comrades was dearer to Hamilton than Laurens, whose untimely death was a very great blow," Hamilton sees no need to address the possibility that the two could have been lovers. He includes the full letter, which contains this provocative passage: "I wish, my dear Laurens, it were in my power, by actions, rather than words, to convince you that I love you."[86]

However, as the new fields of sexology and psychology carved out their place in respected medical thought, same-sex romantic desires became pathologized, as did the *scientific* understanding of homosexuality as an illness. In turn, some Hamilton family biographers delete portions of some letters. The vast majority of biographers simply sidestep the issue by leaving out what they deem to be ambiguously worded letters. Others, such as Miller's 1959 biography, carefully explain away the sentiments expressed as indicative of "the high-flown literary language of the day" and underscore that the two "military men" were also "classical scholars" who in their language alone abided "by the code of the heroes of Plutarch."[87]

But this perceived omission would not do for gay activists and scholars, who looked to the field of history as they fought for political representation, decriminalization of same-sex romantic and sexual love, and social acceptance, riding the crested wave of other civil rights movements of the 1960s and 1970s. Thus, a late 1970s pioneering work in the field of gay and lesbian history includes excerpts of the letters exchanged between Hamilton and Laurens in its documentary record of "Gay Love in American History." Subtitled "'I Wish, My Dear Laurens . . . [to] Convince You That I Love You,'" the section on Hamilton uses his own words to highlight the nature of their bond.[88]

Although most scholars point out that such letters are inconclusive on the question of sexual orientation, some popular audiences claim him as America's gay Founding Father. The Alexander Hamilton Post 448 of the American Legion in San Francisco, a gay veterans group chartered in 1985, takes its name in honor of the perceived homosexual bond between Hamilton and Laurens.[89] Other popular researchers of LGBTQ history have used the exchange between Hamilton and Laurens as evidence of an early, possibly erotic relationship. But despite their efforts, few popular biographies even address the possibility of Hamilton's having fallen in love with another man. As with Washington's infertility and Jefferson's interactions with an adolescent slave girl, only certain handling will do.

The reputation that Hamilton enjoys in certain circles as America's gay Founder has most prominently been built up by award-winning playwright and gay activist Larry Kramer. In a speech given at Yale University, Kramer argues "that George Washington was gay, and that his relationships with Alexander Hamilton and the Marquis de Lafayette were homosexual. And that his feelings for Hamilton led to a government and a country that became Hamiltonian rather than Jeffersonian."[90] Kramer has been at work on a history of the United States that he promises will detail the depictions that are here only provocatively insinuated. But he is not alone; other popular historians have used Hamilton in their historical studies of same-sex sexuality in early America. Archivist William Benemann in his history of same-sex sexuality in early America remarks that "Hamilton's nearly ungovernable libido was legendary." Benemann selects a passage from one of Hamilton's letters to suggest that sexual interest was at play in a letter from Hamilton to Laurens written after Hamilton was engaged to be married: "In spite of Schuyler's black eyes, I have still a part for the public and another for you; so your impatience to have me married is misplaced; a strange cure by the way, as if after matrimony I was to be less devoted than I am now."[91]

Virtually all other biographies ignore the love shared between Laurens and Hamilton. One author, for example, mentions every aspect of Washington's sexual scandals, however untenable, and thereby highlights his virility, but makes no mention of the controversy around how to read the Laurens correspondence or the fact that some historians for decades have been using it as evidence of same-sex love. Indeed, the book, which highlights "intimacy" in the Founders' lives, limits itself to that shared between men and women, despite the fact that the author's conceptualization of intimacy is not solely sexual and includes bonds between parent and daughter and platonic, if flirtatious, male-female friendships. The decision to leave aside intimate bonds between fathers and sons and also between men leads perhaps to Laurens's being cast as a participant in a decidedly heterosexual relationship. Indeed, the author quotes from a letter between the two but uses only the passage where Hamilton asks Laurens to find him a suitable wife.[92] The memory of Hamilton as a gay Founder (a Founder who happened to be same-gender loving, and a forerunner for the gay community) highlights that although the topic of sex is typically taken up by dominant national ideals and identities, it can be used for sexual minorities and subcultures just as meaningfully.

Hamilton was at first the "bastard brat" who "lecherously" "polluted the spotless linen of American politics" by not only engaging in a sexual affair with a "brazen hussy" but also exposing his wife to humiliation by publishing the sordid details for all to read. He quickly became the man of impeccable public "moral integrity" and private honor who defended his and his wife's honor against the false accusations of political enemies and who stood so steadfastly for his honor that he died in a duel (tragically, as had his first-born son only a few years before). The competition for which of these Hamiltons, the immoral or the moral, would capture the American imagination began to develop in his own lifetime and deepened shortly after his being shot to death by Burr. His political enemies worried that his dying young would make him a national hero—and therefore make his policies and vision for the United States more palatable to the public.

Two events contributed to the sympathetic view of Hamilton. First, his death in a duel underscored that he was a man of great personal integrity—thereby further highlighting his affair as a "lapse" and not typical of the true man. Second, the ever-growing centralized power of the U.S. federal government has vindicated his view of the nation and made him seem even more correct in his controversial views.

In contrast to the legacies of other Founders, in the twentieth century, Hamilton's biographers have been forced to dwell more extensively on his personal transgressions in an effort to resurrect his fading popularity. While most biographers of political leaders of the American Revolution seek to assert their subjects as moral public and private role models for Americans by covering up romantic indiscretions, Hamilton's biographers are forced to give quite detailed explanations for his adultery, given that he made it so public in his own lifetime.

As a model man in both public and private realms, Hamilton's own confession hamstrings the ability of his memorializers to ignore his peccadillos and suspend disbelief. Willful ignorance has long benefited Founding Father legacies. As we have seen, the absence of documentation has vindicated Washington's childlessness (what if we had proof that he was impotent?), the nature of Jefferson's relationship with Sally Hemings (we will never know for sure), and Franklin's flirtations with Parisian women (did they or didn't they?)—but there can never be any doubt that Hamilton was born to unwed parents and that he had an extramarital affair. As Hamilton himself explains in his publication detailing the affair, "It is sufficient to say that there is a wide difference between vague rumors and suspicions and the evidence of a positive fact. . . . No man not indelicately unprincipled, with the state of manners in this country, would be willing to have a conjugal infidelity fixed upon him with positive certainty." He continues, "He would know that it would justly injure him with a considerable and respectable portion of the society."[93] Although Hamilton was praised for being forthcoming, his legacy seems to have suffered from the public's inability to avoid his tarnished reputation. His confession, despite his biographers' best efforts, seems to have stalled his position as a model man. Such transgressions can be placed in a positive light for Americans but, like a bell that has been tolled, can never be undone—making him for many biographers the most sympathetic Founding Father of all.

6

GOUVERNEUR MORRIS

We the People of the United States, in order to form a more perfect Union, establish Justice, insure domestic Tranquility. . . .

After Dinner we join in fervent Adoration to the Cyprian Queen, which with Energy repeated conveys to my kind Votary all of mortal Bliss which can be enjoyed.[1]

THESE PASSAGES, both written by Gouverneur Morris (Figure 6.1), point to two aspects of a Founder whose unconventionality challenged his biographers for nearly two centuries. The first, the preamble to the U.S. Constitution, he penned as chairman of the Committee on Style at the Constitutional Convention. It is perhaps his most notable public achievement. The second passage he wrote privately in his diary, detailing with exuberance a sexual encounter with a married woman. When we look at how Americans have remembered Morris, we can see that for most of the nine-

Figure 6.1 (*above*). Portrait of Morris. (*Gouverneur Morris Esq'r., Member of Congress.* Print by Pierre Eugène du Simitière. Published by R. Wilkinson, 1783. Courtesy of the Library of Congress, Washington, D.C., LC-USZ62-45482.)

teenth and twentieth centuries, his personal life was whitewashed. In his most recent incarnation, however, Morris's unconventional sexuality and body have become something to celebrate rather than overlook. Popular and academic biographies fuse these two aspects of Morris's personal life, portraying him as an inspirational figure for today's American—a sexually active bachelor who overcame his disability. His legacy reveals much about the nexus of masculinity, sexuality, and the body—and how it has shifted over time.

Morris spent much of his life in New York, where he was born in 1752 and died in 1816. Despite his many significant contributions to the founding of the nation, Morris has never enjoyed mainstream popularity. While still in his twenties, he signed the Articles of Confederation of 1778 and served in the Constitutional Congress in 1778 and 1779. He represented Pennsylvania at the Constitution Convention of 1787 and served as Minister Plenipotentiary to France from 1792 to 1794. In 1800, he served as a Federalist in the U.S. Senate for the State of New York. He closed his illustrious public career as chairman of the Erie Canal Commission from 1810 to 1813. In the words of one of his earliest biographers, "He made the final draft of the United States Constitution; he first outlined our present system of national coinage; he originated and got under ways the plan for the Erie Canal; as minister to France he successfully performed the most difficult task ever allotted to an American representative at a foreign capital."[2]

Yet as one of his recent biographers laments, "The two-hundred-fiftieth anniversary of Morris's birth in 2002 came and went without a single commemorative gesture by the nation he helped to found; by his native state of New York, whose constitution he helped to write; by the city of New York, whose urban plan can be fairly attributed to his bold vision; or by Columbia University, as one of its most distinguished graduates."[3]

Compared with other Founders, Morris has been relatively neglected by biographers. In the nineteenth and twentieth centuries, only four full-length biographies were published.[4] Perhaps responding to "Founders chic," publishers have put forth three academic works and two popular biographies since 2003.[5] But a veritable mountain of books has been published on other Founders. A recent biographer offers that the "simple answer" to nearly two centuries of neglect is a "persistent problem of mistaken identity," the public's confusing him with the (unrelated) Robert Morris.[6] Others have argued that his aristocratic and antidemocratic sensibilities have made him a less appealing subject than other more easily celebrated Founders.

Morris's multiple disabilities and sexual conduct may also have seemed insurmountable obstacles to memorializing him as a model American man. As a teenager, he was accidentally burned by scalding water in a manner that rendered his right arm "almost fleshless" and his "right side extensively scarred."[7] In his twenties, a carriage accident resulted in the amputation of his left leg just below the knee. Morris lived much of his life as a bachelor, enjoying sexual relationships with married and unmarried women and marrying only at the age of fifty-seven. Even when Morris married, he continued to cross boundaries of propriety. His spouse, Ann Cary Randolph, had a checkered reputation, having been accused of having a child with her brother-in-law, who was tried for and later acquitted of murdering the newborn to cover up the scandal.[8] As we have seen, popular memory of the Founding Fathers has long heralded that cadre as an extraordinary group of individuals whom Americans should emulate, yet whom we could never match in greatness.[9] Morris's nonnormative body and sexuality hardly suited him to serve as a model of American manhood, which has long emphasized both normative bodies and sexuality contained by marital monogamy.[10]

In His Lifetime

Unlike other Founders, Morris left extensive and explicit diaries that reflect on his intimate life. No such documents survive the other Founders, nor do we know whether any of them wrote anything comparable. In his diaries, Morris writes about sexual behavior in a way that emphasizes the pleasure that he shared with a married woman, his main premarital relationship, and fashions it as cosmopolitan and enlightened. Morris expresses a certain degree of pride in his lifestyle, a sense of satisfaction at his ability to combine sexual, romantic, commercial, and political concerns. Typical of the Founders' generation, Morris's writings reveal an attitude toward sexual relations that is unencumbered by the traditional moral framework that would dominate the culture of his nineteenth- and even twentieth-century biographers.[11]

In his own lifetime, Morris was the subject of humor coupled with mild derision. In a classical reference to his sexual appetite, John Jay once quipped that "Gouverneur is daily employed in making oblations to Venus."[12] That he was a disabled man seems to have contributed to his sexual reputation's harmlessness. Most surviving comments on Morris's sexual reputation connect his disability to his intimate affairs—making him very different from Aaron Burr, for example, whose reputation focused on the threat that his sexual activities posed to female virtue and to stable male society.[13] Indeed, much like Benjamin Franklin's old age, Morris's disability seems to have encouraged a more benign assessment of his active sexual life than would have been possible otherwise.

Morris lived in a world that was in transition from viewing disability as a marker of sin to the modern conception of disability as a deviation from the medicalized normative body. Scholars on the body and on disability specifically have shown that the early modern period closely associated disability and deformity with signs from God that deviance had taken place. "The surface of the body," Mary Fissell reminds us, "was supposed to speak truth about aspects of an individual's innermost core."[14] In the early modern period, "deviance," Hal Gladfelder argues, "produces a bodily signature."[15] In particular, there were sexual associations with monstrous births and other marks of illness. Although the "relationship between sin and bodily marking was slow to disappear," it is clear that in Morris's circles, older cultural associations between deviant sex and deformity blended with newer Enlightenment explanations based on reason and pointing to a "diagnosis" and a "cure."[16] Recent scholarship has noted the increased medicalization and discrimination of those defined as disabled in the modern era.

As David M. Turner and Kevin Stagg point out, "In the early modern period, deformity carried moral stigma and could also be a source of laughter and contempt."[17] We do see evidence of Morris's disability clearly eliciting humor in both America and Europe—often with sexual overtones. An oft-told joke recounts his losing his leg while escaping a jealous husband. In a letter to Morris, Jay writes that "a certain married woman after much use of your leg had occasioned your losing one." In a similar vein, Jay writes Robert Morris that it would have been better if Gouverneur Morris had "lost *something* else."[18] In reply to Jay, Gouverneur Morris writes, "Let it pass. The leg is gone, and there is an end of the matter."[19] But such stories continued. A decade later, an Englishman writes in his diary that he had met Gouverneur Morris and describes him as a man who had lost his leg "in consequence of jumping from a window in an affair of gallantry."[20] In another example of humor as a way to deal with difference, Morris records in his Paris diary one day having flirted with a married woman in front of her husband. At the end of that day, among entries about a variety of personal and professional affairs, he writes, "Dress and go at four to Made Foucault's. Dine, & after Dinner, in chatting on one Side, among other Things it is a Question as to the Causes why Children have or have not the Talents and Beauty of those who produce them. I tell her that I wish she loved me enough to let me give her a Child." Her reply indicates his physical body operated as a source of tension. "She asks if I think myself able. I reply that at least I could do my best, and as Monsieur is listening I change the Conversation."[21] Such witty, flirtatious banter was commonplace in Morris's heterosocial world and illustrates an Enlightenment distancing from an earlier era that had situated deformity and illness in a moral Godly framework.

The conceptualization of his disability as a physical indicator of his interior self indicates a social and cultural construction of disability far removed from the medicalized model and harsh stigma of the twentieth century. In one entry, he recounts an exchange with a woman at a dinner party. "How I lost my leg?" She must have asked. "It was, unfortunately, not in the military service of my country." His answer suggests that he at times feigned a cavalier attitude in social situations; he performed as a man comfortable with a disability that was something other than a badge of honor for "service to his country." He notes that she was attracted to him, despite the disability: "'Monsieur, vous avez l'air tres imposant,' and this is accompanied with that look which, without being what Sir John Falstaff calls the 'leer of invitation' amounts to the same thing." However, this repartee goes nowhere, raising the question of sincere interest. For "in the midst of the chat arrive letters, one of which is from her lover . . . now with his regiment. It brings her to a little recollection, which a little time will, I think, again banish, and, in all human probability, a few interviews would stimulate her curiosity to the experiment of what can be effected by the native of a new world who has left one of his legs behind. But, malheureusement, this curiosity cannot now be gratified, and therefore will, I presume, perish." For Morris, perhaps bested in this situation by a man "with his regiment," his only recourse, he believes, is to play the role of "experiment"—to push her beyond a threshold and suggest that his disability makes him unique and specially designed for enjoyment. That it will "perish" because he cannot move the conversation in this direction again suggests that from the outset, he had little hope of overcoming the bias against a man with only one leg.[22] These entries suggest a sense of self in opposition to able-bodied individuals and *their* world.

In the early twentieth century, Morris's disability would have likely rendered him crippled and desexualized—and ostracized him both socially and legally from society. But we see little of that status in the eighteenth century.[23] As an elite man, Morris clearly enjoyed fewer limitations than late-eighteenth-century disabled men of lower status. His mobility and success in his own time suggest less restriction and stigma than would emerge in the twentieth century in both Europe and America. Nonetheless, in his lifetime he experienced an individualized sense of difference—not just physical but also linked to his sexuality.

Morris's Diaries

Morris went to France on personal business in January 1789. By 1792, he was appointed Minister Plenipotentiary of France. After traveling in Europe and being abroad for nearly ten years, Morris returned to America in 1799. When he arrived in Paris, France was still an absolute monarchy under King Louis XVI and Marie Antoinette. Although his diaries and later writings reveal casual intimate encounters with several women, his main relationship before marriage was with a married woman, Adèlaide de Flahaut, who lived in the Louvre. At the time, the Louvre was filled with rooms and apartments that housed those who shared an attachment to the court. They met for the first time on March 21, 1789. She was twenty-eight, and he was thirty-seven. She had been married ten years at the time to Alexandre-Sebastien de Fla- haut de la Billarderie, a sixty-three-year-old Keeper of the King's Gardens. She wrote romantic novels, held a salon, and had a lover—the bishop of Autun, Charles-Maurice de Talleyrand-Périgord, who was rumored to be the father of her son.

Such affairs were not unusual, although, as we have seen, American dip- lomats abroad, such as John Adams, liked to loudly contrast American mor- als with Parisian customs.[24] Yet we know that late-eighteenth-century sexual cultures, especially (though not exclusively) for elites, afforded such men as Morris with ample opportunities for intimacy outside marriage. Although Morris's most detailed reflections were recorded in his diary while in Paris, he conducted an active sexual and romantic life in America as well as Europe. With its larger urban centers, Europe may have offered more opportunities for lovers, but as recent scholarship on late-eighteenth-century New York and Philadelphia has shown, even these relatively smaller American urban centers suffered no shortage of sexual outlets.[25] Morris's relationship with Madame de Flahaut was possible because of the salon culture of eighteenth- century France, but the evidence suggests that we would be mistaken in viewing his time in Paris as a sexual awakening for an American diplomat from a so-called Puritanical New World.

His is no secret diary devoted only to sex. In the pages of his diary, Mor- ris's sexual life melds seamlessly with his salon socializing, his official deal- ings in France, and his assessment of this country's Revolutionary crisis. For Morris, the sexual and the political were part of one Parisian life for him and part of his identity as an American statesman abroad. Nearly all of his diary entries speak to his sense of sexual adventure, appeal, sociability, and politi- cal stature. Given this content, it is difficult to speculate as to his motives for writing the entries. They seem at once part of a process of personal reflection and travel and also useful for recording political, commercial, and social net- works in motion. In one concise entry, for example, he writes about church property, details of finance, bread riots in Paris, and sexual intimacy with Madame de Flahaut. In his diary, political and sexual dealings mingle on the page as the actions did in his daily life. Morris most probably does not write these diaries, with their detailed remarks on sex and flirtation with married women, for the public to read.[26] And as such their musings, reflections, and remembrances should be noted not as public memorializing but as private self-fashioning of an elite unmarried sexually active man with a disability. All activities combined to fill his days, and he clearly positions himself as living the life of a successful gentleman, which for him included a sexual and romantic component.

Shortly after arriving, Morris quickly settled into the salon culture. As we saw with Franklin, unlike the later depoliticized salons of the nineteenth century, by the outbreak of the French Revolution, salons had shifted from an elite social culture to a politicized public sphere for French aristocracy and intellectual elites: "Both salons and *mondanité* (society life) existed in close proximity to the worlds of politics, literature, art, fashion, and business, all of which preoccupied French elites."[27] The salons were part of a broader culture that Morris appears to have enjoyed as he conducted his political and business engagements. Salons included eating and dancing and were generally known for "a luxurious space, feminine governance, a select company, polite conversation" and heterosociability.[28] Morris would not have been out of place at the salons he frequented. As Steven Kale reminds us, "Politicians, diplomats, artists, and journalists frequented the same salons and participated in the same system of social networks."[29] Salons, headed by women, were fully part of the emerging public sphere of the French Revolution.[30]

Unlike Franklin's, Morris's main relationship remained largely secretive. The diaries reveal a social setting with constant entries and exits of diplomats, friends, and salon members. The situation afforded few sustained periods for Morris and Adèle to be alone uninterrupted, yet perhaps as a disabled man, and a foreigner, Morris's liminal position enabled him to take flirtation from erotic banter and wit common to salon culture and pursue it to physical sexual intimacy. His diaries express a certain enjoyment at mixing business and official affairs with clandestine sexual moments. In one entry, for example, he records taking advantage of a moment when he was alone with Madame de Flahaut: "We seize the Opportunity."[31] The following month, he writes of a particular moment that the two shared. After discussing land-purchasing policies in America to shed light on how private property might be preserved, given the circumstances of the Revolution, he attended a dinner party at the Louvre. When his lover's husband went to another room after dinner, Morris stayed behind "with the Ladies," perhaps because his disability made such female space more easily available to him. Shortly thereafter, the women also left him and his lover alone. He wrote,

"And immediately I take Madm on my Lap and at the imminent Risque of Discovery by two Doors and one Window perform the Act. I think of all others Monsr would be least pleasd to behold."[32]

In a number of entries, Morris writes about engaging in sexual relations in the presence of others, unbeknownst to them. A dinner at the Louvre with Adèle and Mademoiselle Duplessy resulted in the following entry: "After Dinner while the latter is playing the fortepiano, as she is near sighted . . . [we] almost perform the genial Act."[33] In another example, he writes, "We perform the Act at Dusk in the Presence of Madlle."[34] In another entry, he writes, "Go to the Louvre, and being disappointed in the Expectation of a clear Stage, Made is so well disposed that we take the Chance of Interruption and celebrate in the Passage while Madlle is at the Harpsichord in the Drawing Room. The husband is below. Visitors are hourly expected. The Doors are all open."[35]

Morris uses an unusually large vocabulary for describing his intimate relations with women. The extent of his vocabulary demonstrates to himself his erudition and sophistication. Some of his terms simply dislocate sexual intimacy from romantic love, focusing on the mechanics of pleasurable erotic interactions. In one entry, he writes, "we perform the usual Exercises." In another, he writes, "[we] performed certain Gesticulations." Often he refers to doing the "Act" or the "operation"—as in, "after Dinner we embrace to mutual Satisfaction and in a few Minutes 'Repeat the Operation.'"[36] But as the above passage illustrates, mutual pleasure was important, and very often Morris's vocabulary demonstrates a pleasure that is rooted in the joy shared equally by intimates. For example, he writes, "as usual communicate the Joy" or "the usual amusement." Other terms include "Love's Disport" or doing the "hymeneal Rights."[37]

In Morris's diaries, sexual intimacy is venerated as a mystery or as a gift passed down from the ancients. This reference to the Greeks and Romans is typical of his era's reverence for that culture. For example, he writes, "[we] celebrate the Misteries," "we celebrate," and "[w]e pay our Adorations." Very often he writes of "Cyprian Mysteries," "Cyprian Rites," or "*join[ing] in fervent Adoration to the Cyprian Queen*." References to the "Cyprian Queen" or versions thereof speak to Aphrodite, the Greek Goddess of Eros, which again emphasizes physical and sexual attraction—not love in a romantic sense, but sexuality and eroticism.[38]

Morris's extensive vocabulary reveals an attitude toward his sexual relations that is unencumbered by the moral framework that dominates nineteenth-century biographers. His understanding of sexual behavior emphasized pleasure, mutually shared between a bachelor and a married woman and fashioned as cosmopolitan and enlightened. Morris expresses a certain degree of pride in his lifestyle, a sense of satisfaction at his ability to combine sexual, romantic, commercial, and political concerns. For Victorian and even twentieth-century biographers, this approach to sexual expression outside marriage would complicate celebration of his legacy. Yet there was (of course) an easy solution.

Remembering Morris as a Chaste Bachelor

Morris's sexual and affective world may have been enjoyable to him, but it would prove undesirable to his few nineteenth-century biographers. Not long after Morris's death in 1816, Jared Sparks wrote a book about his life and accomplishments that includes selections from his personal papers. Sparks, a respected popular historian of the American Revolution, professor, and president of Harvard, is perhaps best known for his published volumes of writings of Franklin and Washington. Beginning in 1832, Sparks published a three-volume work entitled *The Life of Gouverneur Morris, with Selections from his Correspondence and Miscellaneous Papers; Detailing Events in the American Revolution, the French Revolution, and in the Political History of the United States.*

Typical of nineteenth-century biographers of the men identified as Founding Fathers, with their goal of cultivating moral, national character, this earliest biographer makes little mention of Morris's personal life.[39] Despite declaring in his preface, "It has not been my aim to write a panegyric, to conceal defects, or emblazon good qualities, but rather to present traits of character, acts, and opinions, in their genuine light and just bearings, and leave them to make their proper impressions," Sparks is unable to break the conventions of the day that had solidified in the decades after Morris's death. Sparks covers nothing sexual or romantic in his biography, leaving that portion of Morris's life and identity hidden from public eye. Morris's intense romantic and erotic relationship with Madame de Flahaut is not even mentioned, although Sparks could not have avoided reading about it in Morris's diaries and letters. He chooses instead to spend less than two pages on Morris's later-in-life marriage, leaving Morris to appear as a chaste if social bachelor for much of his life.[40]

Some fifty years later, in the absence of biographers stepping forward, Morris's own granddaughter published *The Diary and Letters of Gouverneur Morris*. Echoing Sparks's "sense of propriety," Anne Cary Morris removes all evidence of his romantic relationship with Madame de Flahaut.[41] As we have seen, published volumes of letters and edited diaries—particularly those such as Morris's granddaughter's, which gives no indication that material has been removed—have the disastrous effect of passing off edited material, fashioned with an eye to a particular telling of Morris's life, as unedited and in his own hand. In this way, nineteenth-century volumes by Sparks and Morris's granddaughter use Morris's own words to fashion an individual, the chaste but social bachelor, whom he would scarcely have recognized—or liked, for that matter.

In 1888, Theodore Roosevelt continued the impulse to depict Morris's life as following the early American model of the social and charming bachelor. Such descriptions sidestep questions of extramarital relationships (evidence of which would serve as a direct assault on the institution of marriage) and, with their emphasis on heterosocial interactions, suggest a normative social and presumably sexual interest in women. In his biography, Roosevelt celebrates Morris as a young man in colonial New York, born into wealth and privilege, "a handsome, high-bred young fellow, of easy manners and far from puritanical morals," adding, "He enjoyed it all to the full, and in his bright, chatty letters to his friends pictures himself as working hard, but gay enough also: 'up all night—balls, concerts, assemblies—all of us mad in the pursuit of pleasure.'"[42]

Roosevelt famously conceived of masculinity in both a traditional upper-class model of sociability and his better-known emphasis on the rough and tumble, robust masculinity.[43] In portraying Morris as a success in his political world as well as in the politicized social world of Paris, Roosevelt opens up the possibility of suspect models of masculine deviance. Roosevelt thus protects his subject by explaining Morris's character in that context: "Although Morris entered into the social life of Paris with all the zest natural to his pleasure-loving character, yet he was far too clear-headed to permit it to cast any glamour over him. . . . He enjoyed the life of the salon very much, but it did not in the least awe or impress him; and he was of too virile fibre, too essentially a man, to be long contented with it alone."[44] Given this problematic social world—marked by a stereotyped and nationally infused perception of European decadence as unmanly—Roosevelt explicitly describes Morris's reaction to Paris as properly American.

As for the remarkable three-year affair that Morris had with Madame de Flahaut, Americans would not learn anything about it or what it meant to Morris from Roosevelt. From his biography, readers got the sense that their relationship was a diplomatic one: "'She was thoroughly conversant with the politics of both court and Assembly;' her 'precision and justness of thought was very uncommon in either sex,' and, as time went on, made her a willing and useful helper in some of Morris's plans. . . . She was much flattered by the deference that Morris showed for her judgment, and in return let him into not a few state secrets. She and he together drew up a translation of the outline for a constitution for France, which he had prepared, and through her it was forwarded to the king."[45] In this sense, Roosevelt captures an important part of this relationship that someone focusing purely on the titillating or sexual aspects of his affair could easily overlook. But for Morris, the sexual and the political were part of one Parisian life for him and part of his identity as an American statesman abroad. The extent of their social activities was reduced to dinners with Talleyrand and others—but again seamlessly linked to politics.

Davenport Transcriptions of Original Diaries

It would not be until 1939 that Americans would be able to glimpse Morris's personal life—and even then few would do so. Ann Cary Davenport, Morris's great-granddaughter, edited and published a two-volume set of his writings that have become some of the most famous observations of the French Revolution by an American. Although relatively few individuals had access to the edited volumes, and this was certainly no popular work of biography, the Davenport volumes undoubtedly make Morris's revealing diaries available to later biographers.

The original manuscript diaries themselves had been defaced by someone seeking to shape public memory of Morris by preventing some of what he wrote from ever being seen. In several places, the Davenport transcription preserves words now lost from the original manuscript record. In some cases, only one or two words have been crossed out. On April 15, 1791, for example, Morris writes, "Shortly after Dinner I go to the Louvre and we celebrate." Whoever defaced the original diary understood his sexual code and scribbled out the word "celebrate"—his having ever written it evidenced only by Davenport now. In other places, several lines have been obliterated. In one instance, twenty-two lines of the diary were carefully crossed out, and in one or two places several pages have been torn from the diary—lost for good (Figure 6.2).

In other places, the original manuscript diaries reveal material edited from the Davenport volumes. Despite her contribution to preserving Morris's original words, occasionally Davenport chooses not to include intimate material. Davenport's November 3, 1789, transcription, for example, contains ellipses; it reads, "Go to the Louvre. A long Tete a Tete with Madame de Flahaut. . . . Stay till twelve." But if one consults the original diaries, one learns that removed from this passage is his account of what happened while he was

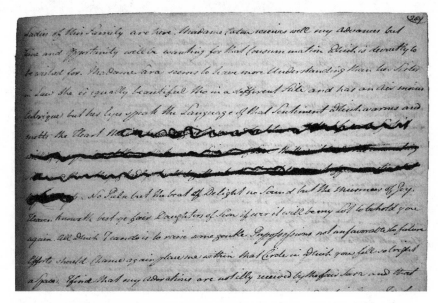

Figure 6.2. Page from Morris's original manuscript diaries showing someone's attempt to shape public memory by eliminating evidence of some of the content. (*The Papers of Gouverneur Morris.* Manuscript Division, Library of Congress, Washington, D.C. Photograph by Melanie R. Miller.)

at the Louvre: "She being yet a little indisposed and I not perfectly well we are chaste tho with strong Inclinations on both sides to be otherwise." To provide another example, Davenport's entry for the following day reads:

> Return to the Louvre and send to see if Mr. Le Couteulx is yet returned. He is not. Endeavor to disswade her from going to see a new Play is wretched, as I am informed, and at the first Representations of which much Disturbance is apprehended. She persists. I tell her that if she will not go I will embrace her, but otherwise not. She tries every Blandishment . . . a very serious Scene which terminates in a Declaration on her Part that she will not go to the Play and will not receive the Pleasure, that she may convince me it is Love, not Desire, which operates on her Conduct.

But if we consult the original diary, we discover that Davenport shies away from a more sexually explicit moment shared between the two and written about by Morris. "She tries every Blandishment," he writes, "and I suffer her to succeed so far as to present myself at the Portal of Loves Temple but will not go beyond the Threshold and finally retire. This induces of course a very serious Scene." Here, Morris presents himself as wholly desired by her, physically and emotionally. He insists that she not go to the play and she takes the initiative in sex, which he halts, leaving her to declare love, not lust. In their lover's quarrel, she then "complains also that I did not forbid her, in which Case she would have obeyed, as she repeatedly assured me. I then offer a new Bargain, which is, to caress her and afterwards permit her to do as she pleases." She then receives a written request for her presence at the play, which she turns down. "This," concludes Morris, "is the Result of that Emotion which follows recent Enjoyment."[46] Davenport, thus, discretely removes five words that attest to what precisely was the "enjoyment" that causes in his mind his lover to cancel her plans and spend the evening with him. The diary reveals that he writes that after offering his "new Bargain" "to caress her and afterwards permit her to do as she pleases. We accordingly proceed to Action."[47]

In a few instances, Davenport is able to discern what has been crossed out in the original diary and includes the information in her transcription. Nearly all the edited material is sexual, but some was cut for other conventions of gentility. For example, on April 12, 1789, Morris writes, "Drinking party in America where the Chamber Pot is set on the table with the Bottles. He sets her right as to the Chamber Pot which is placed in a Corner of the Room."[48] In the original diary now, "Chamber Pot" at both mentions is replaced with emphatic, dark, scribbled crossing-out.

It would not be until the mid–twentieth century, more than one hundred sixty years after the relationship had occurred, that a biographer would directly address Morris's affair with Madame de Flahaut. In the twentieth century, biography, while still, of course, aiming to tell a moral tale, began to focus on psychology and on the individual. Making good use of the Davenport volumes as well as the original manuscript sources, a 1952 biography by Howard Swiggett is surprisingly frank about Morris's sexual life. The author explicitly bemoans the historical shift in standards toward prudery that would not celebrate such an accomplished bachelor.

Swiggett writes while the culture was committed to the idealized, desexualized, nuclear family but also celebrated bachelor culture that was best captured by the debut of *Playboy* magazine in 1953.[49] Swiggett portrays the late eighteenth century as a time of greater freedom of movement and possibilities. For Swiggett, the salon culture of late-eighteenth-century France is far more desirable than the mid-twentieth-century Americans he writes for: "These people are human and familiar today. There was a great deal of fun and gusto about them, and almost a complete absence of that mixture of pious prudery and 'refinement' which appeared sixty-odd years later." For

Swiggett, this trend is lamentable: "Biographies of his adversaries portrayed him as a butterfly and a social climber though not a libertine. In part the false picture arose from the lack of sources now available, but even more from the myth-making process which made of the Founding Fathers men utterly deaf to the uproar of sexual life."[50]

Determined to position himself as of the nonsqueamish world of the eighteenth century and opposed to the prudish Victorian biographers, Swiggett includes passages that speak to this point: "Proceed gently very gently till at last her Lips are prest to mine so much by her Movement as by my Effort. After this I take her in my Arms and in a low voice of interrupted Tenderness exclaim how delightful to press to our Bosom the Being whom we love. I let her enjoy this Sentiment quietly for some Time and find by numerous little Circumstances that her Lips are again disposed to the Expression of Delight." But his account is far more softened and still remarkably romanticized than faithful to the original explicit diaries. The setting is perhaps too much for him to resist: "The melodrama of 1793 began with the King's execution and ended with the Queen's," begins one chapter. Swiggett uses the romance in his breathless depiction of love in the age of Revolution: "Who can say what was in the minds of these two people in the months that followed, each at times so completely recognizable, each so incomprehensible? Their behavior is wanton and flagrant, and one may say, well, this is simply the loose morals of the eighteenth century. But that is frequently not the case at all, when as so often they are as careful of what people may say as any conventional moderns."[51]

Roosevelt comments on Morris's physical attractiveness, but beginning with Swiggett, Morris's body becomes a site of displaced sexual interest—casting a light away from his intimate relationships and focusing it instead on his disability and his desirability, using growing Freudian influences to explain how Morris's psychological and sexual development was affected by the loss of his leg: "Physically he was magnificent, well over six feet tall, a strong, athletic figure without the lankness of Jefferson or Monroe. . . . Even after the loss of a leg his bearing was so splendid that the French sculptor, [Jean-Antoine] Houdon, had him pose for his figure of Washington," writes Swiggett.[52]

Swiggett puts a lot of explanatory weight on Morris's leg: "Whenever a lady, who had once yielded to him, refused to go on, he behaved in the most unreasonable and petty manner, usually leaving at once. It is so unlike his sweet reasonableness in larger matters that the question arises whether it is not the result of sensitiveness about his leg, 'the mark of that misfortune to this hour,' a sensitiveness usually masked, but still representing his only inner uncertainty and sense of inferiority." At other times he notes what he called Morris's "'aggression' complex arising from the inferiority his amputated leg gave him." Writing about Morris being left behind as the army mobilized, Swiggett paints a remarkably sexualized image. "Gouverneur Morris, a stump hanging from his magnificent body," he writes, underscoring his point about being left out of normalized manhood where soldiers are praised and attractive to women. He "had to watch them" leaving as "all the beauties" watched from every door and window.[53]

Public reaction to the Swiggett biography was mixed. Academic reviewers, writing prior to the advent of a subfield of the history of sexuality that would have pointed to the significance of his erotic identity, instead laud the book for not being dishonest about Morris's personal life but criticize the book for neglecting that which was considered more important activities of political leaders of the Revolutionary era—state building. The flagship journal of early American history notes that it was "entertaining" and "lively fare for those who enjoy knowing the peccadilloes of history's magnetic figures" and praises Swiggett's ability to not "quibble with his subject's morals"—but also criticizes the book for not focusing on that which was "serious."[54] The *Yale Law Journal* criticizes Swiggett for giving "tomcattery primary consideration" at the expense of Morris's notable achievements. "Acts of intercourse with Adèle de Flahaut, for example, are analyzed for number, location, and other preliminary and subsequent details on some 73 pages," laments the reviewer, while "the work of the Committee on Style rates something less than a page."[55]

Although academic reviewers were unappreciative, *Time* magazine's reviewer praises the book, embraces the personal life of this unusual Founder, and pitches the melding of psychological and sexual, the personal and political to its middle-class readership of 1950s America. The review in *Time* seems to have been heavily influenced by the cult of the bachelor in mid-twentieth-century America. Calling him a "Merrymaking Forefather," the reviewer praised the overly romantic and psychologized account and includes such lines as "But for Bachelor Morris, the cause of freedom was no reason to neglect the cause of love." Despite this review in *Time* magazine, Morris's place in public memory remained tenuous, allowing him to therefore be "rediscovered" yet again in later years.

In 1970, an academic historian attempts to rescue Morris from lack of recognition in a political biography that focuses on his most notable accomplishments. The book does not hide his affair with Adèle de Flahaut, but in its two-paragraph description, the book does not characterize the relationship as anything other than an affair with a married woman—as it was.[56]

Perhaps this is why academic reviewers called it "clear but unexciting."[57] The author explains the happy marriage using sexual appeal and sexual drive: "He had had his share of conquests, and now, with an appreciation of the practical requirements of marriage, he had selected a compatible woman of youth, good looks, high birth, good education, and, if that much of her enemies' charges was true, lively sexuality." (Anne had been accused of "intimacy with a Negro slave, and of advances to a guest at the home of friends" in addition to giving birth to and destroying a child conceived with her sister's husband.)[58]

At the bicentennial, the popular *American Heritage* magazine ran a story on Morris, noting that he was "one of the most valuable of the Founding Fathers." It also masks his affair with Flahaut as a personal relationship with political overtones. Flahaut's relationship with Talleyrand is described, as is Flahaut's desire to marry Morris. But only someone familiar with this bachelor's relationship would have known of their own intimate connection. Flahaut and Talleyrand are, indeed, described as having an affair. Talleyrand is described as her "official lover," but Morris and Flahaut appear more like social intimates, once again presenting Morris as the chaste, but desirable, bachelor.[59]

A Founder Rediscovered

A recent move to explore and make accessible the lives of the more aristocratic Founders has opened up new public space for memorializing Morris. It is too soon to know the outcome for Morris's reputation from the recent publication of several biographies. In recent years, five biographies have been published about him. Reflecting our current discomfort over viewing the intimate lives of the political Founders of this country, the books capture our culture's tension between the overtly sexualized (yet superficial) and the continued emphasis on depersonalized political views.

Given the cultural shift toward incorporating personal lives into biography, the recent biographies all acknowledge the affair with Madame de Flahaut, although some do so with more emphasis than others. A recent biography by one academic historian attempts to place Morris among the pantheon of great men who founded the nation. Yet Morris's personal life is not obliterated in the hands of this biographer—a full chapter is devoted to explaining his affair with Madame de Flahaut.

At the same time, given its scholarly focus on his political world, James Kirschke's academic account appears to be an unlikely candidate for bringing Morris to the public. It spends few pages discussing the affair and characterizes it as follows: "They entertained each other in an *amitié amoureuse*, a romantic friendship, with the major emphasis on the *amitié* (friendship)." It also uses physical appeal both to capture the reader's attention and to explain his self-indulgences: "As regards female charms, he seems to have felt that the only way to get rid of temptation was to yield to it."[60]

The most popular of these five twenty-first-century books capitalizes on Morris's sexual life. In 2004, a journalist published *Gentleman Revolutionary: Gouverneur Morris, the Rake Who Wrote the Constitution*. With its emphasis on Morris's sexual and romantic life, the account is by the far the more popular read.[61] Yet the characterization of Morris as a "rake" is problematic and underscores the troubling nature of Morris's affair with Madame de Flahaut. If one were to characterize it as mundane, Morris would become the Founder who endorsed nonmarital and extramarital relationships as realistic possibilities for American manhood. To characterize him as a rake is remarkably less subversive, because it mobilizes a sensationalism that one need not take seriously as a model of American life. Robert Lovelace, one of the most famous rakes of the eighteenth century, is a character in the best-selling novel *Clarissa*. Lovelace is typically misogynist, has no intentions of providing joy for his lover, and focuses solely on the quantity of his conquests and his pride—a character type quite far from Morris.

Morris rarely describes himself as a seducer in his writing. It is true that predatory men, then as now, view themselves as merely enacting a model of male sexual prowess that entails seduction and coercion. Yet, Lovelace also continually uses derogatory terms to describe Clarissa (witch), and such men, both fictional and real, nearly always reveal the use of force. The description of Morris as a rake has found its way into other works. Although a recent book on the intimate lives of the Founders does not include a chapter on Morris, he is referenced once—as "Gotham's best known rake" in a chapter on Hamilton.[62] Morris, however, never mentions pleasure at forced conquest, nor does he quantify his experiences in a way that suggests his focus was on numbers of seduced and abandoned partners. At times, he specifically describes himself as unlike other men who cared not for women's interests in them. Describing dinner on one New Year's Eve, for example, he writes, "At Midnight the Gentlemen kiss the Ladies but I do not attempt this Operation because there is some resistance and I like only the yielding Kiss and that from Lips I love."[63] The rake, as a type, self-servingly highlights his ability to bring pleasure, which is generally connected to quantities of women rather than long-term relationships, but notably for Morris, his pride at giving pleasure is not always focused on self but rather emphasizes mutuality ("we perform twice very well the pleasing act").[64] In many diary entries, he uses "we" instead of "I" when referring to having sex.

Emphasizing the debauched headiness of the late eighteenth century, the conservative popular journal the *National Review*, for which Richard Brookhiser writes, loves the depiction of him as a rake in Brookhiser's account. It declares, "There is more good living, more elegant theater, and certainly more documented sexual seduction in Morris's life than in that of any other member of our republic's heroic generation. In feats of voluptuousness Morris was without a superior, perhaps without an equal; only Aaron Burr can possibly compete with him in attested gallantry in bedrooms and Parisian salons. But, unlike Burr, Morris found time, in between what he called his oblations to Venus, to write the Constitution of the United States." Sex makes for, well, sexy biography to contemporary readers. Yet for the reviewer, Morris's explicit writings could be reconciled with the other Founders only if depicted as French. "We are very far, here, from the severe neoclassicism usually associated with the founding generation," quips the reviewer. "Morris had forsaken the examples of Addison's Cato and the American Cincinnatus, General Washington, for the pretty, perfumed classicism of Boucher and Fragonard." Yet Morris was the product not of French culture but of New York and Philadelphia as well as any European urban center. And his diaries reveal that his philandering was not awakened or limited to his time in France. Morris's behavior and identity were the product of the elite cosmopolitan pleasure culture of the late-eighteenth-century Atlantic World that the Founders inhabited.

His Body

The recent popular and academic biographies of Morris self-consciously take as their goal securing public recognition of an overlooked Founder. Writing in an era of skepticism for yet another celebratory account of an elite white man, the authors are also able to use sex and disability to make Morris seem ordinary, vulnerable, and sympathetic. Drawing on earlier depictions, his sexuality and disability are frequently linked, with many accounts celebrating his sexual prowess and portraying his disability as a potential hurdle that he cleared.

Part of this project is that Morris's body is imagined to be an appealing one. Kirschke's recent academic account briefly describes Morris's desirability and his physical attributes: "That many women could not resist his charm quickly becomes apparent to anyone studying the period. By all reports, as well as by the evidence provided in the surviving portraits, Morris was a big man, with a heavy, sensual face, a large nose, a broad forehead, and a worldly manner."[65] Recent popular biography also takes this approach. Brookhiser writes that at six feet tall, Morris had an "imposing physical stature." And he notes, "He rarely paid for sex." This attraction apparently transcends time. Commenting on an image of Morris, the book explains, "Women of the twenty-first century who see the picture say they would like to meet the subject."[66]

Visualizing Morris has also proved to be problematic for biographers. Reinforcing the *able-bodied* image, several works mention that Morris stood in as a body double for Washington as Jean-Antoine Houdon created his famous sculpture of the general. One includes an image of the completed Washington sculpture, so we have an image of Washington, perhaps *the most* able-bodied of Founding Fathers, appearing in a biography on Morris—the statue standing in for Morris's body in effect and the caption reading that Morris "posed for the body."[67]

The images of Morris most often used in his biographies are portraits of only his face. Brookhiser's work sensationally features an image of Morris seated in a chair, his wooden leg in full view (Figure 6.3). The image used was created in 1861 by Alonzo Chappel. Notably, Chappel chose to expand on the Ezra Ames portrait of Morris by adding a peg-leg to draw attention to his distinctiveness. Being featured on the cover of an account that focuses on Morris sexual life and fashions him as the "rake who wrote the constitution" yokes together his sexuality and disability. The image evokes something of a "pirate" model of masculinity. His peg-leg conjures up that deviant counter-norm model of manhood in a way that celebrates the masculine risk-taking and sexual conquests that are vividly highlighted in the book.

Popular resources today continue this view of Morris's disability as a *hurdle* he cleared and link it to his sexual life. The Constitution Center's online biographical sketch euphemistically gestures to his extensive romantic history: "As a young man, Morris lost his leg in a freak carriage accident, but this did not appear to diminish his very active engagement with women. . . . Despite his wooden leg, Morris served in the militia as well."[68] Here the sketch fashions his manly attributes of sexual and military prowess.

The ever-changing Wikipedia has at various times offered versions on a similar theme. For example, one rendition, under "personal life and legacy" once mentioned only his marriage and the following: "Unhampered by his wooden leg, he led a lively life with both married and unmarried women."[69] Yet we know that his mobility and success in his own time suggest less restriction and stigma than would emerge in the twentieth century in both Europe and America. Indeed, it would be just as plausible to state that *because* of his disability he enjoyed romantic relations with a variety of women as it would be to state that *in spite of* his disability he did so—as

Figure 6.3. Portrait of Morris. Relying on a portrait by Ezra Ames, Alonzo Chappel added a peg-leg to his 1861 version. The portrait, used on the cover of an account that fashions Morris as the "rake who wrote the Constitution," links his sexuality and his disability. (Cover of Richard Brookhiser, *Gentleman Revolutionary: Gouverneur Morris, the Rake Who Wrote the Constitution* [New York: Free Press, 2003].)

most accounts anachronistically portray it. Wikipedia later changed it to this: "Morris's public account for the loss of his leg was that it happened in a carriage accident, but there is evidence that this was a story to cover for a dalliance with a woman, during which he jumped from a window to escape a jealous husband. Morris was well-known throughout much of his life for having many affairs, with both married and unmarried women, and recorded many of these in his diary."[70]

That Morris focused largely on one main lover in Paris and wrote extensively about mutual sexual pleasure puts the lie to the image of him as a rake. Yet the image of him as a rake celebrates for today's readers a masculine personal life that is designed to connect with contemporary audiences who may otherwise pull away from the cane-wielding aristocratic Founding Father.

When Morris wrote the preamble to the U.S. Constitution, he cemented his position in American history. Generations of Americans who learned about Morris saw a man who for most of his life remained a bachelor and was active in social circles, diplomacy, and business. For more than a century, if one were to approach Morris as a model of American manhood—one that links national masculinity to historical models of manliness—only the chaste bachelor would be in view.

Relatively few nineteenth- and twentieth-century authors have written about Morris, but for those few who have, his life first has to be recast to fit the early American model of the heterosocial yet chaste bachelor. Morris's transformation from chaste bachelor to the "rake who wrote the Constitution" highlights the enduring problem of publicly remembering and celebrating a sexually active, disabled, bachelor Founding Father.

CONCLUSION

———◦◦◦———

THE POLITICAL LEADERS of the American Revolution and the early
United States were men who lived in a world now lost to us. Seeking to make moral, masculine examples of those men, Americans
have constructed various interpretations of their private lives to stand alongside their celebrated public accomplishments. In examining how sex and
intimacy have operated in the public memory of the Founders' lives, we can
see that sex has long figured in civic identity.

In many ways, the personal lives of the Founding Fathers come down
to us from the subjects themselves. It has often been said that the Founders shaped how their own legacies would develop. Through very conscious
editing of personal papers, through autobiography, and through constant
self-scrutinizing, they performed *themselves* in life and in death. The Founders were acutely, self-consciously aware of their places in history, and they
crafted their images for posterity.[1] The most famous example of this is Benjamin Franklin and his *Autobiography*, which has been used to illustrate his
self-fashioning. As the previous chapters have shown, we can also see the
impact of the Founders' self-fashioning in many of their legacies, including
George Washington's comportment, Alexander Hamilton's published explanation for his adulterous affair, Thomas Jefferson's careful controlling of his
papers, and John Adams's loud Puritanical protestations.

Beginning in the nineteenth century, Americans would not remain content with merely celebrating public and political achievements of the Founders. They also wanted to laud the most famous leaders of the American

Revolution as singularly and uniquely model men in their private lives. This sense of that generation's greatness is today explicitly contrasted with contemporary culture. The love between John and Abigail, for example, is noted for its "unconditional commitment" and held aloft as something that "especially today" "is the exception rather than the rule."[2] In an era of intensive media coverage of celebrity divorces, high-profile political adultery scandals, and controversy over marriage equality for lesbians and gay men, depictions of idealized marriage between George and Martha, John and Abigail, Martha and Thomas, and Alexander and Elizabeth acquire significant resonance. Their relationships become the model of American national virtue—a greatest generation, which modern Americans can never hope to match, a sacred national benchmark against which to castigate contemporary culture.

This book has focused on how the long history of sex in the public memory of the Founders of our nation has generally reflected mainstream ideals. But that history has also shored up sexual minorities as well as political causes. President Bill Clinton's team, for example, pointed to the adultery of Hamilton to attempt to offset some of the criticism he was taking. By gesturing not only to history but also to a Founder, the message was one of legitimacy. Abolitionists used the story of Jefferson as a slave-owning rapist to highlight the corruption of the nation in its refusal to end slavery. Gay activists have pointed to Hamilton to show that LGBTQ people have contributed to the nation without recognition and while enduring unacceptable persecution.

The did he/didn't he question has come up repeatedly in the histories examined here. Although history is full of gaps in the record and lacks many desired smoking guns, Americans have never hesitated to speak definitively about the loves and inner lives of the Founders, despite a lack of documentation. Definitive answers alleviate uncertainty. The desire for them underscores that the stakes are quite high in examinations of the private lives of individuals as important to national identity as are the Founders.

Although my focus here has been on intimate lives, the mythic proportions revealed should give us pause when we read the latest blockbuster biographies of the Founders. In the Middle Ages, hagiographies were written to venerate the saints. Today, the popular biographies that are lately in vogue are sophisticated enough to acknowledge the complexities of race, class, and gender inequity in the past or the ups and downs of married life and the failings of individual men. But such accounts are *warts-and-all hagiography*—ones that present failings only to dismiss them or have them overshadowed by an overarching theme of exceptional greatness. The final lines of a recent biography on John and Abigail Adams illustrate well the tone of exceptionalism in today's popular biographies: "John drew his last breath shortly after six o'clock. Witnesses reported that a final clap of thunder sounded at his passing, and then a bright sun broke through the clouds. . . . [H]is body was laid to rest alongside Abigail's. They have remained together ever since."[3] Many of the great nineteenth-century-derived myths and tales of romantic moments of the Founders are still in circulation today—indeed, arguably more than ever.

The romanticized view of the intimate desires and sexual relationships of the Founders offends our understandings of history and serves only the present. We still glide over uncomfortable historical nuances regarding such matters as the nature of love and marriage in early America.[4] Jefferson was some thirty years older than Sally Hemings, who was enslaved and but sixteen when he "claimed her as his sexual partner."[5] Abigail was barely fourteen when she first met twenty-one-year-old John. George courted Martha before she was even out of mourning for her deceased first husband. But all of these bonds have in some fashion or other been romanticized as modern in their sense of equality and love.

The "Founding Fathers" are constructions of cultural memory. The "Founders," the political leaders of the Revolution and nation's creation, were individuals, flesh and blood, and as such led lives that would not reflect later ideals of manly sexual behaviors and desires. It is, of course, quite ironic that the political leaders of the American Revolution would come to serve as role models of personal life for American masculinity in the Victorian era—and today. Although a segment of our contemporary culture continues to hold the Founding Fathers aloft as more moral and virtuous than today's generation, doing so requires ignoring what the Founders themselves told us about their lives. It has often been pointed out that the men associated with freedom and liberty held others in bondage and viewed democracy with skepticism. What is less often acknowledged is that the men associated with an era of supposed morality and Christian values of monogamy and marriage have nearly all been linked to infidelity and sex out of wedlock.[6]

There is still a certain degree of ambivalence about the relevance of private behavior for an assessment of public figures. On the one hand, we want to know more than can be known given the historical record and the private nature of the questions asked of individuals long gone. On the other hand, we do not want to know everything, because we do not want public figures and national heroes to exhibit anything other than positive attributes, and their sexual expressions must somehow conform to that depiction.[7] Thus, even the most negative of behaviors must be explained away. Unlike contemporary sex-scandalized politicians who can be removed from office and disappear from public view, we are stuck with the Founding Fathers. They are going nowhere, and so we rewrite and respin and reremember them in various ways to present them in a positive light. Biographers generally laud their subjects (albeit with more sophistication than those of the early nineteenth century). Rarely is a biography of a Founding Father written to disgrace the individual or remove him from the pantheon. The recent trend has been to expand only that top circle of important Founders.

This book, with its examination of how Americans have created and re-created the sexual histories of the most famous of the political leaders of the American Revolution, shows how sex has long been a component of civic and national identity. It should also challenge us to avoid superficially characterizing the complex personal lives of famous individuals, including political leaders, in society today. And it should make us ask ourselves what we are hoping to accomplish by mobilizing familiar tropes and stock depictions of romantic life. Such portrayals draw on a centuries-old history in America of connecting personal to public personas—and often rest on a host of tropes informed by a range of prescribed characteristics. By focusing on cultural constructions of the intimate lives of the Founders, this book challenges how we configure sex and gender in our public evaluations of prominent Americans—and perhaps should also give us pause about private considerations of ourselves and each other. What future generations will make of these men and their private lives remains to be seen, but given the longtime interest in this aspect of their lives, one thing seems certain: They will take an interest in the men's private lives. But those private lives, as remembered by future generations, will likely not be the ones we know today.

NOTES

INTRODUCTION

1. Indeed, in recognition of this issue, several museums of Founding Fathers' homes have launched efforts to circulate more youthful, vital images in an effort to connect to modern audiences. And recent biographies that strive to make the Founders more appealing (dubbed "Founders chic" by friend and foe alike) likewise frequently highlight the heights and musculature of the men in their youth in efforts to dispel the dusty old images held in most American's minds. The term "Founders chic" comes from Evan Thomas ("Founders Chic: Live from Philadelphia," *Newsweek*, July 9, 2001). But "Founders chic" "is really "'Federalist chic,'" according to Jeffrey L. Pasley, who observes that the increased interest in Founders often focuses on conservatives who did not embrace democracy or the "expansion of individual rights," such as Washington, Adams, and Hamilton. Pasley, "Federalist Chic," Common-place.org, February 2002, available at www.common-place. org/publick/200202.shtml.

2. Mason Weems, *A History of the Life and Death, Virtues and Exploits of General George Washington* (New York: Grosset and Dunlap, 1927), 8; italics original.

3. This book, therefore, builds on my earlier work on sex and masculinity and on the long history of sexual identities in America. See, for example, Thomas A. Foster, *Sex and the Eighteenth-Century Man: Massachusetts and the History of Sexuality in America* (Boston: Beacon Press, 2006); and Thomas A. Foster, ed., *Long before Stonewall: Histories of Same-Sex Sexuality in Early America* (New York: New York University Press, 2007). See also George Chauncey, *Gay New York: Gender, Urban Culture, and the Making of the Gay Male World, 1890–1940* (New York: Basic Books, 1995); and Regina G. Kunzel, *Criminal Intimacy: Prison and the Uneven History of Modern American Sexuality* (Chicago: University of Chicago Press, 2008).

4. Michael Kammen, *Mystic Chords of Memory: The Transformation of Tradition in American Culture* (New York: Vintage, 1993), 3. See also Eric Hobsbawm and Terence Ranger, eds., *The Invention of Tradition* (Cambridge, UK: Cambridge University Press, 1992); David Glassberg, "Public History and the Study of Memory," *Public Historian* 18,

no. 2 (Spring 1996): 7–23; and Patrick Hutton, "Recent Scholarship on Memory and History," *History Teacher* 33, no. 4 (August 2000): 533–548.

5. Gore Vidal, *Imperial America: Reflections on the United States of Amnesia* (New York: Nation Books, 2004).

6. Jill Lepore has argued that "historical fundamentalism" is used by the Tea Party and others to support their contemporary political claims. This viewpoint posits the Founders and the "sacred texts" of the nation as "ageless and sacred and to be worshipped" and the Founders as "prophets." Jill Lepore, *The Whites of Their Eyes: The Tea Party's Revolution and the Battle over American History* (Princeton, NJ: Princeton University Press, 2010), 6. See also François Furstenberg, *In the Name of the Father: Washington's Legacy, Slavery, and the Making of a Nation* (New York: Penguin, 2006); and Pauline Maier, *American Scripture: Making the Declaration of Independence* (New York: Knopf, 1997). In her study of biography, Paula R. Backscheider argues that "nations have modeled themselves on and understood each other through the great, lasting subjects of their biographies." Paula R. Backscheider, *Reflections on Biography* (Oxford, UK: Oxford University Press, 1999), 167.

7. Although academic historians have moved "beyond the Founders" in their understanding of the vital role that ordinary people played in the establishment of the United States, including non-elites and political minorities, such as women, African Americans, and a host of immigrants, the public largely has not. In political history, see Jeffrey Pasley, Andrew W. Robertson, and David Waldstreicher, eds., *Beyond the Founders: New Approaches to the Political History of the Early American Republic* (Chapel Hill: University of North Carolina Press, 2004). See also Alfred F. Young, Gary B. Nash, and Ray Raphael, eds., *Revolutionary Founders: Rebels, Radicals, and Reformers in the Making of the Nation* (New York: Knopf, 2011).

Trevor Burnard argues that to the public, the Founders are all the more important because of the later development of the United States as a world power. Trevor Burnard, "The Founding Fathers in Early American Historiography: A View from Abroad," *William and Mary Quarterly* 62, no. 4 (October 2005): 745–763.

Lauren Berlant argues that in contemporary society, "intimacy, sexuality, reproduction, and the family . . . are properly interrelated with these questions of identity, inequality, and national existence." See Lauren Berlant, *The Queen of America Goes to Washington City: Essays on Sex and Citizenship* (Durham, NC: Duke University Press, 1997), 8. Other scholarship in LGBTQ history and Queer Studies has expanded our recognition of how heteronormativity figures in national discussions of sexual citizenship. *Sex and the Founding Fathers* contributes to this growing body of literature that examines how sex figures in the national identity. For other examples, see Margot Canaday, *The Straight State: Sexuality and Citizenship in Twentieth-Century America* (Princeton, NJ: Princeton University Press, 2009); David K. Johnson, *The Lavender Scare: The Cold War Persecution of Gays and Lesbians in the Federal Government* (Chicago: University of Chicago Press, 2004); and Gayle S. Rubin, *Deviations: A Gayle Rubin Reader* (Durham, NC: Duke University Press, 2011). See also Robert O. Self, *All in the Family: The Realignment of American Democracy since the 1960s* (New York: Hill and Wang, 2012); and Nayan Shah, *Stranger Intimacy: Contesting Race, Sexuality, and the Law in the North American West* (Berkeley: University of California Press, 2012).

8. As Berlant argues, Americans have been engaged in an accelerated "process of collapsing the political and the personal into a world of public intimacy." Berlant, *The Queen of America*, 1.

9. Headlined a "Self-Portrait of Founding Father's Penis Discovered in 18th Century Letter to Woman," it explains, "Painted with oil paint on canvas, the 220 year-old pic-

ture features a fully erect Washington standing beside his horse, the fabric of his trousers straining to accommodate the force of his engorged phallus, and was accompanied by a letter peppered with arcane sexual references." Attempting to shock, the article continues by quoting from the alleged document: "'My hickory stick yearns for the purchase of your fertile soil'"; see www.newsmutiny.com/pages/Founding-Fathers-Penis.html.

10. Alyssa Bereznak, "Christopher Hitchens on *The Daily Show*: Sparring with Jon Stewart over the Years," *VF Daily*, December 16, 2011, available at www.vanityfair.com/online/daily/2011/11/Christopher-Hitchens-on-iThe-Daily-Showi-Sparring-with-Jon-Stewart-Over-the-Years.

11. Larry Flynt and David Eisenbach, *One Nation under Sex: How the Private Lives of Presidents, First Ladies, and Their Lovers Changed the Course of American History* (New York: Palgrave Macmillan, 2011); Virginia Scharff, *The Women Jefferson Loved* (New York: HarperCollins, 2010); Charles Callan Tansill, *The Secret Loves of the Founding Fathers: The Romantic Side of George Washington, Thomas Jefferson, Benjamin Franklin, Gouverneur Morris, Alexander Hamilton* (New York: Devin-Adair, 1964). On the eroticization of modern culture, see Paul Rutherford, *A World Made Sexy: Freud to Madonna* (Toronto, Canada: University of Toronto Press, 2007); on normative sexuality, see Gayle S. Rubin, "Thinking Sex: Notes for a Radical Theory of the Politics of Sexuality," in *Deviations*, 137–181.

Scharff focuses on women whom Jefferson loved because it "informed his greatest achievements and glowed at the heart of his vision of life, liberty, and the pursuit of happiness." Scharff, *The Women Jefferson Loved*, 384. On love between men in Jefferson's time, see Caleb Crain, *American Sympathy: Men, Friendship, and Literature in the New Nation* (New Haven, CT: Yale University Press, 2001); Caleb Crain, "Leander, Lorenzo, and Castalio: An Early American Romance," in Foster, *Long before Stonewall*, 217–252; Richard Godbeer, *The Overflowing of Friendship: Love between Men and the Creation of the American Republic* (Baltimore: Johns Hopkins University Press, 2009); and John Salliant, "The Black Body Erotic and the Republican Body Politic, 1790–1820," in Foster, *Long before Stonewall*, 303–330.

12. Thomas Fleming, *The Intimate Lives of the Founding Fathers* (Washington, DC: Smithsonian Books, 2009).

13. Wesley O. Hagood, *Presidential Sex: From the Founding Fathers to Bill Clinton* (1996; repr., New York: Citadel Press, 1998).

14. Michael Farquhar, *A Treasury of Great American Scandals: Tantalizing True Tales of Historic Misbehavior by the Founding Fathers and Others Who Let Freedom Swing* (New York: Penguin, 2003), xi.

15. Roy Rosenzweig and David Thelen, *The Presence of the Past: Popular Uses of History in American Life* (New York: Columbia University Press, 1998), 13, 115–146, 234–259.

16. Lois W. Banner, "'Biography as History' Roundtable: Historians and Biography," *American Historical Review* 114, no. 3 (June 2009): 583.

17. Available at http://constitutioncenter.org/FoundersQuiz/.

18. Michel Foucault, *The History of Sexuality: An Introduction*, trans. Robert Hurley (New York: Vintage Books, 1990). For a counter to the narrative of progress that Americans hold, see, for example, John D'Emilio and Estelle Freedman, *Intimate Matters: A History of Sexuality in America*, 3rd ed. (Chicago: University of Chicago Press, 2012).

19. As a cultural history of popular memory, this book is a history of the stories that Americans have told themselves about the intimate lives of the Founders. Scholars have also referred to this approach as the study of "historical consciousness," "historical memory," and "popular historymaking." See Rosenzweig and Thelen, *The Presence of the Past*, 3. See also Joyce Appleby, *A Restless Past: History and the American Public* (New York: Rowman

and Littlefield, 2005); Christopher Castiglia and Christopher Reed, *If Memory Serves: Gay Men, AIDS, and the Promise of the Queer Past* (Minneapolis: University of Minnesota Press, 2011), 2, 11, 27; and Foucault, *The History of Sexuality*. On memory and on cultural uses of history, see also, for example, Mark C. Carnes, ed., *Novel History: Historians and Novelists Confront America's Past (and Each Other)* (New York: Simon and Schuster, 2001); Jean M. Humez, *Harriet Tubman: The Life and the Life Stories* (Madison: University of Wisconsin Press, 2003); Kammen, *Mystic Chords of Memory*; Michael Kammen, *A Season of Youth: The American Revolution and the Historical Imagination* (Ithaca, NY: Cornell University Press, 1978); Lepore, *The Whites of Their Eyes*; Milton C. Sernett, *Harriet Tubman: Myth, Memory, and History* (Durham, NC: Duke University Press, 2007); Warren I. Susman, *Culture as History: The Transformation of American Society in the Twentieth Century* (1973; repr., New York: Pantheon Books, 1984); David D. Van Tassel, *Recording America's Past: An Interpretation of the Development of Historical Studies in America, 1607–1884* (Chicago: University of Chicago Press, 1960); and Alfred F. Young, *The Shoemaker and the Tea Party: Memory and the American Revolution* (Boston: Beacon Press, 1999).

20. Van Tassel, *Recording America's Past*, 75.

21. On a nineteenth-century "ideology of heroism" and the later development of trading heroes for celebrities, see, for example, Peter H. Gibbon, *A Call to Heroism: Renewing America's Vision of Greatness* (New York: Atlantic Monthly Press, 2002), 18–35, 90–100.

Traditionally, the genre has been derided by academic historians for being "insufficiently analytical." See Scott E. Casper, *Constructing American Lives: Biography and Culture in Nineteenth-Century America* (Chapel Hill: University of North Carolina Press, 1999), 327. See also Jill Lepore, "Historians Who Love Too Much: Reflections on Microhistory and Biography," *Journal of American History* 88, no. 1 (June 2001), available at www.historycooperative.org/cgi-bin/justtop.cgi?act=justtop&url=http://www.historycooperative.org/journals/jah/88.1/lepore.html (accessed February 26, 2010). On academic historians and biography, see AHR Roundtable, "Historians and Biography," *American Historical Review* (June 2009): 573–614.

22. On the history of sexuality in America, see, for example, D'Emilio and Freedman, *Intimate Matters*; and Kevin White, *Sexual Liberation or Sexual License? The American Revolt against Victorianism* (Chicago: Dee, 2000).

23. Nancy Isenberg, "The 'Little Emperor': Aaron Burr, Dandyism, and the Sexual Politics of Treason," in Pasley, Robertson, and Waldstreicher, *Beyond the Founders*, 130.

24. Lepore, *The Whites of Their Eyes*, 16.

25. Paul M. Zall, *Benjamin Franklin's Humor* (Lexington: University Press of Kentucky, 2006).

26. Richard Brookhiser, *Gentleman Revolutionary: Gouverneur Morris, the Rake Who Wrote the Constitution* (New York: Free Press, 2003).

CHAPTER 1

1. David Hackett Fischer, *Washington's Crossing* (Oxford, UK: Oxford University Press, 2006).

2. Richard Lacayo, with an introduction by Joseph J. Ellis, "George Washington: How the Great Uniter Helped Create the United States," *Time* (special issue, 2011): 40–41.

3. Michael King, "The Battle of Washington's Bulge," *Austin Chronicle*, November 22, 2002.

4. The literature on George Washington is enormous. A number of books focus on the construction of his image. See, for example, Marcus Cunliffe, *George Washington, Man and*

Monument (Boston: Little, Brown, 1958); François Furstenberg, *In the Name of the Father: Washington's Legacy, Slavery, and the Making of a Nation* (New York: Penguin, 2006); Don Higginbotham, ed., *George Washington Reconsidered* (Charlottesville: University of Virginia Press, 2001); Barry Schwartz, *George Washington: The Making of an American Symbol* (New York: Free Press, 1987); and Harlow G. Unger, *The Unexpected George Washington: His Private Life* (Hoboken, NJ: Wiley, 2006).

See also John E. Ferling, *The First of Men: A Life of George Washington* (Knoxville: University of Tennessee Press, 1988); Paul Leland Haworth, *George Washington: Country Gentleman* (1915; repr., Indianapolis: Bobbs-Merrill, 1925); Rupert Hughes, *George Washington: The Human Being and the Hero, 1732–1762* (New York: William Morrow, 1926); and Elswyth Thane, *Washington's Lady* (New York: Dodd, Mead, 1960).

5. *Daily Advertiser* (London), January 25, 1783; image from *Rambler's Magazine* (London), April 1, 1783. See also Patricia Bonomi, *Lord Cornbury Scandal: The Politics of Reputation in British America* (Chapel Hill: University of North Carolina Press, 1998), 25–26; and John C. Fitzpatrick, "The George Washington Scandals," Bulletin No. 1 of the Washington Society of Alexandria, 1929.

6. James Thomas Flexner, "Washington Mythology," *American Heritage* 41, no. 1 (February 1990): 107.

7. Fitzpatrick, "The George Washington Scandals."

8. See Alice Curtis Desmond, *Martha Washington: Our First Lady* (New York: Dodd, 1942), 142.

9. By the end of the eighteenth century, items still appeared in newspapers that suggested a link between Freemasonry and a deviant sexual disposition. Critics of the Freemasons denigrated them as men who lacked a normative desire for women and deviated from heterosociability. See Thomas A. Foster, *Sex and the Eighteenth-Century Man: Massachusetts and the History of Sexuality in America* (Boston: Beacon Press, 2006), 169–173.

10. See for example, Thomas A. Foster, "Deficient Husbands: Manhood, Sexual Incapacity, and Male Marital Sexuality in Seventeenth-Century New England," *William and Mary Quarterly* 56 (October 1999): 723–744; Foster, *Sex and the Eighteenth-Century Man*; Anne S. Lombard, *Making Manhood: Growing Up Male in Colonial New England* (Cambridge, MA: Harvard University Press, 2003); Elaine Tyler May, *Barren in the Promised Land: Childless Americans and the Pursuit of Happiness* (New York: Basic Books, 1995); Anthony Rotundo, *American Manhood: Transformations in Masculinity from the Revolution to the Modern Era* (New York: Basic Books, 1994); and Lisa Wilson, *Ye Heart of a Man: The Domestic Life of Men in Colonial New England* (New Haven, CT: Yale University Press, 1999).

11. Kathleen M. Brown, *Good Wives, Nasty Wenches, and Anxious Patriarchs: Gender, Race, and Power in Colonial Virginia* (Chapel Hill: University of North Carolina Press, 1996), 303, 337; Foster, "Deficient Husbands."

12. On Washington and political self-fashioning, see, for example, Paul K. Longmore, *The Invention of George Washington* (Berkeley: University of California Press, 1988).

13. Letter to George Augustine Washington, October 25, 1786, in Theodore J. Crackel, ed., *The Papers of George Washington, Digital Edition*, available at http://rotunda.upress.virginia.edu/founders/GEWN.html; William M. S. Rasmussen and Robert S. Tilton, *George Washington: The Man behind the Myths* (Charlottesville: University of Virginia Press, 1999), 99.

14. Karen Lystra, *Searching the Heart: Women, Men, and Romantic Love in Nineteenth-Century America* (New York: Oxford University Press, 1989), 3.

15. Gordon S. Wood, *Revolutionary Characters: What Made the Founders Different* (New York: Penguin, 2006), 51.

16. Richard Brookhiser, *Founding Father: Rediscovering George Washington* (New York: Free Press, 1996), 164–165.

17. Charles Moore, *The Family Life of George Washington* (Boston: Houghton Mifflin, 1926), 123.

18. Ruth Miller Elson, *Guardians of Tradition: American Schoolbooks of the Nineteenth Century* (Lincoln: University of Nebraska, 1972), 194–195.

19. Gouverneur Morris, *An Oration Upon the Death of General Washington* (New York: John Furman, 1800), 8. On early veneration of Washington, see, for example, Andrew S. Trees, *The Founding Fathers and the Politics of Character* (Princeton, NJ: Princeton University Press, 2004), 135–146.

20. Mason Weems, *A History of the Life and Death Virtues and Exploits of General George Washington* (New York: Grosset and Dunlap, 1927), 8.

21. Furstenberg, *In the Name of the Father*, 75–76.

22. Elson, *Guardians of Tradition*, 201–202.

23. James Kirk Paulding, *The Life of Washington* (Aberdeen, UK: Clark, 1848), 60.

24. Weems, *A History of the Life and Death*, 90.

25. Scott E. Casper, *Constructing American Lives: Biography and Culture in Nineteenth-Century America* (Chapel Hill: University of North Carolina Press, 1999), 12.

26. Ibid., 69.

27. Ibid., 29, 35.

28. On public reception of the statue of Washington by Horatio Greenough, see Peter H. Gibbon, *A Call to Heroism: Renewing America's Vision of Greatness* (New York: Atlantic Monthly Press, 2002), 87–89.

29. Casper, *Constructing American Lives*, 8–9.

30. R. B. Bernstein, *The Founding Fathers Reconsidered* (Oxford, UK: Oxford University Press, 2009), 125.

31. Jared Sparks, *The Writings of George Washington*, 2 vols. (New York: Harper and Brothers, 1837), 1:78.

32. Ibid., 1:106.

33. John Marshall, *The Life of George Washington, Commander in Chief of the American Forces, during the War Which Established the Independence of His Country, and First President of the United States*, 5 vols. (1804; repr. Fredericksburg, VA: The Citizen's Guild of Washington's Boyhood Home, 1926), 2:52.

34. Washington Irving, *Life of George Washington*, 4 vols. (New York: Putnam, 1856), 1: 211, 1:253.

35. Casper, *Constructing American Lives*, 20.

36. Irving, *Life of George Washington*, 1:pref.

37. *New York Herald*, March 30, 1877. Letter to Sarah Cary Fairfax, September 12, 1758, in Crackel, *The Papers of George Washington, Digital Edition*, available at http://rotunda.upress.virginia.edu/founders/GEWN.html.

38. Weems, *A History of the Life and Death*, 373–374.

39. Benson John Lossing, *Mary and Martha: The Mother and the Wife of George Washington* (New York: Harper and Brothers, 1886), 121–122.

40. Rosemarie Zagarri, ed., *David Humphreys' "Life of General Washington"* (Athens: University of Georgia Press, 1991), 37.

41. Henry Cabot Lodge, *George Washington* (Boston: Houghton Mifflin, 1889), 107–108.

42. Paul Leicester Ford, *The True George Washington* (Philadelphia: Lippincott, 1898), 96.

43. Rasmussen and Tilton, *George Washington*, 93.

44. Woodrow Wilson, *George Washington* (New York: Harper and Brothers, 1896), 93.

45. Casper, *Constructing American Lives*, 9.

46. *Daily Commercial* (Cincinnati), March 28, 1871.

47. "The Son of Washington," St. Louis (MO) *Daily Globe-Democrat*, April 21, 1886. See also Fitzpatrick, "The George Washington Scandals."

48. Fitzpatrick, "The George Washington Scandals."

49. Wilson, *George Washington*, 101.

50. Ford, *The True George Washington*, 84.

51. Lodge, *George Washington*, 92.

52. Ibid., 96–97.

53. Casper, *Constructing American Lives*, 315.

54. Fitzpatrick, "The George Washington Scandals."

55. Kevin White, *The First Sexual Revolution: The Emergence of Male Heterosexuality in Modern America* (New York: New York University Press, 1993), 13. See also John D'Emilio and Estelle Freedman, *Intimate Matters: A History of Sexuality in America*, 3rd ed. (Chicago: University of Chicago Press, 2012).

56. Lacayo, "George Washington," 14, 22.

57. Letter to Sarah Cary Fairfax, May 16, 1798, in Crackel, *The Papers of George Washington, Digital Edition*, available at http://rotunda.upress.virginia.edu/founders/GEWN .html.

58. Rebecca Earle, ed., *Epistolary Selves: Letters and Letter-Writers, 1600–1945* (Aldershot, UK: Ashgate, 1999), 7. Historians and literary scholars have argued that letters are performative and illustrate the construction of a self, rather than being simply transparent "documents" to be taken at face value. They are "texts" full of multiple layers of meaning and production of meaning. See, for example, Toby L. Ditz, "Formative Ventures: Eighteenth-Century Commercial Letters and the Articulation of Experience," in Earle, *Epistolary Selves*, 59–78.

59. See, for example, Thomas Fleming, *The Intimate Lives of the Founding Fathers* (Washington, DC: Smithsonian Books, 2009), 4–5.

60. Hughes, *George Washington*, 178.

61. Meade Minnigerode, *Some American Ladies: Seven Informal Biographies* (1926; repr., Freeport, NY: Books for Libraries Press, 1969), 9.

62. Sally Nelson Robins, *Love Stories of Famous Virginians*, 2nd ed. (Richmond, VA: Dietz Printing, 1925), 21, 23, 34; italics original.

63. Peter Gay, ed., introduction and "Three Essays on the Theory of Sexuality," in *The Freud Reader* (New York: Norton, 1989), 239–292. See also D'Emilio and Freedman, *Intimate Matters*.

64. Hughes, *George Washington*, 410, 488–489.

65. Eugene E. Prussing, *George Washington in Love and Otherwise* (Chicago: Pascal Covici, 1925), 3, 21.

66. John C. Fitzpatrick, *George Washington Himself: A Commonsense Biography Written from His Manuscripts* (Indianapolis: Bobbs-Merrill, 1933), 42.

67. Prussing, *George Washington*, 32–33.

68. Douglas Southall Freeman, *George Washington: A Biography*, 7 vols. (New York: Scribner, 1948–1957), 2:338n75.

69. Fitzpatrick, *George Washington Himself*, 113–114, 110, 41.

70. Moore, *The Family Life of George Washington*, 84.

71. Hughes, *George Washington*, 477.

72. Prussing, *George Washington*, 22.

73. Moore, *The Family Life of George Washington*, 84.

74. Desmond, *Martha Washington*, 188. An earlier account claims that "the marriage was a failure in that there were no children" (Haworth, *George Washington*, 222).

75. Robins, *Love Stories of Famous Virginians*, 29. In 1960, Elswyth Thane's *Washington's Lady* implies that Martha may have become infertile after having measles (28).

76. May, *Barren in the Promised Land*, 61; White, *The First Sexual Revolution*.

77. White, *The First Sexual Revolution*, 57.

78. May, *Barren in the Promised Land*, 11–12, 131–134, 136.

79. Fitzpatrick, *George Washington Himself*, 119.

80. Hughes, *George Washington*, 351.

81. Moore, *The Family Life of George Washington*, 55.

82. Minnigerode, *Some American Ladies*, 8.

83. Freeman, *George Washington*, 2:np (caption to photo between 285 and 286).

84. Cunliffe, *George Washington*, 47.

85. Desmond, *Martha Washington*, 77, 64, 220.

86. May, *Barren in the Promised Land*, 134.

87. It was rereleased in 2002 as Mary Higgins Clark, *Mount Vernon Love Story: A Novel of George and Martha Washington* (New York: Pocket Books, 2003).

88. Unger, *The Unexpected George Washington*, 1.

89. Gore Vidal, *Burr: A Novel* (1973; repr. New York: Vintage, 2000), 23.

90. Patricia Brady, *Martha Washington: An American Life* (New York: Viking, 2005), 57.

91. Fleming, *Intimate Lives*, 10.

92. Willard Sterne Randall, *George Washington: A Life* (New York: Holt, 1997), 53. Randall adds yet another woman to Washington's list of "loves" with his discussion of Betty Fauntleroy, whom he claims Washington fell in "love" with (62–63).

93. Ibid., 53.

94. Joseph J. Ellis, *His Excellency: George Washington* (New York: Vintage, 2004), 37.

95. Brady, *Martha Washington*, 232.

96. Fleming, *Intimate Lives*, 18.

97. James MacGregor Burns and Susan Dunn, *George Washington* (New York: Times Books, 2004), 134; Randall, *George Washington*, 179.

98. Desmond, *Martha Washington*, 90. On the association of the white male body with modernity, see, for example, John F. Kasson, *Houdini, Tarzan, and the Perfect Man: The White Male Body and the Challenge of Modernity in America* (New York: Hill and Wang, 2001).

99. Susan Bordo, *The Male Body: A New Look at Men in Public and in Private* (New York: Farrar, Straus, and Giroux, 1999).

100. Clark, *Mount Vernon Love Story*, preface.

101. Ellis, *His Excellency*, 12.

102. Wood, *Revolutionary Characters*, 33.

103. Randall, *George Washington*, 3.

104. Fleming, *Intimate Lives*, 19, 7.

105. Fischer, *Washington's Crossing*, 7–8.

106. Clark, *Mount Vernon Love Story*, preface.

107. Unger, *The Unexpected George Washington*, 1.

108. Brookhiser, *Founding Father*, 107–109, 111.

109. Brady, *Martha Washington*, 59.

110. Fleming, *Intimate Lives*, 19, 7.

111. Ellis, *His Excellency*, 11.

112. On being "flat chested," see Fitzpatrick, *George Washington Himself*, 147. On being "wide across the hips," see Ferling, *The First of Men*, 19.

113. John Ferling, *The Ascent of George Washington: The Hidden Political Genius of an American Icon* (New York: Bloomsbury, 2009), 13–14.

114. Zagarri, *David Humphreys' "Life of General Washington,"* 7.

115. Ellis, *His Excellency*, 40.

116. Bernhard Knollenberg, *George Washington, the Virginia Period, 1732–1775* (Durham, NC: Duke University Press, 1964), 72.

117. Ellis, *His Excellency*, 42.

118. Wood, *Revolutionary Characters*, 60. Similarly, Ferling notes, "Their union began as a virtual marriage of convenience" and that "economically it was a good match" (Ferling, *The First of Men*, 78).

119. Ellis, *His Excellency*, 42.

120. Ibid.

121. Clark, *Mount Vernon Love Story*, preface.

122. Brady, *Martha Washington*, 99, 114–115.

123. Joseph E. Fields, *"Worthy Partner": The Papers of Martha Washington* (Westport, CT: Greenwood Press, 1994), xx.

124. Brady, *Martha Washington*, 233. A film produced by the History Channel and narrated by Glenn Close that plays at the Mount Vernon visitor center focuses on the relationship of George and Martha and assures visitors that despite his many years away from her during the Revolution, Martha never suspected that he was unfaithful to her.

125. Fleming, *Intimate Lives*, 37, 18, 57.

126. Bruce Chadwick, *The General and Mrs. Washington: The Untold Story of a Marriage and a Revolution* (Naperville, IL: Sourcebooks, 2007), 134.

127. This desire to fill in the record has forced biographers to go out on limbs that would otherwise be unacceptable to most historians. In the absence of much evidence, one recent biographer claims to understand how Washington *felt* about not having children of his own. In describing Mount Vernon, the Washingtons' plantation, he writes, "Another aspect of his life revealed in this room is the absence of portraits of Washington's own children. He and Martha were childless, and that failure saddened him." Henry Wiencek, *An Imperfect God: George Washington, His Slaves, and the Creation of America* (New York: Farrar, Straus, and Giroux, 2003), 10.

Similarly, the C-SPAN website AmericanPresidents.org, which is designed for student education and for the general public, also styles Washington as a father. In a chart entitled "Life Facts," the website notes two under "number of children"—counting Martha's children in a manner that makes it appear that he did, indeed, sire children. This accounting style is not uniformly employed, however. Under James Madison, for example, the website notes "none"—even though Dolley and James raised her son John Payne Todd.

On Washington, see www.americanpresidents.org/presidents/gwashington.asp (accessed April 20, 2009). On Madison, see www.americanpresidents.org/presidents/president.asp?PresidentNumber=4 (accessed April 20, 2009).

128. Brookhiser, *Founding Father*, 163.

129. Available at http://en.wikipedia.org/wiki/George_washington (accessed July 21, 2007).

130. Arnold A. Rogow, *A Fatal Friendship: Alexander Hamilton and Aaron Burr* (New York: Hill and Wang, 1998), 7.

131. Flexner, "Washington Mythology," 107.

132. Marcus Cunliffe, *George Washington: Man and Monument*, rev. ed. (New York: NAL, 1982), 147–148.

133. Randall, *George Washington*, 196.

134. Fleming, *Intimate Lives*, 25.

135. John K. Amory, "George Washington's Infertility: Why Was the Father of Our Country Never a Father?" *Fertility and Sterility* 81, no. 3 (March 2004): 497. Dr. Amory concludes that Washington was most likely sterile due to tuberculosis epididymitis.

136. Edward O. Laumann, Anthony Paik, and Raymond C. Rosen, "Sexual Dysfunction in the United States: Prevalence and Predictors," *Journal of the American Medical Association* 281, no. 6 (1999): 537–544; John E. Anderson, et al., "Infertility Services Reported by Men in the United States: National Survey Data," *Fertility and Sterility* 91, no. 6 (June 2009): 2466–2470.

137. Rasmussen and Tilton, *George Washington*, 99.

138. Clark, *Mount Vernon Love Story*, 240.

139. Foster, "Deficient Husbands." See also Angus McLaren, *Impotence: A Cultural History* (Chicago: University of Chicago Press, 2007).

140. May, *Barren in the Promised Land*, 34.

141. Wiencek, *An Imperfect God*, 294, 12.

142. Linda Allen Bryant, *I Cannot Tell a Lie: The True Story of George Washington's African American Descendants* (New York: iUniverse Star, 2001).

143. Unger, *The Unexpected George Washington*, 272.

CHAPTER 2

1. Available at www.presidency.ucsb.edu/ws/index.php?pid=45697#axzz1ld4W8iFM. See also Francis D. Cogliano, *Thomas Jefferson: Reputation and Legacy* (Charlottesville: University of Virginia Press, 2006), 170.

2. C-SPAN 2000 and 2009 survey of historians, available at www.c-span.org/PresidentialSurvey/Overall-Ranking.aspx.

3. Annette Gordon-Reed, *The Hemingses of Monticello: An American Family* (New York: Norton, 2008); Charles Haid, *Sally Hemings: An American Scandal* (Echo Bridge Home Entertainment Studio, 2004); and Marlon Wayans, *Scary Movie* (Burbank, CA: Dimension Home Video, 2000).

4. For recent work on Thomas Jefferson, see Joyce Appleby, *Thomas Jefferson* (New York: Times Books, 2003); Joseph J. Ellis, *American Sphinx: The Character of Thomas Jefferson* (New York: Knopf, 1997); and Peter S. Onuf, *The Mind of Thomas Jefferson* (Charlottesville: University of Virginia Press, 2007). See also Paul Finkelman, *Slavery and the Founders: Race and Liberty in the Age of Jefferson* (London: Sharpe, 1996).

5. *Thomas Jefferson Papers* Series 1, General Correspondence, 1651–1827 Henry Lee, 1805, John Walker Affair, available at http://hdl.loc.gov/loc.mss/mtj.mtjbib014530. See also Fawn M. Brodie, *Thomas Jefferson: An Intimate History* (New York: Norton, 1975), 83.

6. *Richmond Recorder*, September 1, 1802; italics original.

7. [Joseph Dennie and Asbury Dickens] Oliver Oldschool, *Port Folio*, vol. 2 (Philadelphia: H. Maxwell, 1802), 312. On *Port Folio*, see Linda K. Kerber and Walter John Morris, "Politics and Literature: The Adams Family and the Port Folio," *William and Mary Quarterly* 23, no. 3 (July 1966): 450–476; and Jonathan Daniels, *Ordeal of Ambition: Jefferson, Hamilton, Burr* (New York: Doubleday, 1970), 267.

8. James Akin, *"A Philosophic Cock,"* Newburyport, MA, 1804.

9. Quoted in Virginius Dabney and Jon Kukla, "The Monticello Scandals: History and Fiction," *Virginia Cavalcade* 29, no. 2 (Autumn 1979): 54.

10. Henry Stephens Randall, *The Life of Thomas Jefferson*, 3 vols. (New York: Derby and Jackson, 1857–1858).

11. Sarah N. Randolph, *The Domestic Life of Thomas Jefferson* (1871; repr., Charlottesville: Thomas Jefferson Memorial Foundation by the University Press of Virginia, 1978), preface, 34.

12. James Parton, *Life of Thomas Jefferson* (Boston: Osgood, 1874), 34.

13. William Eleroy Curtis, *The True Thomas Jefferson* (Philadelphia: Lippincott, 1901), 29–31.

14. Thomas E. Watson, *The Life and Times of Thomas Jefferson* (New York: Appleton, 1903), 17, 87.

15. Albert Jay Nock, *Jefferson* (New York: Hill and Wang, 1926), 15.

16. Sally Nelson Robins, *Love Stories of Famous Virginians*, 2nd ed. (Richmond, VA: Dietz Printing, 1925), 51.

17. Brodie, *Thomas Jefferson*, 64.

18. Phillips Russell, *Jefferson: Champion of the Free Mind* (New York: Dodd, Mead, 1956), 11.

19. Nock, *Jefferson*, 11.

20. Francis W. Hirst, *Life and Letters of Thomas Jefferson* (New York: Macmillan, 1926), 30.

21. Claude G. Bowers, *The Young Jefferson, 1743–1789* (Boston: Houghton Mifflin, 1945), 27, 28, 14, 24–25.

22. John C. Miller, *The Wolf by the Ears: Thomas Jefferson and Slavery* (New York: Free Press, 1977), 192.

23. Charles Callan Tansill, *The Secret Loves of the Founding Fathers: The Romantic Side of George Washington, Thomas Jefferson, Benjamin Franklin, Gouverneur Morris, Alexander Hamilton* (New York: Devin-Adair, 1964), 81. Joseph Ellis similarly states that Jefferson's "most sensual statements were aimed at beautiful buildings rather than beautiful women." See Ellis, *American Sphinx*, 307.

24. Tansill, *The Secret Loves of the Founding Fathers*, 86.

25. Randall, *Thomas Jefferson*, 28, 59.

26. Christopher Hitchens, *Thomas Jefferson: Author of America* (New York: Harper Perennial, 2009), 8–9.

27. T.P.H. Lyman, *The Life of Thomas Jefferson, Esq, L.L.D. late ex president of the United States* (Philadelphia: Neall, 1826); for another example, see B. L. Rayner, *Life of Thomas Jefferson* (Boston: Lilly, Wait, Colman, and Holden, 1834).

28. George Tucker, *The Life of Thomas Jefferson, Third President of the United States*, 2 vols. (Philadelphia: Carey, Lea, and Blanchard, 1837), 1:67. Tucker quotes a traveler who described Jefferson as a man with a "mild and amiable wife." See also William Linn, *Life of Thomas Jefferson*, 3rd ed. (Ithaca, NY: Andrus, Woodruff, and Gauntlett, 1843), 215.

29. Linn, *Life of Thomas Jefferson*, 15.

30. Randolph, *The Domestic Life of Thomas Jefferson*, 44.

31. Ibid., 44–45.

32. Parton, *Life of Thomas Jefferson*.

33. Scott E. Casper, *Constructing American Lives: Biography and Culture in Nineteenth-Century America* (Chapel Hill: University of North Carolina Press, 1999), 5.

34. Milton E. Flower, *James Parton: The Father of Modern Biography* (New York: Greenwood Press, 1968).

35. Parton, *Life of Thomas Jefferson*, 102.

36. John T. Morse, ed., *Thomas Jefferson* (Boston: Houghton Mifflin, 1883), 9–10.

37. Parton, *Life of Thomas Jefferson*, 102–103.

38. Ibid., 104, 265–256.

39. Rev. Hamilton W. Pierson, *Jefferson at Monticello: The Private Life of Thomas Jefferson* (New York: Scribner, 1862), 107.

40. Linn, *Life of Thomas Jefferson*, 15.

41. Nock, *Jefferson*, 16.

42. Tansill, *The Secret Loves of the Founding Fathers*, 99.

43. Watson, *The Life and Times of Thomas Jefferson*, 90.

44. Bowers, *The Young Jefferson*, 48.

45. Tansill, *The Secret Loves of the Founding Fathers*, 121.

46. Bowers, *The Young Jefferson*, 228.

47. William K. Bottorff, *Thomas Jefferson* (Boston: Twayne Publishers, 1979), 17. For other examples, see Bowers, *The Young Jefferson*, 48; Brodie, *Thomas Jefferson*, 85; Hirst, *Life and Letters of Thomas Jefferson*, 51; and Randolph, *The Domestic Life of Thomas Jefferson*, 44–45.

48. Bowers, *The Young Jefferson*, 47.

49. Nock, *Jefferson*, 20–21; Curtis, *The True Thomas Jefferson*, 29–31.

50. Tansill, *The Secret Loves of the Founding Fathers*, 99.

51. Randall, *Thomas Jefferson*, 158–160, 348.

52. Edmund S. Morgan and Marie Morgan, "Jefferson's Concubine," *New York Review of Books*, October 9, 2008.

53. Virginia Scharff, *The Women Jefferson Loved* (New York: HarperCollins, 2010), 154.

54. Brodie, *Thomas Jefferson*, 207.

55. Ibid., 203.

56. Bowers, *The Young Jefferson*, 447.

57. Brodie, *Thomas Jefferson*, 200.

58. Bowers, *The Young Jefferson*, 450.

59. Brodie, *Thomas Jefferson*, 203, 200.

60. Scharff, *The Women Jefferson Loved*, 204–205.

61. Tansill, *The Secret Loves of the Founding Fathers*, 102, 107.

62. Ellis, *American Sphinx*, 95.

63. Tansill, *The Secret Loves of the Founding Fathers*, 107–108.

64. Thomas Fleming, *The Intimate Lives of the Founding Fathers* (Washington, DC: Smithsonian Books, 2009), 270, 289, 300, 265.

65. Tansill, *The Secret Loves of the Founding Fathers*, 107–108.

66. Willard Sterne Randall, *Thomas Jefferson: A Life* (New York: Harper Perennial, 1993), 403, 438. Randall, in contrast to many authors in the 1990s, characterizes the stories of romantic connections to Betsey Walker and to Sally Hemings as purely the product of political enemies. For him, Jefferson's only true loves were his wife and Maria Cosway.

67. Hitchens, *Thomas Jefferson*, 62–64. See also John P. Kaminski, *Jefferson in Love: The Love Letters between Thomas Jefferson and Maria Cosway* (New York: Rowman and Littlefield, 1999).

68. Parton, *Life of Thomas Jefferson*.

69. Hirst, *Life and Letters of Thomas Jefferson*.

70. Bowers, *The Young Jefferson*, 46.

71. Ibid.

72. Quoted in Tansill, *The Secret Loves of the Founding Fathers*, 88. Tansill cites Dumas Malone, *Jefferson, the Virginian*, vol. 1 of *Jefferson and His Time* (Boston: Little, Brown, 1948), 154–155.

73. Russell, *Jefferson*, 278.

74. Fleming, *Intimate Lives*, 270, 289, 300, 265.

75. Hitchens, *Thomas Jefferson*, 8–9.

76. Pauline Maier, *American Scripture: Making the Declaration of Independence* (New York: Knopf, 1997).

77. Onuf, *The Mind of Thomas Jefferson*, 3.

78. Nock, *Jefferson*, 20.

79. Dumas Malone, *Jefferson and Our Times* (Pasadena, CA: Fund for Adult Education, 1955), 26.

80. Russell, *Jefferson*, 10.

81. Ellis, *American Sphinx*, 25.

82. Brodie, *Thomas Jefferson*, 30.

83. After all, as historian Joyce Appleby notes, Meriwether Lewis "lived with Jefferson in the President's House, remarking to a friend that they were like two mice in a church." Joyce Appleby, *Thomas Jefferson* (New York: Times Books, 2003), 38.

84. See, for example, Jon Kukla, *Mr. Jefferson's Women* (New York: Knopf, 2007); and Kenneth A. Lockridge, *On the Sources of Patriarchal Rage: The Commonplace Books of William Byrd and Thomas Jefferson and the Gendering of Power in the Eighteenth Century* (New York: New York University Press, 1992).

85. Winthrop Jordan, *White over Black: American Attitudes toward the Negro, 1550–1812* (Chapel Hill: University of North Carolina Press, 1968), 462.

86. Miller, *The Wolf by the Ears*, 177.

87. Ellis, *American Sphinx*, 97.

88. Bottorff, *Thomas Jefferson*, 16.

89. See John D'Emilio and Estelle Freedman, *Intimate Matters: A History of Sexuality in America*, 3rd ed. (Chicago: University of Chicago Press, 2012), 223.

90. Howard Swiggett, *The Extraordinary Mr. Morris* (New York: Doubleday, 1952), 151.

91. Brodie, *Thomas Jefferson*, 28, 30–31.

92. *Liberator*, September 21, 1838.

93. *Liberator*, May 26, 1848.

94. Max Cavitch, "Slavery and Its Metrics," in *The Cambridge Companion to Nineteenth-Century American Poetry*, ed. Kerry Larson (Cambridge, UK: Cambridge University Press, 2011), 94–112. See also William Wells Brown, *Clotel; or, The President's Daughter: A Narrative of Slave Life in the United States*, ed. and introd. M. Giulia Fabi (1853; repr., New York: Penguin, 2004).

95. "Life among the Lowly, No. 1," *Pike County (Ohio) Republican*, March 13, 1873.

96. Casper, *Constructing American Lives*, 186–187.

97. Morse, *Thomas Jefferson*, 225, 228.

98. Excellent accounts include Annette Gordon-Reed, *Thomas Jefferson and Sally Hemings: An American Controversy* (Charlottesville: University of Virginia Press, 1997); and Jan Ellen Lewis and Peter S. Onuf, eds., *Sally Hemings and Thomas Jefferson: History, Memory, and Civic Culture* (Charlottesville: University of Virginia Press, 1999).

99. Watson, *The Life and Times of Thomas Jefferson*, 22–23.

100. Curtis, *The True Thomas Jefferson*, 313.

101. Hirst, *Life and Letters of Thomas Jefferson*, 387.

102. See Douglass Adair, *Fame and the Founding Fathers* (Indianapolis: Liberty Fund, 1974), 237–239.

103. Dabney and Kukla, "The Monticello Scandals," 54–55; Merrill D. Peterson, *The Jefferson Image in the American Mind* (New York: Oxford University Press, 1960), 182–183.

104. Quoted in Adair, *Fame and the Founding Fathers*, 237.

105. Dabney and Kukla, "The Monticello Scandals," 54. Jerry Knudson takes to task the biographers (virtually all) who merely repeat the original stories about Jefferson. He singles out Brodie for special criticism: "Thus, Brodie speaks repeatedly of Callender's 'expose' of the Jefferson-Hemings liaison, a word that was not used at that time and that implies Callender uncovered the truth. It is also stretching the meaning of words to refer to *editor* rather than *printer* (for the most part), *reporter* or *journalist* rather than *writer*, the public's *right to know*, *investigating the news*, or to Callender as one of the *muckrakers*, that little band of reform journalists who flourished between 1902 and 1912." Jerry W. Knudson, *Jefferson and the Press: Crucible of Liberty* (Columbia: University of South Carolina Press, 2006), 44–45.

106. Russell, *Jefferson*, 278.

107. Tansill, *The Secret Loves of the Founding Fathers*, 89. This approach echoes the scholarly interpretations of the day that argue that Jefferson had been the victim of political sabotage and that his nephew Peter Carr had fathered Sally Hemings's children. See, for example, Adair, *Fame and the Founding Fathers*, 227–273.

108. Malone, *Jefferson and Our Times*, 42.

109. Frank L. Mott, *Jefferson and the Press* (Baton Rouge: Louisiana State University Press, 1943), 35.

110. Dabney and Kukla, "The Monticello Scandals," 57.

111. Miller, *The Wolf by the Ears*, 164, 177, 185.

112. Ibid., 171.

113. Ibid., 193.

114. Ibid., 167, 179.

115. Carlyle C. Douglas, "The Dilemma of Thomas Jefferson," *Ebony* (August 1975): 60–66.

116. Barbara Chase-Riboud, *Sally Hemings: A Novel* (New York: Viking, 1979).

117. Winthrop D. Jordan, *White over Black: Attitudes toward the American Negro, 1550–1812* (Chapel Hill: University of North Carolina Press, 1968; New York: Penguin, 1969).

118. On the anachronism of this portrayal, see Andrew Burstein, *Jefferson's Secrets: Death and Desire at Monticello* (New York: Basic Books, 2005), 4, 151–188.

119. Brodie, *Thomas Jefferson*, 32.

120. Bottorff, *Thomas Jefferson*, 24.

121. Fergus M. Bordewich, "Holiday Guide," *Washington Post*, December 7, 2008.

122. Morgan and Morgan, "Jefferson's Concubine."

123. Richard Godbeer, *Sexual Revolution in Early America* (Baltimore: Johns Hopkins University Press, 2001); Deborah Gray White, *Ar'n't I a Woman: Female Slaves in the Plantation South*, rev. ed. (1987; rev.: New York: Norton, 1999).

124. Ellis, *American Sphinx*, 21.

125. See, for example, David Barton at Liberty University, available at www.youtube.com/watch?v=A5jnKuQIDHE (accessed January 23, 2013). See also Mark Tooley, "Challenging the Jefferson Hemings Orthodoxy," *American Spectator*, September 7, 2011, available at http://spectator.org/archives/2011/09/07/challenging-the-jefferson-hemi (accessed April 20, 2009).

126. Ellis, *American Sphinx*, 22.

127. Scharff, *The Women Jefferson Loved*, 103, 218.

128. Some cracks have begun to appear in this young façade of total acceptance of the Jefferson-Hemings affair in popular writing. Fleming, for example, points out that Callender called Hemings "'a slut as common as the pavement,'" casting doubt not only on the relationship but on the view of their relationship as entirely monogamous. Notably, Fleming, in a book that uses every tale possible to talk about love and romance, frames this particular story not in such terms but instead as scandal and focuses on the "guilt" or innocence. And he is explicitly skeptical that it could have occurred as "thirty-eight years of furtive sex in a house swarming with visitors and grandchildren." He moves away from earlier defenses based on Jefferson's character. In the end, he suggests no love across the color line, asserting that "we should not allow differences about Sally Hemings to obscure the other women in Jefferson's life." See Fleming, *Intimate Lives*, 312, 352.

129. William Howard Adams, *The Paris Years of Thomas Jefferson* (New Haven, CT: Yale University Press, 1997), 221.

130. Appleby, *Thomas Jefferson*, 75.

131. Chase-Riboud, *Sally Hemings*.

132. Bottorff, *Thomas Jefferson*, 52–53.

133. Hitchens, *Thomas Jefferson*, 60.

134. Roger Wilkins, *Jefferson's Pillow: The Founding Fathers and the Dilemma of Black Patriotism* (Boston: Beacon Press, 2001), 99.

135. Clarence E. Walker, *Mongrel Nation: The America Begotten by Thomas Jefferson and Sally Hemings* (Charlottesville: University of Virginia Press, 2009), 39.

136. Annette Gordon-Reed, "'The Memories of a Few Negroes': Rescuing America's Future at Monticello," in Lewis and Onuf, *Sally Hemings and Thomas Jefferson*, 251.

137. Joseph J. Ellis, *American Sphinx: The Character of Thomas Jefferson* (New York: Vintage, 1998), xx.

138. Wilkins, *Jefferson's Pillow*, 136. See also Henry Wiencek, *Master of the Mountain: Thomas Jefferson and His Slaves* (New York: Farrar, Straus, and Giroux, 2012). On the issue of Hemings and Jefferson, Wiencek limits his examination to the issue of paternity and does not make substantial claims about the dynamic of relationship.

139. Garry Wills, *"Negro President": Jefferson and the Slave Power* (Boston: Beacon Press, 2003), xii–xiii; italics original.

140. Bottorff, *Thomas Jefferson*, 28, 52.

141. Joshua D. Rothman, *Notorious in the Neighborhood: The Color Line in Virginia 1787–1861* (Chapel Hill: University of North Carolina Press, 2003), 25.

142. Ellis, *American Sphinx* (1998), 26.

143. Miller, *The Wolf by the Ears*, 176.

144. Onuf, *The Mind of Thomas Jefferson*, 7. See also Shannon Lanier and Jane Feldman, *Jefferson's Children: The Story of One American Family* (New York: Random House, 2002).

CHAPTER 3

1. Available at www.imdb.com/title/tt0472027/awards.

2. David McCullough, *John Adams* (New York: Simon and Schuster, 2001), 56.

3. Available at www.tvguide.com/PhotoGallery/7-Unsexiest-Sex-1850/4984 (accessed February 5, 2012). According to the Internet Movie Database, NPR ran a piece that explained the scene as the product of the imagination of the two main actors: "During an interview on NPR's 'Fresh Air,' Paul Giamatti told interviewer Dave Davies that the scene in which Abigail and John have sex upon being reunited after many years apart was not writ-

ten as a sex scene. The script only called for John and Abigail to kiss, but Giamatti said that he and Laura Linney discussed between themselves that they thought the characters would go farther in that situation, and they decided to 'keep going' and hope the director and camera person would follow them, which they did. The scene they improvised and shot was originally much longer than what ended up in the finished film"; available at www.imdb .com/title/tt0472027/trivia (accessed February 5, 2012). For an example of a blog about the "unwatchable" scene, see www.historiann.com/2010/07/05/1776-c/#more-11604 (accessed February 5, 2012).

4. Matthew Gilbert, "No Sex Scandals Taint This Power Couple in HBO's John Adams," *Denver Post*, March 27, 2008, available at www.denverpost.com/ci_8707240?source=rss (accessed February 5, 2012).

5. Available at http://naturalresources.house.gov/UploadedFiles/AdamsTestimony07 .30.09.pdf.

6. *John and Abigail Adams*, documentary film, *American Experience* series (PBS, 2006).

7. Recent biographies include John Ferling, *John Adams: A Life* (Knoxville: University of Tennessee Press, 1992), 53; and McCullough, *John Adams*.

8. On Puritan culture and sexual expression, see, for example, Richard Godbeer, *Sexual Revolution in Early America* (Baltimore: Johns Hopkins University Press, 2001).

9. Thomas A. Foster, ed., "John Adams and the Choice of Hercules: Manliness and Sexual Virtue in Eighteenth-Century British America," in *New Men: Manliness in Early America* (New York: New York University Press, 2011), 217–235. On Adams and virtue, see also, for example, G. J. Barker-Benfield, *Abigail and John Adams: The Americanization of Sensibility* (Chicago: University of Chicago Press, 2010); Andrew S. Trees, *The Founding Fathers and the Politics of Character* (Princeton, NJ: Princeton University Press, 2004), 75–106. On John Adams, see, for example, Joseph J. Ellis, *Passionate Sage: The Character and Legacy of John Adams* (New York: Norton, 1994).

10. Quoted in Walter Stahr, *John Jay: Founding Father* (New York: Continuum International Publishing Group, 2006), 131.

11. Quoted in ibid., 139.

12. John Adams autobiography, part 2, "Travels, and Negotiations," 1777–1778, sheet 9 of 37, April 1–3, 1778 [electronic edition], *Adams Family Papers: An Electronic Archive*, Massachusetts Historical Society, available at www.masshist.org/digitaladams/.

13. Letter from John Adams to Abigail Adams, April 25, 1778 [electronic edition], *Adams Family Papers: An Electronic Archive*, Massachusetts Historical Society, available at www.masshist.org/digitaladams/.

14. June 23, 1779. John Adams diary 29, March 12–July 31, 1779 [electronic edition], *Adams Family Papers: An Electronic Archive*, Massachusetts Historical Society, available at www.masshist.org/digitaladams/.

15. Letter from John Adams to Abigail Adams, January 9, 1797 [electronic edition], *Adams Family Papers: An Electronic Archive*, Massachusetts Historical Society, available at www.masshist.org/digitaladams/. On his "hatred" of Hamilton, see Ellis, *Passionate Sage*, 21–25.

16. On the rivalry and comment, see, for example, Gore Vidal, *Inventing a Nation: Washington, Adams, Jefferson* (New Haven, CT: Yale University Press, 2003), 17.

17. Mercy Otis Warren, *History of the Rise, Progress and Termination of the American Revolution*, 2 vols. (Indianapolis: Liberty Classics, 1988), 2:677.

18. Charles Francis Adams, *The Works of John Adams*, 10 vols. (Boston: Little, Brown, 1856).

19. March 15, 1756. John Adams diary 1, November 18, 1755–August 29, 1756 [electronic edition], *Adams Family Papers: An Electronic Archive*, Massachusetts Historical Society, available at www.masshist.org/digitaladams/.

20. John Adams diary 3, 1759 [electronic edition], *Adams Family Papers: An Electronic Archive*, Massachusetts Historical Society, available at www.masshist.org/digitaladams/.

21. John Adams autobiography, part 1, "John Adams," through 1776, sheet 3 of 53 [electronic edition], *Adams Family Papers: An Electronic Archive*, Massachusetts Historical Society, available at www.masshist.org/digitaladams/.

22. John Adams autobiography, part 2, "Travels, and Negotiations," 1777–1778, sheet 11 of 37 [electronic edition], *Adams Family Papers: An Electronic Archive*, Massachusetts Historical Society, available at www.masshist.org/digitaladams/.

23. John T. Morse, *John Adams* (Boston: Houghton Mifflin, 1884), 6–7.

24. Mellen Chamberlain, *John Adams: The Statesman of the American Revolution* (Boston: Houghton Mifflin, 1898), 5–6.

25. Ibid., 96.

26. Adams, *The Works of John Adams*, 1:61–62.

27. L. H. Butterfield, *The Book of Abigail and John: Selected Letters of the Adams Family, 1762–1784* (Cambridge, MA: Harvard University Press, 1975), 11.

28. Kevin White, *The First Sexual Revolution: The Emergence of Male Heterosexuality in Modern America* (New York: New York University Press, 1993).

29. Quoted in Meade Minnigerode, *Some American Ladies: Seven Informal Biographies* (1926; repr., Freeport, NY: Books for Libraries Press, 1969), 55.

30. Quoted in ibid.

31. Quoted in Samuel McCoy, *This Man Adams: The Man Who Never Died* (New York: Bretano's, 1928), 49; italics original.

32. Quoted in ibid., 50–51.

33. Alfred Steinberg, *John Adams* (New York: Putnam, 1969), 39–40.

34. Page Smith, *John Adams*, 2 vols. (New York: Doubleday, 1962), 1:20.

35. Robert A. East, *John Adams* (Boston: Twayne Publishers, 1979), 20.

36. Ibid., 57.

37. Ferling, *John Adams*, 53, 172, 203.

38. Ibid., 26–27.

39. Ibid., 234.

40. McCullough, *John Adams*, 36, 48, 51.

41. Stahr, *John Jay*, 162; Thomas Fleming, *The Intimate Lives of the Founding Fathers* (Washington, DC: Smithsonian Books, 2009), 195.

42. Letter from John Adams to Abigail Adams, June 3, 1778 [electronic edition], *Adams Family Papers: An Electronic Archive*, Massachusetts Historical Society, available at www.masshist.org/digitaladams/.

43. John Adams diary 44, March 27–July 21, 1786 [electronic edition], *Adams Family Papers: An Electronic Archive*, Massachusetts Historical Society, available at www.masshist.org/digitaladams/.

44. Judith St. George, *John and Abigail Adams: An American Love Story* (New York: Holiday House, 2001), 46.

45. John P. Diggins, *John Adams* (New York: Times Books, 2003), 21–22.

46. Ibid., 30.

47. James Grant, *John Adams: Party of One* (New York: Farrar, Straus, and Giroux, 2005), 21–22, 43, 203.

48. Fleming, *Intimate Lives*, 125–129.

49. John Adams diary 3, includes commonplace book entries, spring and summer 1759 [electronic edition], *Adams Family Papers: An Electronic Archive*, Massachusetts Historical Society, available at www.masshist.org/digitaladams/.

50. Fleming, *Intimate Lives*, 125–129.

51. John Adams diary 3, includes commonplace book entries, spring and summer 1759 [electronic edition], *Adams Family Papers: An Electronic Archive*, Massachusetts Historical Society, available at www.masshist.org/digitaladams/.

52. Morse, *John Adams*, 20.

53. Letter from John Adams to Abigail Adams, April 28, 1776 [electronic edition], *Adams Family Papers: An Electronic Archive*, Massachusetts Historical Society, available at www.masshist.org/digitaladams/.

54. Minnigerode, *Some American Ladies*, 56.

55. Ibid., 65.

56. Although we should, of course, read these letters as genuine and heartfelt, we must also recognize that, given the postal system of the day, writers also recognized the distinct possibility that mail could be read by others. Additionally, in some instances, letters would be shared. In at least one instance, the sharing of Abigail's letters resulted in gains for her. "The other Day, after I had received a Letter of yours, with one or two others, Mr. William Barrell desired to read them. I put them into his Hand," writes John to Abigail, "and the next Morning had them returned in a large Bundle packed up with two great Heaps of Pins, with a very polite Card requesting Portias Acceptance of them." Letter from John Adams to Abigail Adams, July 7, 1775 [electronic edition], *Adams Family Papers: An Electronic Archive*, Massachusetts Historical Society, available at www.masshist.org/digitaladams/.

57. Letter from Abigail Adams to John Adams, September 17, 1777 [electronic edition], *Adams Family Papers: An Electronic Archive*, Massachusetts Historical Society, available at www.masshist.org/digitaladams/.

58. Letter from Abigail Adams to John Adams, May 4, 1796 [electronic edition], *Adams Family Papers: An Electronic Archive*, Massachusetts Historical Society, available at www.masshist.org/digitaladams/.

59. Letter from Abigail Adams to John Adams, September 14, 1774 [electronic edition], *Adams Family Papers: An Electronic Archive*, Massachusetts Historical Society, available at www.masshist.org/digitaladams/.

60. Letter from John Adams to Abigail Adams, May 17, 1776 [electronic edition], *Adams Family Papers: An Electronic Archive*, Massachusetts Historical Society, available at www.masshist.org/digitaladams/.

61. Letter from John Adams to Abigail Adams, October 1, 1775 [electronic edition], *Adams Family Papers: An Electronic Archive*, Massachusetts Historical Society, available at www.masshist.org/digitaladams/.

62. Letter from Abigail Adams to John Adams, September 14, 1767 [electronic edition], *Adams Family Papers: An Electronic Archive*, Massachusetts Historical Society, available at www.masshist.org/digitaladams/.

63. Letter from John Adams to Abigail Adams, February 21, 1779 [electronic edition], *Adams Family Papers: An Electronic Archive*, Massachusetts Historical Society, available at www.masshist.org/digitaladams/.

64. On the significance of sibling relationships in early America, see C. Dallett Hemphill, *Siblings: Brothers and Sisters in American History* (Oxford: Oxford University Press, 2011).

65. Edith B. Gelles, *Portia: The World of Abigail Adams* (Bloomington: Indiana University Press, 1992), 1–23, 25, 26, 59–71, chaps. 7 and 9. Writers who wish to highlight the sexuality of the Founding Fathers have consistently applied a double standard to interpreting love letters written between Founding Fathers' wives and other men and those letters written between Founding Fathers and other women. Letters between Franklin and women, as we have seen, are readily served as evidence of his libido in a full voyeurism. Yet, the same authors describe the correspondence of Abigail and James Lovell in qualified terms. Fleming, for example, calls him her "literary lover" and conveniently uses Gelles to point out that "historians" have referred to it as a "'virtuous affair.'" Fleming, *Intimate Lives*, 148. See also Joseph Ellis, *First Family: Abigail and John* (New York: Vintage, 2010), 72–73; Smith, *John Adams*, 1:407–409.

66. Anne Husted Burleigh, *John Adams* (New Rochelle, NY: Arlington House, 1969), 36–37.

67. Ibid., 38–39.

68. East, *John Adams*, 30, 35–36, 76, 68.

69. Ferling, *John Adams*, 321.

70. Richard Brookhiser, *America's First Dynasty: The Adamses, 1735–1918* (New York: Free Press, 2002), 17, 37.

71. Grant, *John Adams*, 215, 217.

72. Available at www.clarencedarrowgaryanderson.com/law_liberty_passion.html.

73. Diggins, *John Adams*, 22–23.

74. Smith, *John Adams*, 1:167.

75. Ellis, *First Family*, 16, 79.

76. Available at www.pbs.org/wgbh/amex/adams/sfeature/sf_letters.html.

77. Letter from Abigail Adams to John Adams, October 16, 1774 [electronic edition], *Adams Family Papers: An Electronic Archive*, Massachusetts Historical Society, available at www.masshist.org/digitaladams/.

78. Letter from John Adams to Abigail Adams, February 10, 1777 [electronic edition], *Adams Family Papers: An Electronic Archive*, Massachusetts Historical Society, available at www.masshist.org/digitaladams/.

79. Letter from Abigail Adams to John Adams, December 27, 1778 [electronic edition], *Adams Family Papers: An Electronic Archive*, Massachusetts Historical Society, available at www.masshist.org/digitaladams/.

80. Letter from John Adams to Abigail Adams, May 14, 1789 [electronic edition], *Adams Family Papers: An Electronic Archive*, Massachusetts Historical Society, available at www.masshist.org/digitaladams/.

81. Stahr, *John Jay*, 187, 191. See, for example, Anya Jabour, *Marriage in the Early Republic: Elizabeth and William Wirt and the Companionate Ideal* (Baltimore: Johns Hopkins University Press, 1998).

82. Available at http://harvardpress.typepad.com/off_the_page/2008/02/the-romance-of.html (accessed February 5, 2012).

83. Available at http://clarencedarrowfoundation.org/lovers_and_patriots.html. In Cokie and Steve Roberts's biography of their marriage, they include a section on John and Abigail, referring to their union as "one of the most remarkable" marriages. Cokie and Steve Roberts, *From This Day Forward* (New York: William Morrow, 2001), 38.

84. Available at www.rememberingtheladies.com/Rememberingtheladies/Abigail_Adams.html.

85. Ellis, *First Family*, 3, 108.

CHAPTER 4

1. H. W. Brands, *The First American: The Life and Times of Benjamin Franklin* (New York: Doubleday, 2000); Walter Isaacson, *Benjamin Franklin: An American Life* (New York: Simon and Schuster, 2003), 216–217; and Gordon S. Wood, *The Americanization of Benjamin Franklin* (New York: Penguin, 2005). For an analysis of slavery figured into Franklin's Americanness, see David Waldstreicher, *Runaway America: Benjamin Franklin, Slavery, and the American Revolution* (New York: Hill and Wang, 2004).

2. Isaacson, *Benjamin Franklin*.

3. Ibid., 2.

4. Thomas Fleming, *The Intimate Lives of the Founding Fathers* (Washington, DC: Smithsonian Books, 2009), 77, 103.

5. Paul M. Zall, *Benjamin Franklin's Humor* (Lexington: University Press of Kentucky, 2005), 1. For an early-twentieth-century biography that depicts Franklin's flirtatiousness as charming and nonthreatening, see Benjamin Franklin, *Dr. Benjamin Franklin and the Ladies: Being Various Letters, Essays, and Bagatelles and Satires to and about the Fair Sex* (Mount Vernon, NY: Peter Pauper Press, 1939). The title page reads, "collected for the Public Delight." The text includes the at-times controversial "Speech of Polly Baker" and "Choice of a Mistress."

6. Claude-Anne Lopez, *My Life with Benjamin Franklin* (New Haven, CT: Yale University Press, 2000), 24.

7. Larry E. Tise, ed., *Benjamin Franklin and Women* (University Park: Pennsylvania State University Press, 2000), ix–x.

8. On Franklin, see, for example, Carla Mumford, ed., *The Cambridge Companion to Benjamin Franklin* (Cambridge, UK: Cambridge University Press, 2008).

9. Gordon S. Wood, *Revolutionary Characters: What Made the Founders Different* (New York: Penguin, 2006), 101.

10. Quoted in Isaacson, *Benjamin Franklin*, 216–217. See J. Philip Gleason, "A Scurrilous Colonial Election and Franklin's Reputation," *William and Mary Quarterly* 18 (January 1961): 79–80.

11. Quoted in Sydney George Fisher, *The True Benjamin Franklin* (1898; repr., Philadelphia: Lippincott, 1900), 107–108.

12. Isaacson, *Benjamin Franklin*, 329.

13. On the Chevalier D'Eon, see Gary Kates, *Monsieur D'Eon Is a Woman: A Tale of Political Intrigue and Sexual Masquerade* (Baltimore: Johns Hopkins University Press, 2001).

14. John Jay's Correspondence, vol. 1, April 27, 1780, 311.

15. David Schoenbrun, *Triumph in Paris: The Exploits of Benjamin Franklin* (New York: Harper and Row, 1976), 197.

16. Ruth Miller Elson, *Guardians of Tradition: American Schoolbooks of the Nineteenth Century* (Lincoln: University of Nebraska Press, 1964), 191–192.

17. Scott E. Casper, *Constructing American Lives: Biography and Culture in Nineteenth-Century America* (Chapel Hill: University of North Carolina Press, 1999), 90–91.

18. Leonard W. Labaree et al., eds., *The Autobiography of Benjamin Franklin*, 2nd ed. (New Haven, CT: Yale University Press, 2003), 125–126; italics original.

19. Wood, *Revolutionary Characters*, 88.

20. Although, as Ruth Miller Elson argues, Franklin is often used in schoolbooks to depict the self-made man, other scholars are correct to point out that Franklin is not universally celebrated. Political scientist Jerry Weinberger reminds us that his "reputation did

not always fly so high." Among his most famous early critics are such influential writers as Max Weber, D. H. Lawrence, and Charles Angoff, who considered him to be "shallow at best and as a full-blown philistine at worst." Jerry Weinberger, *Benjamin Franklin Unmasked: On the Unity of His Moral, Religious, and Political Thought* (Lawrence: University of Kansas Press, 2005), ix.

21. Edwin S. Gaustad, *Benjamin Franklin* (Oxford, UK: Oxford University Press, 2006), 11–12.

22. Introduction to *Memoirs of the Late Dr. Franklin* (London: 1790).

23. Carla Mulford, "Franklin, Women, and American Cultural Myths," in *Benjamin Franklin and Women*, ed. Larry E. Tise (University Park: Pennsylvania State University Press, 2000), 105–106.

24. The next several paragraphs draw on Nian-Sheng Huang, *Benjamin Franklin in American Thought and Culture, 1790–1990* (Philadelphia: American Philosophical Society, 1994); and Tise, *Benjamin Franklin and Women*, introduction.

25. Quoted in Tise, *Benjamin Franklin and Women*, 9.

26. Ibid.

27. Ellen Carol DuBois, ed., *Elizabeth Cady Stanton, Susan B. Anthony: Correspondence, Writings, Speeches* (New York: Schocken Books, 1981), 137; Mulford, "Franklin, Women, and American Cultural Myths," 115–117.

28. Quoted in Fisher, *The True Benjamin Franklin*, 127–128.

29. Tise, *Benjamin Franklin and Women*, 7.

30. M. L. Weems, *The Life of Benjamin Franklin* (1829; repr., Philadelphia: Hunt, 1845), 155.

31. John T. Morse, *Benjamin Franklin* (1889; repr., Boston: Houghton Mifflin, 1897), 15.

32. Ibid., 16.

33. John Bach McMaster, *Benjamin Franklin as a Man of Letters* (Boston: Houghton Mifflin, 1887), 45.

34. John Stevens Cabot Abbott, *Benjamin Franklin* (New York: University Society, 1876), 80; italics original.

35. Quoted in ibid., 99.

36. Ibid., 111–112. For earlier accounts that are also explicit, see Orville Luther Holley, *The Life of Benjamin Franklin* (New York: Cooledge, 1848); Henry Stueber, *The Works of Dr. Benjamin Franklin* (Boston: Bedlington, 1825); and Horatio Hastings Weld, *Benjamin Franklin: His Autobiography* (New York: Harper, 1856).

37. Frank Strong, *Benjamin Franklin: A Character Sketch* (Dansville, NY: Instructor Publishing, 1898).

38. George Canning Hill, *Benjamin Franklin: A Biography* (New York: Worthington, 1888), 29.

39. Frederick Jackson Turner, "Franklin in France," *Dial*, May 1887, 7, available at http://babel.hathitrust.org/cgi/pt?view=image;size=100;id=mdp.39015030979556;page=root;seq=19;num=7 (accessed February 14, 2012).

40. Quoted in J. A. Leo Lemay and P. M. Zall, eds., *Benjamin Franklin's Autobiography: An Authoritative Text, Backgrounds, Criticism* (New York: Norton, 1986), 276.

41. Phillips Russell, *Benjamin Franklin: The First Civilized American* (1926; repr., New York: Brentano's, 1927).

42. Ibid., 1.

43. Morse, *Benjamin Franklin*, 420.

44. Fisher, *The True Benjamin Franklin*, 121–122.

45. Carl Van Doren, *Benjamin Franklin* (New York: Viking Press, 1938), 90–94.

46. E. Lawrence Dudley, *Benjamin Franklin* (New York: Macmillan, 1915).

47. Frank Woodworth Pine, ed., *The Autobiography of Benjamin Franklin* (New York: Holt, 1916), 39.

48. Paul Elmer More, *Benjamin Franklin* (Boston: Houghton Mifflin, 1900).

49. Russell, *Benjamin Franklin*, 222–223.

50. John D'Emilio and Estelle Freedman, *Intimate Matters: A History of Sexuality in America*, 3rd ed. (Chicago: University of Chicago Press, 2012), 234.

51. Russell, *Benjamin Franklin*, 138.

52. Tise, *Benjamin Franklin and Women*, 3.

53. Charles Callan Tansill, *The Secret Loves of the Founding Fathers: The Romantic Side of George Washington, Thomas Jefferson, Benjamin Franklin, Gouverneur Morris, Alexander Hamilton* (New York: Devin-Adair, 1964), 44–46.

54. Schoenbrun, *Triumph in Paris*, 145.

55. Russell, *Benjamin Franklin*, 31.

56. Claude-Anne Lopez, *Mon Cher Papa: Franklin and the Ladies of Paris* (New Haven, CT: Yale University Press, 1966), 19–20.

57. Schoenbrun, *Triumph in Paris*, 59.

58. Robert Middlekauff, *Benjamin Franklin and His Enemies* (Berkeley: University of California Press, 1996), 14.

59. Lopez, *Mon Cher Papa*, x.

60. Ibid., vii–viii. For an excellent analysis of this issue and an outline of how to remedy it, see Susan E. Klepp, "Benjamin Franklin and Women," in David Waldstreicher, *A Companion to Benjamin Franklin* (Oxford, UK: Wiley-Blackwell, 2011), 237–252.

61. Schoenbrun, *Triumph in Paris*, 137, 60.

62. Quoted in Isaacson, *Benjamin Franklin*, 348.

63. Tansill, *The Secret Loves of the Founding Fathers*, 51. For other examples of relatively recent popular depictions of a highly sexual Franklin, see Andrew M. Schocket, "Benjamin Franklin in Memory and Popular Culture," in Waldstreicher, *A Companion to Benjamin Franklin*, 479–498.

64. Tansill, *The Secret Loves of the Founding Fathers*, 39–40.

65. Fleming, *Intimate Lives*, 82.

66. Weinberger, *Benjamin Franklin Unmasked*, 102–103.

67. Paul M. Zall, *Franklin on Franklin* (Lexington: University Press of Kentucky, 2000), 100.

68. Blaine McCormick, *Ben Franklin, America's Original Entrepreneur: Franklin's Autobiography Adapted for Modern Times* (Irvine, CA: Entrepreneur Press, 2005), 106.

69. Isaacson, *Benjamin Franklin*, 72.

70. Wood, *The Americanization of Benjamin Franklin*, 32.

71. Edmund S. Morgan, *Benjamin Franklin* (New Haven, CT: Yale University Press, 2002), 45.

72. Ibid., 112.

73. Claude-Anne Lopez, "Three Women, Three Styles: Catharine Ray, Polly Hewson, and Georgiana Shipley," in Tise, *Benjamin Franklin and Women*, 51–52.

74. "Ben Franklin Myths and Facts. An Interview with Historian J. A. Leo Lemay in the University of Delaware U Daily." Available at www.udel.edu/PR/UDaily/2005/mar/franklin061605.html (accessed April 10, 2009).

75. Claude-Anne Lopez, "Why He Was a Babe Magnet," *Time Magazine*, July 7, 2003.

76. Ibid.

77. Tansill, *The Secret Loves of the Founding Fathers*, 78.

78. Quoted in ibid., 79.

79. Middlekauff, *Benjamin Franklin and His Enemies*, 15.

80. Isaacson, *Benjamin Franklin*, 357.

81. Quoted in ibid.

82. Schoenbrun, *Triumph in Paris*, 143.

83. Isaacson, *Benjamin Franklin*, 365.

84. Lopez, "Why He Was a Babe Magnet."

85. Lopez, *Mon Cher Papa*, 243.

86. Middlekauff, *Benjamin Franklin and His Enemies*, 19.

87. Ruth H. Bloch, *Gender and Morality in Anglo-American Culture, 1650–1800* (Berkeley: University of California Press, 2003), 114–115.

88. Mulford, "Franklin, Women, and American Cultural Myths," in Tise, *Benjamin Franklin and Women*, 111; italics original.

89. Gaustad, *Benjamin Franklin*, 101–102.

90. Middlekauff, *Benjamin Franklin and His Enemies*, 20, 116, 115.

91. Isaacson, *Benjamin Franklin*, 357.

92. Lopez, "Three Women, Three Styles," in Tise, *Benjamin Franklin and Women*, 51–52.

CHAPTER 5

1. Ron Chernow, *Alexander Hamilton* (New York: Penguin, 2004); John Lamberton Harper, *American Machiavelli: Alexander Hamilton and the Origins of U.S. Foreign Policy* (Cambridge, UK: Cambridge University Press, 2004); Willard Sterne Randall, *Alexander Hamilton: A Life* (New York: HarperCollins, 2003).

2. *Alexander Hamilton*, documentary film, *American Experience* series (PBS, 2007).

3. Ibid.

4. Available at www.alexanderhamiltonexhibition.org/index.html (accessed February 9, 2009).

5. Jacob Katz Cogan, "The Reynolds Affair and the Politics of Character," *Journal of the Early Republic* 16, no. 3 (1996): 389–417. On Hamilton and honor, see Andrew S. Trees, *The Founding Fathers and the Politics of Character* (Princeton, NJ: Princeton University Press, 2004), 45–72.

6. Alexander Hamilton, *The Reynolds Pamphlet* (Philadelphia, 1797).

7. On the sexual culture of the late eighteenth century, see, for example, Richard Godbeer, *Sexual Revolution in Early America* (Baltimore: Johns Hopkins University Press, 2001); and Clare A. Lyons, *Sex among the Rabble: An Intimate History of Gender and Power in the Age of the Revolution, Philadelphia, 1730–1830* (Chapel Hill: University of North Carolina Press for the Omohundro Institute of Early American History and Culture, 2006).

8. Cogan, "The Reynolds Affair," 390, 392. On Hamilton's changing historiography, see Stephen F. Knott, *Alexander Hamilton and the Persistence of Myth* (Lawrence: University Press of Kansas, 2002).

9. See, for example, Stanley Elkins and Eric McKitrick, *The Age of Federalism: The Early American Republic, 1788–1800* (New York: Oxford University Press, 1993); and John Chester Miller, *The Federalist Era, 1789–1801* (New York: Harper & Row, 1960).

10. Cogan, "The Reynolds Affair," 398.

11. John Wood, *A Correct Statement* (New York: Hopkins, 1802), 9, as cited in Cogan, "The Reynolds Affair," 399. Cogan's analysis of the Reynolds affair highlights the gendered rhetoric of the controversy: "Republican reaction focused on the supposedly private

concern of his alleged adultery," while "Federalists stressed Hamilton's masculine public virtue, his disinterested service to the nation, and feminine licentiousness" (400).

12. Henry Jones Ford, *Alexander Hamilton* (New York: Scribner, 1920), 310.

13. Johan Jacob Smertenko, *Alexander Hamilton* (New York: Greenberg, 1932), 105, 232, 107–108.

14. Quoted in ibid., 105, 232, 107–108; italics original.

15. Richard Godbeer, *The Overflowing of Friendship: Love between Men and the Creation of the American Republic* (Baltimore: Johns Hopkins University Press, 2009), 128.

16. Fawn M. Brodie, *Thomas Jefferson: An Intimate History* (New York: Norton, 1975), 265. On Jefferson-Hamilton, see, for example, Thomas J. DiLorenzo, *Hamilton's Curse: How Jefferson's Archenemy Betrayed the American Revolution—And What It Means for Americans Today* (New York: Crown Forum, 2008).

17. Forrest McDonald, *Alexander Hamilton: A Biography* (New York: Norton, 1979), 15.

18. John C. Miller, *Alexander Hamilton and the Growth of the New Nation* (New York: Harper Torchbooks, 1959), 463–465.

19. Smertenko, *Alexander Hamilton*, xii.

20. McDonald, *Alexander Hamilton*, 229.

21. John C. Hamilton, *The Life of Alexander Hamilton*, 2 vols. (New York: Appleton, 1840–1841), 1:2.

22. Henry Brevoort Renwick and James Renwick, *Lives of John Jay and Alexander Hamilton* (New York: Harper, 1840), 151

23. Lewis Henry Boutell, *Alexander Hamilton: The Constructive Statesman* (Chicago: Privately Printed, 1890), 15. There is no mention of bastard status in Edward Sylvester Ellis, Graeme Mercer Adam, and Bernard John Cigrand, *Alexander Hamilton: A Character Sketch* (Chicago: Union School Furnishing, 1899); James Edward Graybill, *Alexander Hamilton: Nevis-Weehawken* (Lansing, MI: Press of Wynkoop Hallenbeck Crawford, 1898), 7; and George Shea, *Alexander Hamilton: A Historical Study* (New York: Hurd and Houghton, 1877).

24. William Graham Sumner, *Alexander Hamilton* (New York: Dodd, Mead, 1890), 1.

25. Henry Cabot Lodge, *Alexander Hamilton* (Boston: Houghton Mifflin, 1898), 1.

26. Charles Arthur Conant, *Alexander Hamilton* (Boston: Houghton Mifflin, 1901), 5–6.

27. Allan McLane Hamilton, *The Intimate Life of Alexander Hamilton* (New York: Scribner, 1910), 1–2, 7, 10–11, 48.

28. Quoted in ibid., 1–2, 7, 10–11, 48.

29. William S. Culbertson, *Alexander Hamilton: An Essay* (New Haven, CT: Yale University Press, 1911), preface.

30. Smertenko, *Alexander Hamilton*, 9.

31. Ralph Edward Bailey, *An American Colossus: The Singular Career of Alexander Hamilton* (Boston: Lothrop, Lee, and Shepard, 1933), 18.

32. Smertenko, *Alexander Hamilton*, preface, xii, xiii.

33. Miller, *Alexander Hamilton and the Growth of the New Nation*, 62.

34. McDonald, *Alexander Hamilton*, 6.

35. Arnold A. Rogow, *A Fatal Friendship: Alexander Hamilton and Aaron Burr* (New York: Hill and Wang, 1998).

36. Chernow, *Alexander Hamilton*, 367–368, 363.

37. Renwick and Renwick, *Lives of John Jay and Alexander Hamilton*, 303–304.

38. Knott, *Alexander Hamilton and the Persistence of Myth*.

39. James Parton, *Life of Thomas Jefferson* (Boston: Osgood, 1874), 539.

40. Debby Applegate, *The Most Famous Man in America: The Biography of Henry Ward Beecher* (New York: Doubleday, 2006).

41. Parton, *Life of Thomas Jefferson*, 534.

42. Ibid., 539, 534.

43. Shea, *Alexander Hamilton*, 406, 405–407.

44. John T. Morse, *The Life of Alexander Hamilton*, 2 vols. (Boston: Little Brown, 1882), 2:336–338.

45. Lodge, *Alexander Hamilton*, 276.

46. On folly, see Miller, *Alexander Hamilton and the Growth of the New Nation*, 463.

47. Smertenko, *Alexander Hamilton*, 231.

48. Bailey, *An American Colossus*, 213.

49. Charles Callan Tansill, *The Secret Loves of the Founding Fathers: The Romantic Side of George Washington, Thomas Jefferson, Benjamin Franklin, Gouverneur Morris, Alexander Hamilton* (New York: Devin-Adair, 1964), 179–182, 186.

50. Broadus Mitchell, *Heritage from Hamilton* (New York: Columbia University Press, 1957), 39.

51. Smertenko, *Alexander Hamilton*, 233.

52. Tansill, *The Secret Loves of the Founding Fathers*, 204–205.

53. Hamilton, *Intimate Life*, 116–117.

54. Bailey, *An American Colossus*, 272–273.

55. Richard B. Morris, ed., *The Basic Ideas of Alexander Hamilton* (New York: Washington Square Press, 1956), 427.

56. Tansill, *The Secret Loves of the Founding Fathers*, 210.

57. Gertrude Franklin Horn Atherton, *The Conqueror: Being the True and Romantic Story of Alexander Hamilton* (Toronto, Canada: Morang, 1902), 371–372.

58. Hamilton, *Intimate Life*, 60.

59. Eugene E. Prussing, *George Washington in Love and Otherwise* (Chicago: Pascal Covici, 1925), 173–177.

60. Bailey, *An American Colossus*, 272.

61. Tansill, *The Secret Loves of the Founding Fathers*, 197–198, 209.

62. Michel Foucault, *The History of Sexuality: An Introduction*, trans. Robert Hurley (New York: Vintage Books, 1990), 58–61.

63. Frederick Scott Oliver, *Alexander Hamilton, an Essay on American Union* (New York: G. P. Putnam's Sons, 1907), 389.

64. Ford, *Alexander Hamilton*, 310.

65. Ibid., 312–313. For another early-twentieth-century biography that lauds Hamilton's "moral courage" and points to his having "vindicated his official honor" by confessing to the affair, see Claude Gernade Bowers, *Jefferson and Hamilton: The Struggle for Democracy in America* (New York: Houghton Mifflin, 1925), 34, 190.

66. Nathan Schachner, *Alexander Hamilton, Nation Builder* (New York: McGraw-Hill, 1952), 174.

67. Morse, *The Basic Ideas of Alexander Hamilton*, 427.

68. Ibid., 426. See also Richard B. Morse, ed., *Alexander Hamilton and the Founding of the Nation* (New York: Dial Press, 1957), which is a longer version and contains all the same editor's explanations.

69. *Alexander Hamilton* (2007).

70. Chernow, *Alexander Hamilton*, 367. Mrs. Hamilton's devotion and the story of her not letting Monroe sit down when he came to visit her years later is the final passage of Randall's 2003 account. Randall, *Alexander Hamilton*, 424.

71. *Alexander Hamilton* (2007).

72. Chernow, *Alexander Hamilton*, 363, 203.

73. Joseph A. Murray, *Alexander Hamilton: America's Forgotten Founder* (New York: Algora, 2007), preface.

74. *Alexander Hamilton* (2007).

75. Ibid.

76. Murray, *Alexander Hamilton*, preface.

77. Richard Brookhiser, *Alexander Hamilton: American* (New York: Free Press, 1999), 99.

78. Murray, *Alexander Hamilton*, preface.

79. *Alexander Hamilton* (2007).

80. Murray, *Alexander Hamilton*, preface.

81. Ibid.

82. Thomas Fleming, *The Intimate Lives of the Founding Fathers* (Washington, DC: Smithsonian Books, 2009), 229.

83. Randall, *Alexander Hamilton*, 409. Notably, given Randall's depiction of Hamilton's affair as the product of his ego, he does not need to fall back on the portrayal of Hamilton as purely devoted to his wife (save for one "lapse"), and thus he writes freely of other "loves," including one Kitty Livingston from his youth and a nearly lifelong affair with his sister-in-law, Angelica Church.

84. Godbeer, *The Overflowing of Friendship*, 127; see chap. 4.

85. Sumner, *Alexander Hamilton*, 252, 105.

86. Hamilton, *Intimate Life*, 242.

87. Miller, *Alexander Hamilton and the Growth of the New Nation*, 22.

88. Jonathan Katz, *Gay American History: Lesbians and Gay Men in the U.S.A.* (New York: Crowell, 1976), 452–456.

89. Linda Rapp, "Alexander Hamilton," available at www.glbtq.com/social-sciences/hamilton_a,3.html December 20, 2007; Hamilton, *Intimate Life*, 245, 241–242. See Caleb Crain, "Leander, Lorenzo, and Castalio: An Early American Romance," in *Long before Stonewall: Histories of Same-Sex Sexuality in Early America*, ed. Thomas A. Foster (New York: New York University Press, 2007), 229. On same-sex romantic friendships in early America, see also Godbeer, *The Overflowing of Friendship*.

90. Available at www.thedailybeast.com/blogs-and-stories/2009–04–24/my-apology-to-yale/full/.

91. William Benemann, *Male-Male Intimacy in Early America: Beyond Romantic Friendships* (New York: Harrington Park Press, 2006), 100.

92. Fleming, *Intimate Lives*, 219.

93. Hamilton, *The Reynolds Pamphlet*.

CHAPTER 6

1. *Papers of Gouverneur Morris,* original diary entry for October 11, 1789, Manuscript Division, Library of Congress, Washington, DC (hereafter Diary, LOC).

2. Theodore Roosevelt, *Gouverneur Morris* (Boston: Houghton Mifflin, 1899), 364.

3. William Howard Adams, *Gouverneur Morris: An Independent Life* (New Haven, CT: Yale University Press, 2003), xvi.

4. Max M. Mintz, *Gouverneur Morris and the American Revolution* (Norman: University of Oklahoma Press, 1970); Roosevelt, *Gouverneur Morris*; Jared Sparks, *The life of Gouverneur Morris: with selections from his correspondence and miscellaneous papers; detailing*

events in the American Revolution, the French Revolution, and in the political history of the United States, 3 vols. (Boston: Gray and Bowen, 1832); Howard Swiggett, *The Extraordinary Mr. Morris* (New York: Doubleday, 1952).

Morris's granddaughter and great-granddaughter published selected letters and edited diaries. Gouverneur Morris, *A Diary of the French Revolution,* ed. Beatrix Cary Davenport, 2 vols. (Boston: Houghton Mifflin, 1939); Anne Cary Morris, ed., *The Diary and Letters of Gouverneur Morris, Minister of the United States to France; Member of the Constitutional Convention,* 2 vols. (New York: Scribner, 1888).

5. Adams, *Gouverneur Morris*; Richard Brookhiser, *Gentleman Revolutionary: Gouverneur Morris, the Rake Who Wrote the Constitution* (New York: Free Press, 2003); James J. Kirschke, *Gouverneur Morris: Author, Statesman, and Man of the World* (New York: Thomas Dunne Books, 2005); Melanie Miller, *Envoy to the Terror: Gouverneur Morris and the French Revolution* (Dulles, VA: Potomac Books, 2006); and Melanie Miller, *An Incautious Man: The Life of Gouverneur Morris* (Wilmington, DE: ISI Books, 2008).

6. Adams, *Gouverneur Morris,* xi.

7. Kirschke, *Gouverneur Morris,* 13.

8. See Alan Crawford, *Unwise Passions—A True Story of a Remarkable Woman—and the First Great Scandal of Eighteenth-Century America* (New York: Simon and Schuster, 2005). See also Christopher L. Doyle, "The Randolph Scandal in Early National Virginia, 1792–1815: New Voices in the "Court of Honour," *Journal of Southern History* 69 (2003): 283–318.

9. For a recent example, see Gordon S. Wood, *Revolutionary Characters: What Made the Founders Different* (New York: Penguin, 2006). For an overview of the controversy over what some see as a renewed hagiography of the Founding Fathers, see David Waldstreicher, "Founders Chic as Culture War," *Radical History Review* 84 (Fall 2002): 185–194.

10. Thomas A. Foster, *Sex and the Eighteenth-Century Man: Massachusetts and the History of Sexuality in America* (Boston: Beacon Press, 2006); Christopher Looby, "Republican Bachelorhood: Sex and Citizenship in the Early United States," *Historical Reflections/Reflexions Historiques* 33 (Spring 2007): 89–100; Laura Mandell, "What's Sex Got to Do with It? Marriage versus Circulation in the *Pennsylvania Magazine,* 1775–76," in *Long before Stonewall: Histories of Same-Sex Sexuality in Early America,* ed. Thomas A. Foster (New York: New York University Press, 2007), 331–356; Dana D. Nelson, *National Manhood: Capitalist Citizenship and the Imagined Fraternity of White Men* (Durham, NC: Duke University Press, 1998); Anthony Rotundo, *American Manhood: Transformations in American Masculinity from the Revolution to the Modern Era* (New York: Basic Books, 1994); Bryce Traister, "The Wandering Bachelor: Irving, Masculinity, and Authorship," *American Literature* 74 (2002): 111–137; and Scott Slawinski, *Validating Bachelorhood: Audience, Patriarchy and Charles Brockden Brown's Editorship of the Monthly Magazine and American Review* (New York: Routledge, 2005). On disability and sexuality, see, for example, Robert McRuer and Anna Mollow, eds., *Sex and Disability* (Durham, NC: Duke University Press, 2012).

On bachelors in American culture, see, for example, Howard P. Chudacoff, *The Age of the Bachelor: Creating an American Subculture* (Princeton, NJ: Princeton University Press, 1999); Barbara Ehrenreich, *The Hearts of Men: American Dreams and the Flight from Commitment* (New York: Anchor, 1987).

11. Thomas A. Foster, "Reconsidering Libertines and Early Modern Heterosexuality: Sex and American Founder Gouverneur Morris," *Journal of the History of Sexuality* 22, no. 1 (January 2013): 65–84.

12. Quoted in Brookhiser, *Gentleman Revolutionary,* 260.

13. Nancy Isenberg, *Fallen Founder: The Life of Aaron Burr* (New York: Penguin, 2008).

14. Mary E. Fissell, "Hairy Women and Naked Truths: Gender and the Politics of Knowledge in *Aristotle's Masterpiece*," *William and Mary Quarterly* 60 (January 2003): 60. See also Elaine Forman Crain, "'I Have Suffer'd Much Today': The Defining Force of Pain in Early America," in *Through a Glass Darkly: Reflections on Personal Identity in Early America*, ed. Ronald Hoffman, Mechal Sobel, and Fredrika J. Teute (Chapel Hill: University of North Carolina Press, 1997), 370–403; Thomas A. Foster, "Recovering Washington's Body-Double: Disability and Manliness in the Life and Legacy of a Founding Father," *Disability Studies Quarterly* 2, no. 1 (January 2012); and David Waldstreicher, "The Long Arm of Benjamin Franklin," in *Artificial Parts, Practical Lives: Modern Histories of Prosthetics*, ed. Katherine Ott, David Serlin, and Stephen Mihm (New York: New York University Press, 2002), 300–326; and Thomas A. Foster, "Recovering Washington's Body-Double: Disability and Manliness in the Life and Legacy of a Founding Father," *Disability Studies Quarterly* 2, no. 1 (January 2012).

15. Hal Gladfelder, "Plague Spots," in Turner and Stagg, *Social Histories of Disability*, 56.

16. David M. Turner and Kevin Stagg, eds., *Social Histories of Disability and Deformity* (London: Routledge, 2006), 4–8, 57.

17. Turner and Stagg, *Social Histories*, 57.

18. Kirschke, *Gouverneur Morris*, 119 ; italics original.

19. Mintz, *Gouverneur Morris*, 141.

20. Morris, *A Diary of the French Revolution*, 2:247.

21. Diary, LOC, March 19, 1791.

22. Morris, *Diary and Letters*, 1:165.

23. Paul Longmore, *Why I Burned My Book and Other Essays on Disability* (Philadelphia: Temple University Press, 2003), 20. Disability scholars remind us, for example, that places like Chicago in the twentieth century passed ordinances restricting the movement of disabled individuals in public, most notably the poor and homeless.

24. See, for example, William L. Chew, III, "'Straight' Sam Meets 'Lewd' Louis: American Perceptions of French Sexuality, 1775–1815," in *Revolutions and Watersheds: Transatlantic Dialogues, 1775–1815,* ed. W. M. Verhoeven and Beth Dolan Kautz (Amsterdam: Rodopi, 1999), 61–86.

25. Morris enjoyed a reputation for being a ladies' man even in his early twenties in America. See, for example, Adams, *Gouverneur Morris*, 29. On late-eighteenth-century urban centers, see, for example, Richard Godbeer, *Sexual Revolution in Early America* (Baltimore: Johns Hopkins University Press, 2001); and Clare A. Lyons, *Sex among the Rabble: An Intimate History of Gender and Power in the Age of Revolution, Philadelphia, 1730–1830* (Chapel Hill: University of North Carolina Press for the Omohundro Institute of Early American History and Culture, 2006). See also Isenberg, *Fallen Founder*, 233–235.

26. Miller, *Envoy to the Terror*, xi.

27. Steven Kale, *French Salons: High Society and Political Sociability from the Old Regime to the Revolution of 1848* (Baltimore: Johns Hopkins University Press, 2004), 2; Lynn Hunt, *Politics, Culture, and Class in the French Revolution* (Berkeley: University of California Press, 2004). On connections between politics and sexuality, see, for example, Lynn Hunt, ed., *Eroticism and the Body Politic* (Baltimore: Johns Hopkins University Press, 1991).

28. Kale, *French Salons*, 3.

29. Ibid., 7.

30. On women, salons, and the development of the public sphere in France, see, for example, Roger Chartier, ed., *The Cultural Origins of the French Revolution*, trans. Lydia G. Cochrane (Durham, NC: Duke University Press, 1991); Robert Darnton, *The Literary Underground of the Old Regime* (Cambridge, MA: Harvard University Press, 1982); Dena Goodman, *The Republic of Letters: A Cultural History of the French Enlightenment* (Ithaca, NY: Cornell University Press, 1994); Jürgen Habermas, *The Structural Transformation of the Public Sphere: An Inquiry into a Category of Bourgeois Society*, trans. Thomas Burger (Cambridge, MA: MIT Press, 1989); Joan B. Landes, *Women and the Public Sphere in the Age of the French Revolution* (Ithaca, NY: Cornell University Press, 1988); and Sarah Maza, *Private Lives and Public Affairs: The Causes Célèbres of Prerevolutionary France* (Berkeley: University of California Press, 1993).

31. Morris, *A Diary of the French Revolution,* 2:165.

32. *The Papers of Gouverneur Morris,* original diary entry for May 18, 1791, Manuscript Division, Library of Congress, Washington, DC (hereafter Diary, LOC). All of this is deleted by Davenport and only available to us from the original diaries.

33. Diary, LOC, February 12, 1791.

34. Diary, LOC, August 10, 1791. For other examples, see also entries for October 10, 16, 1791; December 9, 1791; and January 1, 1792.

35. Diary, LOC, July 30, 1791.

36. Diary, LOC, June 15, 1792.

37. Diary, LOC, May 18, 1791.

38. The Cyprian Queen is a reference to Venus or Aphrodite; italics original.

39. John H. Summers, "What Happened to Sex Scandals? Politics and Peccadilloes, Jefferson to Kennedy," *Journal of American History* 87, no. 3 (December 2000): 825–854. On biography, see Scott E. Casper, *Constructing American Lives: Biography and Culture in Nineteenth-Century America* (Chapel Hill: University of North Carolina Press, 1999). On print culture and national identity in the early Republic, see, for example, Jay Fliegelman, *Declaring Independence: Jefferson, Natural Language, and the Culture of Performance* (Palo Alto, CA: Stanford University Press, 1993); Christopher Looby, *Voicing America: Language, Literary Form, and the Origins of the United States* (Chicago: University of Chicago Press, 1998); and Michael Warner, *The Letters of the Republic: Publication and the Public Sphere in Eighteenth-Century America* (1990; repr., Cambridge, MA: Harvard University Press, 2006).

40. Sparks, *The Life of Gouverneur Morris,* 1:295.

41. Henry Bertram Hill, review of Gouverneur Morris, *A Diary of the French Revolution*, ed. Beatrix Cary Davenport, *Journal of Modern History* 12 (March 1940): 103–104. Yet this reviewer could not refrain from adding his own moralizing, remarking that the affair was "a thing which robbed him of a part of his character."

42. Roosevelt, *Gouverneur Morris*, 26–27.

43. See, for example, Gail Bederman, *Manliness and Civilization: A Cultural History of Gender and Race in the United States, 1880–1917* (Chicago: University of Chicago Press, 1995).

44. Roosevelt, *Gouverneur Morris*, 197.

45. Ibid., 204–205.

46. Morris, *Diary of the French Revolution*, 1:284–285.

47. Diary LOC, November 4, 1789.

48. Diary LOC, April 12, 1789.

49. Chudacoff, *The Age of the Bachelor*; John D'Emilio and Estelle Freedman, *Intimate Matters: A History of Sexuality in America,* 3rd ed. (Chicago: University of Chicago Press, 2012); Ehrenreich, *The Hearts of Men.*

50. Swiggett, *The Extraordinary Mr. Morris,* 2, 5.

51. Ibid., 258, 179.

52. Ibid., 4.

53. Ibid., 209, 317, 319, 181, 92.

54. *The Extraordinary Mr. Morris* by Howard Swiggett, reviewed by Gordon B. Turner, *William and Mary Quarterly* 9, no. 4 (October 1952): 571–572. See also the review by Burke M. Hermann, *Pennsylvania History* 20 (January 1953): 108–109.

55. John P. Frank, review of *The Extraordinary Mr. Morris* by Howard Swiggett, *Yale Law Journal* 61 (1952): 1227–1231.

56. Mintz, *Gouverneur Morris and the American Revolution.*

57. Charles W. Akers, review of *Gouverneur Morris and the American Revolution, Journal of American History* 58 (Fall 1971): 440–441.

58. Mintz, *Gouverneur Morris,* 234, 236.

59. Arnold Whitridge, "A Representative of America," *American Heritage* 27 (June 1976).

60. Kirschke, *Gouverneur Morris,* 209, xxiv.

61. Brookhiser misunderstands some of Davenport's ellipses. Combining the desperate events of the French Revolution with the budding romance, he remarks, "Less than a week after his encounter with Foulon's dismembered corpse, Morris made love for the first time to Adèle de Flahaut. Recording the event in his diary, he was unusually laconic, slipping behind the mask of three dots." Brookhiser, *Gentleman Revolutionary,* 111.

62. Thomas Fleming, *The Intimate Lives of the Founding Fathers* (Washington, DC: Smithsonian Books, 2009), 225.

63. Diary, LOC, December 31, 1789. Melanie Miller similarly points out that Morris "liked and respected women." Miller, *An Incautious Man,* 97.

64. Diary, LOC, May 28, 1791.

65. Kirschke, *Gouverneur Morris,* xxiv.

66. Brookhiser, *Gentleman Revolutionary,* 11, 61.

67. Mintz, *Gouverneur Morris and the American Revolution.*

68. Available at www.constitutioncenter.org/explore/FoundingFathers/Pennsylvania.shtml.

(accessed July 8, 2008).

69. Available at http://en.wikipedia.org/wiki/Gouverneur_Morris (accessed January 17, 2007).

70. Available at http://en.wikipedia.org/wiki/Gouverneur_Morris (accessed April 16, 2009).

CONCLUSION

1. See, for example, Joseph Ellis, *Founding Brothers: The Revolutionary Generation* (New York: Vintage Books, 2000), 18; and Douglass Adair, *Fame and the Founding Fathers* (Indianapolis: Liberty Fund, 1974), ch. 1.

2. Joseph Ellis, *First Family: Abigail and John* (New York: Vintage, 2010), ix.

3. Ibid., 255.

4. For an excellent example of work that carefully reminds readers that love and marriage are historically contingent, see Virginia Scharff, *The Women Jefferson Loved* (New York: HarperCollins, 2010).

5. Ibid., 217.

6. Thomas Jefferson, for example, has most recently been the subject of discussion about sexual relations between slave-owning Founding Fathers and their slaves—but oral histories also testify to George Washington and James Madison as fathers of enslaved descendants. On Washington, see, for example, Henry Wiencek, *An Imperfect God: George Washington, His Slaves, and the Creation of America* (New York: Farrar, Straus, and Giroux, 2003). On James Madison, see, for example, the work of Betty Kearse. Jonathan Mummolo, "African American Seeks to Prove a Genetic Link to James Madison," *Washington Post Monday,* June 11, 2007.

7. On the eroticization of modern culture, see Paul Rutherford, *A World Made Sexy: Freud to Madonna* (Toronto, Canada: University of Toronto Press, 2007). On normative sexuality, see Gayle S. Rubin, "Thinking Sex: Notes for a Radical Theory of the Politics of Sexuality," in *Deviations: A Gayle Rubin Reader* (Durham, NC: Duke University Press, 2011), 137–181.

BIBLIOGRAPHY

Abbott, John Stevens Cabot. *Benjamin Franklin.* New York: University Society, 1876.

Adair, Douglass. *Fame and the Founding Fathers.* Indianapolis: Liberty Fund, 1974.

Adams, Charles Francis. *The Works of John Adams.* Boston: Little, Brown, 1856.

Adams, William Howard. *Gouverneur Morris: An Independent Life.* New Haven, CT: Yale University Press, 2003.

———. *The Paris Years of Thomas Jefferson.* New Haven, CT: Yale University Press, 1997.

Alexander Hamilton. Documentary film. *American Experience* series. PBS, 2007.

Amory, John K. "George Washington's Infertility: Why Was the Father of Our Country Never a Father?" *Fertility and Sterility* 81, no. 3 (March 2004): 495–499.

Anderson, John E., et al., "Infertility Services Reported by Men in the United States: National Survey Data." *Fertility and Sterility* 91, no. 6 (June 2009): 2466–2470.

Appleby, Joyce. *A Restless Past: History and the American Public.* New York: Rowman and Littlefield, 2005.

———. *Thomas Jefferson.* New York: Times Books, 2003.

Applegate, Debby. *The Most Famous Man in America: The Biography of Henry Ward Beecher.* New York: Doubleday, 2006.

Atherton, Gertrude Franklin Horn. *The Conqueror: Being the True and Romantic Story of Alexander Hamilton.* Toronto, Canada: Morang, 1902.

Backscheider, Paula R. *Reflections on Biography.* Oxford, UK: Oxford University Press, 1999.

Bailey, Ralph Edward. *An American Colossus: The Singular Career of Alexander Hamilton.* Boston: Lothrop, Lee, and Shepard, 1933.

Banner, Lois W. "'Biography as History' Roundtable: Historians and Biography." *American Historical Review* 114, no. 3 (June 2009): 583.

Barker-Benfield, G. J. *Abigail and John Adams: The Americanization of Sensibility.* Chicago: University of Chicago Press, 2010.

Bederman, Gail. *Manliness and Civilization: A Cultural History of Gender and Race in the United States, 1880–1917.* Chicago: University of Chicago Press, 1995.

Berlant, Lauren. *The Queen of America Goes to Washington City: Essays on Sex and Citizenship*. Durham, NC: Duke University Press, 1997.

Bernstein, R. B. *The Founding Fathers Reconsidered*. Oxford, UK: Oxford University Press, 2009.

Bonomi, Patricia. *Lord Cornbury Scandal: The Politics of Reputation in British America*. Chapel Hill: University of North Carolina Press, 1998.

Bordo, Susan. *The Male Body: A New Look at Men in Public and in Private*. New York: Farrar, Straus, and Giroux, 1999.

Bottorff, William K. *Thomas Jefferson*. Boston: Twayne Publishers, 1979.

Boutell, Lewis Henry. *Alexander Hamilton: The Constructive Statesman*. Chicago: Privately Printed, 1890.

Bowers, Claude G. *Jefferson and Hamilton: The Struggle for Democracy in America*. New York: Houghton Mifflin, 1925.

———. *The Young Jefferson, 1743–1789*. Boston: Houghton Mifflin, 1945.

Brady, Patricia. *Martha Washington: An American Life*. New York: Viking, 2005.

Brands, H. W. *The First American: The Life and Times of Benjamin Franklin*. New York: Doubleday, 2000.

Brodie, Fawn M. *Thomas Jefferson: An Intimate History*. New York: Norton, 1975.

Brookhiser, Richard. *Alexander Hamilton: American*. New York: Free Press, 1999.

———. *America's First Dynasty: The Adamses, 1735–1918*. New York: Free Press, 2002.

———. *Founding Father: Rediscovering George Washington*. New York: Free Press, 1996.

———. *Gentleman Revolutionary: Gouverneur Morris, the Rake Who Wrote the Constitution*. New York: Free Press, 2003.

Brown, Kathleen M. *Good Wives, Nasty Wenches, and Anxious Patriarchs: Gender, Race, and Power in Colonial Virginia*. Chapel Hill: University of North Carolina Press, 1996.

Brown, William Wells. *Clotel; or, The President's Daughter: A Narrative of Slave Life in the United States*. Edited and with an introduction by M. Giulia Fabi. 1853. Reprint, New York: Penguin, 2004.

Bryant, Linda Allen. *I Cannot Tell a Lie: The True Story of George Washington's African American Descendants*. New York: iUniverse Star, 2001.

Burleigh, Anne Husted. *John Adams*. New Rochelle, NY: Arlington House, 1969.

Burnard, Trevor. "The Founding Fathers in Early American Historiography: A View from Abroad." *William and Mary Quarterly* 62, no. 4 (October 2005): 745–763.

Burns, James MacGregor, and Susan Dunn, *George Washington*. New York: Times Books, 2004.

Burstein, Andrew. *Jefferson's Secrets: Death and Desire at Monticello*. New York: Basic Books, 2005.

Butterfield, L. H. *The Book of Abigail and John: Selected Letters of the Adams Family, 1762–1784*. Cambridge, MA: Harvard University Press, 1975.

Canaday, Margot. *The Straight State: Sexuality and Citizenship in Twentieth-Century America*. Princeton, NJ: Princeton University Press, 2009.

Carnes, Mark C., ed. *Novel History: Historians and Novelists Confront America's Past (and Each Other)*. New York: Simon and Schuster, 2001.

Casper, Scott E. *Constructing American Lives: Biography and Culture in Nineteenth-Century America*. Chapel Hill: University of North Carolina Press, 1999.

Castiglia, Christopher, and Christopher Reed. *If Memory Serves: Gay Men, AIDS, and the Promise of the Queer Past*. Minneapolis: University of Minnesota Press, 2011.

Chadwick, Bruce. *The General and Mrs. Washington: The Untold Story of a Marriage and a Revolution*. Naperville, IL: Sourcebooks, 2007.

Chamberlain, Mellen. *John Adams: The Statesman of the American Revolution.* Boston: Houghton Mifflin, 1898.

Chase-Riboud, Barbara. *Sally Hemings: A Novel.* New York: Viking, 1979.

Chauncey, George. *Gay New York: Gender, Urban Culture, and the Making of the Gay Male World, 1890–1940.* New York: Basic Books, 1995.

Chernow, Ron. *Alexander Hamilton.* New York: Penguin, 2004.

Clark, Mary Higgins. *Mount Vernon Love Story: A Novel of George and Martha Washington.* New York: Pocket Books, 2003.

Cogan, Jacob Katz. "The Reynolds Affair and the Politics of Character." *Journal of the Early Republic* 16, no. 3 (1996): 389–417.

Cogliano, Francis D. *Thomas Jefferson: Reputation and Legacy.* Charlottesville: University of Virginia Press, 2006.

Conant, Charles Arthur. *Alexander Hamilton.* Boston: Houghton Mifflin, 1901.

Crackel, Theodore J., ed. *The Papers of George Washington. Digital edition.* Available at http://rotunda.upress.virginia.edu/founders/GEWN.html.

Crain, Caleb. *American Sympathy: Men, Friendship, and Literature in the New Nation.* New Haven, CT: Yale University Press, 2001.

———. "Leander, Lorenzo, and Castalio: An Early American Romance." In *Long before Stonewall: Histories of Same-Sex Sexuality in Early America,* edited by Thomas A. Foster, 217–252. New York: New York University Press, 2007.

Crawford, Alan. *Unwise Passions—A True Story of a Remarkable Woman—and the First Great Scandal of Eighteenth-Century America.* New York: Simon and Schuster, 2005.

Culbertson, William S. *Alexander Hamilton: An Essay.* New Haven, CT: Yale University Press, 1911.

Cunliffe, Marcus. *George Washington: Man and Monument.* Boston: Little, Brown, 1958. Revised edition, New York: NAL, 1982.

Curtis, William Eleroy. *The True Thomas Jefferson.* Philadelphia: Lippincott, 1901.

Dabney, Virginius, and Jon Kukla. "The Monticello Scandals: History and Fiction." *Virginia Cavalcade* 29, no. 2 (Autumn 1979): 52–61.

Daniels, Jonathan. *Ordeal of Ambition: Jefferson, Hamilton, Burr.* New York: Doubleday, 1970.

D'Emilio, John, and Estelle Freedman. *Intimate Matters: A History of Sexuality in America.* 3rd edition. Chicago: University of Chicago Press, 2012.

Dennie, Joseph, and Asbury Dickens. *Port Folio.* Vol. 2. Philadelphia: Maxwell, 1802.

Desmond, Alice Curtis. *Martha Washington: Our First Lady.* New York: Dodd, 1942.

Diggins, John P. *John Adams.* New York: Times Books, 2003.

Douglas, Carlyle C. "The Dilemma of Thomas Jefferson." *Ebony* (August 1975): 60–66.

Doyle, Christopher L. "The Randolph Scandal in Early National Virginia, 1792–1815: New Voices in the 'Court of Honour.'" *Journal of Southern History* 69 (2003): 283–318.

Dudley, E. Lawrence. *Benjamin Franklin.* New York: Macmillan, 1915.

Earle, Rebecca, ed. *Epistolary Selves: Letters and Letter-Writers, 1600–1945.* Aldershot, UK: Ashgate, 1999.

East, Robert A. *John Adams.* Boston: Twayne Publishers, 1979.

Ehrenreich, Barbara. *The Hearts of Men: American Dreams and the Flight from Commitment.* New York: Anchor, 1987.

Elkins, Stanley, and Eric McKitrick. *The Age of Federalism: The Early American Republic, 1788–1800.* New York: Oxford University Press, 1993.

Ellis, Edward Sylvester, Graeme Mercer Adam, and Bernard John Cigrand. *Alexander Hamilton: A Character Sketch.* Chicago: Union School Furnishing, 1899.

Ellis, Joseph J. *American Sphinx: The Character of Thomas Jefferson.* New York: Knopf, 1997; New York: Vintage 1998.

———. *First Family: Abigail and John.* New York: Vintage, 2010.

———. *Founding Brothers: The Revolutionary Generation.* New York: Vintage, 2000.

———. *His Excellency: George Washington.* New York: Vintage, 2004.

———. *Passionate Sage: The Character and Legacy of John Adams.* New York: Norton, 1994.

Elson, Ruth Miller. *Guardians of Tradition: American Schoolbooks of the Nineteenth Century.* Lincoln: University of Nebraska Press, 1964.

Farquhar, Michael. *A Treasury of Great American Scandals: Tantalizing True Tales of Historic Misbehavior by the Founding Fathers and Others Who Let Freedom Swing.* New York: Penguin, 2003.

Ferling, John. *The Ascent of George Washington: The Hidden Political Genius of an American Icon.* New York: Bloomsbury, 2009.

———. *The First of Men: A Life of George Washington.* Knoxville: University of Tennessee Press, 1988.

———. *John Adams: A Life.* Knoxville: University of Tennessee Press, 1992.

Fields, Joseph E. *"Worthy Partner": The Papers of Martha Washington.* Westport, CT: Greenwood Press, 1994.

Finkelman, Paul. *Slavery and the Founders: Race and Liberty in the Age of Jefferson.* London: Sharpe, 1996.

Fischer, David Hackett. *Washington's Crossing.* Oxford, UK: Oxford University Press, 2006.

Fisher, Sydney George. *The True Benjamin Franklin.* 1898. Reprint, Philadelphia: Lippincott, 1900.

Fitzpatrick, John C. *George Washington Himself: A Commonsense Biography Written from His Manuscripts.* Indianapolis: Bobbs-Merrill, 1933.

———. "The George Washington Scandals." Bulletin No. 1 of the Washington Society of Alexandria, 1929.

Fleming, Thomas. *The Intimate Lives of the Founding Fathers.* Washington, DC: Smithsonian Books, 2009.

Flexner, James Thomas. "Washington Mythology," *American Heritage* 41, no. 1 (February 1990): 107.

Fliegelman, Jay. *Declaring Independence: Jefferson, Natural Language, and the Culture of Performance.* Palo Alto, CA: Stanford University Press, 1993.

Flint, Larry, and David Eisenbach. *One Nation under Sex: How the Private Lives of Presidents, First Ladies, and Their Lovers Changed the Course of American History.* New York: Palgrave Macmillan, 2011.

Flower, Milton E. *James Parton: The Father of Modern Biography.* New York: Greenwood Press, 1968.

Ford, Henry Jones. *Alexander Hamilton.* New York: Scribner, 1920.

Ford, Paul Leicester. *The True George Washington.* Philadelphia: Lippincott, 1898.

Foster, Thomas A., "Deficient Husbands: Manhood, Sexual Incapacity, and Male Marital Sexuality in Seventeenth-Century New England." *William and Mary Quarterly* 56 (October 1999): 723–744.

———. "John Adams and the Choice of Hercules: Manliness and Sexual Virtue in Eighteenth-Century British America." In *New Men: Manliness in Early America,* edited by Thomas A. Foster, 217–235. New York: New York University Press, 2011.

———, ed. *Long before Stonewall: Histories of Same-Sex Sexuality in Early America.* New York: New York University Press, 2007.

———. "Reconsidering Libertines and Early Modern Heterosexuality: Sex and American Founder Gouverneur Morris." *Journal of the History of Sexuality* 22, no. 1 (2013): 65–84.

———. "Recovering Washington's Body-Double: Disability and Manliness in the Life and Legacy of a Founding Father." *Disability Studies Quarterly* 2, no. 1 (2012). Available at http://dsq-sds.org/article/view/3028/3064.

———. *Sex and the Eighteenth-Century Man: Massachusetts and the History of Sexuality in America.* Boston: Beacon Press, 2006.

Foucault, Michel. *The History of Sexuality: An Introduction.* Translated by Robert Hurley. New York: Vintage Books, 1990.

Franklin, Benjamin. *Dr. Benjamin Franklin and the Ladies: Being Various Letters, Essays, and Bagatelles and Satires to and about the Fair Sex.* Mount Vernon, NY: Peter Pauper Press, 1939.

Freeman, Douglas Southall. *George Washington: A Biography.* 7 vols. New York: Scribner, 1948–1957.

Furstenberg, François. *In the Name of the Father: Washington's Legacy, Slavery, and the Making of a Nation.* New York: Penguin, 2006.

Gaustad, Edwin S. *Benjamin Franklin.* Oxford, UK: Oxford University Press, 2006.

Gelles, Edith B. *Portia: The World of Abigail Adams.* Bloomington: Indiana University Press, 1992.

Gibbon, Peter H. *A Call to Heroism: Renewing America's Vision of Greatness.* New York: Atlantic Monthly Press, 2002.

Gilbert, Matthew. "No Sex Scandals Taint This Power Couple in HBO's *John Adams.*" *Denver Post,* March 27, 2008.

Glassberg, David. "Public History and the Study of Memory." *Public Historian* 18, no. 2 (Spring 1996): 7–23.

Gleason, J. Philip. "A Scurrilous Colonial Election and Franklin's Reputation." *William and Mary Quarterly* 18 (January 1961): 68–84.

Godbeer, Richard. *The Overflowing of Friendship: Love between Men and the Creation of the American Republic.* Baltimore: Johns Hopkins University Press, 2009.

———. *Sexual Revolution in Early America.* Baltimore: Johns Hopkins University Press, 2001.

Gordon-Reed, Annette. *The Hemingses of Monticello: An American Family.* New York: Norton, 2008.

———. *Thomas Jefferson and Sally Hemings: An American Controversy.* Charlottesville: University of Virginia Press, 1997.

Grant, James. *John Adams: Party of One.* New York: Farrar, Straus, and Giroux, 2005.

Graybill, James Edward. *Alexander Hamilton: Nevis-Weehawken.* Lansing, MI: Press of Wynkoop Hallenbeck Crawford, 1898.

Hagood, Wesley O. *Presidential Sex: From the Founding Fathers to Bill Clinton.* 1996. Reprint, New York: Citadel Press, 1998.

Haid, Charles, dir. *Sally Hemings: An American Scandal.* TV miniseries. Echo Bridge Home Entertainment Studio, 2004.

Hamilton, Alexander. *The Reynolds Pamphlet.* Philadelphia, 1797.

Hamilton, Allan McLane. *The Intimate Life of Alexander Hamilton.* New York: Scribner, 1910.

Hamilton, John C. *The Life of Alexander Hamilton.* 2 vols. New York: Appleton, 1840–1841.

Harper, John Lamberton. *American Machiavelli: Alexander Hamilton and the Origins of U.S. Foreign Policy.* Cambridge, UK: Cambridge University Press, 2004.

Haworth, Paul Leland. *George Washington: Country Gentleman*. 1915. Reprint, Indianapolis: Bobbs-Merrill, 1925.

Higginbotham, Don, ed. *George Washington Reconsidered*. Charlottesville: University of Virginia Press, 2001.

Hill, George Canning. *Benjamin Franklin: A Biography*. New York: Worthington, 1888.

Hirst, Francis W. *Life and Letters of Thomas Jefferson*. New York: Macmillan, 1926.

Hitchens, Christopher. *Thomas Jefferson: Author of America*. New York: Harper Perennial, 2009.

Hobsbawm, Eric, and Terence Ranger, eds. *The Invention of Tradition*. Cambridge, UK: Cambridge University Press, 1992.

Holley, Orville Luther. *The Life of Benjamin Franklin*. New York: Cooledge, 1848.

Huang, Nian-Sheng. *Benjamin Franklin in American Thought and Culture, 1790–1990*. Philadelphia: American Philosophical Society, 1994.

Hughes, Rupert. *George Washington: The Human Being and the Hero, 1732–1762*. New York: William Morrow, 1926.

Humez, Jean M. *Harriet Tubman: The Life and the Life Stories*. Madison: University of Wisconsin Press, 2003.

Hunt, Lynn. *Politics, Culture, and Class in the French Revolution*. Berkeley: University of California Press, 2004.

Hutton, Patrick. "Recent Scholarship on Memory and History." *History Teacher* 33, no. 4 (August 2000): 533–548.

Irving, Washington. *Life of George Washington*. New York: Putnam, 1856.

Isaacson, Walter. *Benjamin Franklin: An American Life*. New York: Simon and Schuster, 2003.

Isenberg, Nancy. *Fallen Founder: The Life of Aaron Burr*. New York: Penguin, 2008.

———. "The 'Little Emperor': Aaron Burr, Dandyism, and the Sexual Politics of Treason." In *Beyond the Founders,* edited by Jeffrey Pasley, Andrew W. Robertson, and David Waldstreicher, 129–158. Chapel Hill: University of North Carolina Press, 2004.

Jabour, Anya. *Marriage in the Early Republic: Elizabeth and William Wirt and the Companionate Ideal*. Baltimore: Johns Hopkins University Press, 1998.

John and Abigail Adams. Documentary film. *American Experience* series. PBS, 2006.

Johnson, David K. *The Lavender Scare: The Cold War Persecution of Gays and Lesbians in the Federal Government*. Chicago: University of Chicago Press, 2004.

Jordan, Winthrop. *White over Black: American Attitudes toward the Negro, 1550–1812*. Chapel Hill: University of North Carolina Press, 1968.

Kale, Steven. *French Salons: High Society and Political Sociability from the Old Regime to the Revolution of 1848*. Baltimore: Johns Hopkins University Press, 2004.

Kaminski, John P. *Jefferson in Love: The Love Letters between Thomas Jefferson and Maria Cosway*. New York: Rowman and Littlefield, 1999.

Kammen, Michael. *Mystic Chords of Memory: The Transformation of Tradition in American Culture*. New York: Vintage, 1993.

———. *A Season of Youth: The American Revolution and the Historical Imagination*. Ithaca, NY: Cornell University Press, 1978.

Kasson, John F. *Houdini, Tarzan, and the Perfect Man: The White Male Body and the Challenge of Modernity in America*. New York: Hill and Wang, 2001.

Kerber, Linda K., and Walter John Morris. "Politics and Literature: The Adams Family and the Port Folio." *William and Mary Quarterly* 23, no. 3 (July 1966): 450–476.

Kirschke, James J. *Gouverneur Morris: Author, Statesman, and Man of the World*. New York: Thomas Dunne Books, 2005.

Knollenberg, Bernhard. *George Washington, the Virginia Period, 1732–1775*. Durham, NC: Duke University Press, 1964.

Knott, Stephen F. *Alexander Hamilton and the Persistence of Myth*. Lawrence: University Press of Kansas, 2002.

Knudson, Jerry W. *Jefferson and the Press: Crucible of Liberty*. Columbia: University of South Carolina Press, 2006.

Kukla, Jon. *Mr. Jefferson's Women*. New York: Knopf, 2007.

Kunzel, Regina G. *Criminal Intimacy: Prison and the Uneven History of Modern American Sexuality*. Chicago: University of Chicago Press, 2008

Labaree, Leonard W., et al., eds., *The Autobiography of Benjamin Franklin*. 2nd edition. New Haven, CT: Yale University Press, 2003.

Lacayo, Richard. With an introduction by Joseph J. Ellis. "George Washington: How the Great Uniter Helped Create the United States." *Time*. Special issue, 2011.

Landes, Joan B. *Women and the Public Sphere in the Age of the French Revolution*. Ithaca, NY: Cornell University Press, 1988.

Lanier, Shannon, and Jane Feldman. *Jefferson's Children: The Story of One American Family*. New York: Random House, 2002.

Laumann, Edward O., Anthony Paik, and Raymond C. Rosen. "Sexual Dysfunction in the United States: Prevalence and Predictors." *Journal of the American Medical Association* 281, no. 6 (1999): 537–544.

Lemay, J. A. Leo, and P. M. Zall, eds. *Benjamin Franklin's Autobiography: An Authoritative Text, Backgrounds, Criticism*. New York: Norton, 1986.

Lepore, Jill. *The Whites of Their Eyes: The Tea Party's Revolution and the Battle over American History*. Princeton, NJ: Princeton University Press, 2010.

Lewis, Jan Ellen, and Peter S. Onuf, eds. *Sally Hemings and Thomas Jefferson: History, Memory, and Civic Culture*. Charlottesville: University of Virginia Press, 1999.

Linn, William. *Life of Thomas Jefferson*. 3rd edition. Ithaca, NY: Andrus, Woodruff, and Gauntlett, 1843.

Lockridge, Kenneth A. *On the Sources of Patriarchal Rage: The Commonplace Books of William Byrd and Thomas Jefferson and the Gendering of Power in the Eighteenth Century*. New York: New York University Press, 1992.

Lodge, Henry Cabot. *Alexander Hamilton*. Boston: Houghton Mifflin, 1898.

———. *George Washington*. Boston: Houghton Mifflin, 1889.

Lombard, Anne S. *Making Manhood: Growing Up Male in Colonial New England*. Cambridge, MA: Harvard University Press, 2003.

Longmore, Paul K. *The Invention of George Washington*. Berkeley: University of California Press, 1988.

Looby, Christopher. "Republican Bachelorhood: Sex and Citizenship in the Early United States." *Historical Reflections/Reflexions Historiques* 33 (Spring 2007): 89–100.

———. *Voicing America: Language, Literary Form, and the Origins of the United States*. Chicago: University of Chicago Press, 1998.

Lopez, Claude-Anne. *Mon Cher Papa: Franklin and the Ladies of Paris*. New Haven, CT: Yale University Press, 1966.

———. *My Life with Benjamin Franklin*. New Haven, CT: Yale University Press, 2000.

Lossing, Benson John. *Mary and Martha: The Mother and the Wife of George Washington*. New York: Harper and Brothers, 1886.

Lyman, T.P.H. *The Life of Thomas Jefferson, Esq, L.L.D. late ex president of the United States*. Philadelphia: Neall, 1826.

Lyons, Clare A. *Sex among the Rabble: An Intimate History of Gender and Power in the Age of*

Revolution, Philadelphia, 1730–1830. Chapel Hill: University of North Carolina Press for the Omohundro Institute of Early American History and Culture, 2006.

Lystra, Karen. *Searching the Heart: Women, Men, and Romantic Love in Nineteenth-Century America*. New York: Oxford University Press, 1989.

Maier, Pauline. *American Scripture: Making the Declaration of Independence*. New York: Knopf, 1997.

Malone, Dumas. *Jefferson and Our Times*. Pasadena, CA: Fund for Adult Education, 1955.

———. *Jefferson, the Virginian*. Vol. 1 of *Jefferson and His Time*. Boston: Little, Brown, 1948.

Marshall, John. *The Life of George Washington, Commander in Chief of the American Forces, during the War Which Established the Independence of His Country, and First President of the United States*. 1804. Reprint, New York: Wise, 1926.

May, Elaine Tyler. *Barren in the Promised Land: Childless Americans and the Pursuit of Happiness*. New York: Basic Books, 1995.

Maza, Sarah. *Private Lives and Public Affairs: The Causes Célèbres of Prerevolutionary France*. Berkeley: University of California Press, 1993.

McCormick, Blaine. *Ben Franklin, America's Original Entrepreneur: Franklin's Autobiography Adapted for Modern Times*. Irvine, CA: Entrepreneur Press, 2005.

McCoy, Samuel. *This Man Adams: The Man Who Never Died*. New York: Bretano's, 1928.

McCullough, David. *John Adams*. New York: Simon and Schuster, 2001.

McDonald, Forrest. *Alexander Hamilton: A Biography*. New York: Norton, 1979.

McLaren, Angus. *Impotence: A Cultural History*. Chicago: University of Chicago Press, 2007.

McMaster, John Bach. *Benjamin Franklin as a Man of Letters*. Boston: Houghton Mifflin, 1887.

Middlekauff, Robert. *Benjamin Franklin and His Enemies*. Berkeley: University of California Press, 1996.

Miller, John C. *Alexander Hamilton and the Growth of the New Nation*. New York: Harper Torchbooks, 1959.

———. *The Wolf by the Ears: Thomas Jefferson and Slavery*. New York: Free Press, 1977.

Miller, Melanie. *Envoy to the Terror: Gouverneur Morris and the French Revolution*. Dulles, VA: Potomac Books, 2006.

———. *An Incautious Man: The Life of Gouverneur Morris*. Wilmington, DE: ISI Books, 2008.

Minnigerode, Meade. *Some American Ladies: Seven Informal Biographies*. 1926. Reprint, Freeport, NY: Books for Libraries Press, 1969.

Mintz, Max M. *Gouverneur Morris and the American Revolution*. Norman: University of Oklahoma Press, 1970.

Mitchell, Broadus. *Heritage from Hamilton*. New York: Columbia University Press, 1957.

Moore, Charles. *The Family Life of George Washington*. Boston: Houghton Mifflin, 1926.

More, Paul Elmer. *Benjamin Franklin*. Boston: Houghton Mifflin, 1900.

Morgan, Edmund S. *Benjamin Franklin*. New Haven, CT: Yale University Press, 2002.

Morris, Anne Cary, ed. *The Diary and Letters of Gouverneur Morris, Minister of the United States to France; Member of the Constitutional Convention*. 2 vols. New York: Scribner, 1888.

Morris, Gouverneur. *A Diary of the French Revolution*. Edited by Beatrix Cary Davenport. 2 vols. Boston: Houghton Mifflin, 1939.

———. *An Oration Upon the Death of General Washington*. New York: John Furman, 1800.

Morris, Richard B., ed. *Alexander Hamilton and the Founding of the Nation*. New York: Dial Press, 1957.

———. *The Basic Ideas of Alexander Hamilton*. New York: Washington Square Press, 1956.

Morse, John T. *Benjamin Franklin*. 1889. Reprint, Boston: Houghton Mifflin, 1897.

———. *John Adams*. Boston: Houghton Mifflin, 1884.

———. *The Life of Alexander Hamilton*. 2 vols. Boston: Little Brown, 1882.

———, ed. *Thomas Jefferson*. Boston: Houghton Mifflin, 1883.

Mott, Frank L. *Jefferson and the Press*. Baton Rouge: Louisiana State University Press, 1943.

Mumford, Carla, ed. *The Cambridge Companion to Benjamin Franklin*. Cambridge, UK: Cambridge University Press, 2008.

Murray, Joseph A. *Alexander Hamilton: America's Forgotten Founder*. New York: Algora, 2007.

Nock, Albert Jay. *Jefferson*. New York: Hill and Wang, 1926.

Oliver, Frederick Scott, *Alexander Hamilton, an Essay on American Union*. New York: G. P. Putnam's Sons, 1907.

Onuf, Peter S. *The Mind of Thomas Jefferson*. Charlottesville: University of Virginia Press, 2007.

Papers of Gouverneur Morris, Manuscript Division, Library of Congress, Washington, DC.

Parton, James. *Life of Thomas Jefferson*. Boston: Osgood, 1874.

Pasley, Jeffrey, Andrew W. Robertson, and David Waldstreicher, eds., *Beyond the Founders: New Approaches to the Political History of the Early American Republic*. Chapel Hill: University of North Carolina Press, 2004.

———. "Federalist Chic." February 2002. Available at http://common-place.org.

Paulding, James Kirk. *The Life of Washington*. Aberdeen, UK: Clark, 1848.

Peterson, Merrill D. *The Jefferson Image in the American Mind*. New York: Oxford University Press, 1960.

Pierson, Hamilton W. *Jefferson at Monticello: The Private Life of Thomas Jefferson*. New York: Scribner, 1862.

Pine, Frank Woodworth, ed. *The Autobiography of Benjamin Franklin*. New York: Holt, 1916.

Prussing, Eugene E. *George Washington in Love and Otherwise*. Chicago: Pascal Covici, 1925.

Randall, Henry Stephens. *The Life of Thomas Jefferson*. 3 vols. New York: Derby and Jackson, 1857–1858.

Randall, Willard Sterne. *Alexander Hamilton: A Life*. New York: HarperCollins, 2003.

———. *George Washington: A Life*. New York: Holt, 1997.

———. *Thomas Jefferson: A Life*. New York: Harper Perennial, 1993.

Randolph, Sarah N. *The Domestic Life of Thomas Jefferson*. Charlottesville: 1871. Reprint, Thomas Jefferson Memorial Foundation by the University Press of Virginia, 1978.

Rasmussen, William M. S., and Robert S. Tilton. *George Washington: The Man behind the Myths*. Charlottesville: University of Virginia Press, 1999.

Rayner, B. L. *Life of Thomas Jefferson*. Boston: Lilly, Wait, Colman, and Holden, 1834.

Renwick, Henry Brevoort, and James Renwick. *Lives of John Jay and Alexander Hamilton*. New York: Harper, 1840.

Roberts, Cokie, and Steve Roberts. *From This Day Forward*. New York: Morrow, 2001.

Robins, Sally Nelson. *Love Stories of Famous Virginians*. 2nd edition. Richmond, VA: Dietz Printing, 1925.

Rogow, Arnold A. *A Fatal Friendship: Alexander Hamilton and Aaron Burr*. New York: Hill and Wang, 1998.

Roosevelt, Theodore. *Gouverneur Morris.* Boston: Houghton Mifflin, 1899.

Rosenzweig, Roy, and David Thelen. *The Presence of the Past: Popular Uses of History in American Life.* New York: Columbia University Press, 1998.

Rothman, Joshua D. *Notorious in the Neighborhood: The Color Line in Virginia 1787–1861.* Chapel Hill: University of North Carolina Press, 2003.

Rotundo, Anthony. *American Manhood: Transformations in Masculinity from the Revolution to the Modern Era.* New York: Basic Books, 1994.

Rubin, Gayle S. *Deviations: A Gayle Rubin Reader.* Durham, NC: Duke University Press, 2011.

Russell, Phillips. *Benjamin Franklin: The First Civilized American.* 1926. Reprint, New York: Brentano's, 1927.

———. *Jefferson: Champion of the Free Mind.* New York: Dodd, Mead, 1956.

Rutherford, Paul. *A World Made Sexy: Freud to Madonna.* Toronto, Canada: University of Toronto Press, 2007.

Salliant, John. "The Black Body Erotic and the Republican Body Politic, 1790–1820." In *Long before Stonewall,* edited by Thomas A. Foster, 303–330. New York: New York University Press, 2007.

Schachner, Nathan. *Alexander Hamilton, Nation Builder.* New York: McGraw-Hill, 1952.

Scharff, Virginia. *The Women Jefferson Loved.* New York: HarperCollins, 2010.

Schoenbrun, David. *Triumph in Paris: The Exploits of Benjamin Franklin.* New York: Harper and Row, 1976.

Schwartz, Barry. *George Washington: The Making of an American Symbol.* New York: Free Press, 1987.

Self, Robert O. *All in the Family: The Realignment of American Democracy since the 1960s.* New York: Hill and Wang, 2012.

Sernett, Milton C. *Harriet Tubman: Myth, Memory, and History.* Durham, NC: Duke University Press, 2007.

Shah, Nayan. *Stranger Intimacy: Contesting Race, Sexuality, and the Law in the North American West.* Berkeley: University of California Press, 2012.

Shea, George. *Alexander Hamilton: A Historical Study.* New York: Hurd and Houghton, 1877.

Smertenko, Johan Jacob. *Alexander Hamilton.* New York: Greenberg, 1932.

Smith, Page. *John Adams.* 2 vols. New York: Doubleday, 1962.

Sparks, Jared. *The life of Gouverneur Morris: with selections from his correspondence and miscellaneous papers; detailing events in the American Revolution, the French Revolution, and in the political history of the United States.* 3 vols. Boston: Gray and Bowen, 1832.

———. *The Writings of George Washington.* 2 vols. New York: Harper and Brothers, 1837.

Stahr, Walter. *John Jay: Founding Father.* New York: Continuum International, 2006.

Steinberg, Alfred. *John Adams.* New York: Putnam, 1969.

St. George, Judith. *John and Abigail Adams: An American Love Story.* New York: Holiday House, 2001.

Strong, Frank. *Benjamin Franklin: A Character Sketch.* Dansville, NY: Instructor Publishing, 1898.

Stueber, Henry. *The Works of Dr. Benjamin Franklin.* Boston: Bedlington, 1825.

Summers, John H. "What Happened to Sex Scandals? Politics and Peccadilloes, Jefferson to Kennedy." *Journal of American History* 87, no. 3 (2000): 825–854.

Sumner, William Graham. *Alexander Hamilton.* New York: Dodd, Mead, 1890.

Susman, Warren I. *Culture as History: The Transformation of American Society in the Twentieth Century.* 1973. Reprint, New York: Pantheon Books, 1984.

Swiggett, Howard. *The Extraordinary Mr. Morris.* New York: Doubleday, 1952.

Tansill, Charles Callan. *The Secret Loves of the Founding Fathers: The Romantic Side of George Washington, Thomas Jefferson, Benjamin Franklin, Gouverneur Morris, Alexander Hamilton.* New York: Devin-Adair, 1964.

Thane, Elswyth. *Washington's Lady.* New York: Dodd, Mead, 1960.

Thomas, Evan. "Founders Chic: Live from Philadelphia." *Newsweek,* July 9, 2001.

Tise, Larry E., ed. *Benjamin Franklin and Women.* University Park: Pennsylvania State University Press, 2000.

Trees, Andrew S. *The Founding Fathers and the Politics of Character.* Princeton, NJ: Princeton University Press, 2004.

Tucker, George. *The Life of Thomas Jefferson, Third President of the United States.* 2 vols. Philadelphia: Carey, Lea, and Blanchard, 1837.

Unger, Harlow G. *The Unexpected George Washington: His Private Life.* Hoboken, NJ: Wiley, 2006.

Van Doren, Carl. *Benjamin Franklin.* New York: Viking Press, 1938.

Van Tassel, David D. *Recording America's Past: An Interpretation of the Development of Historical Studies in America, 1607–1884.* Chicago: University of Chicago Press, 1960.

Vidal, Gore. *Burr: A Novel.* 1973. Reprint, New York: Vintage, 2000.

———. *Imperial America: Reflections on the United States of Amnesia.* New York: Nation Books, 2004.

———. *Inventing a Nation: Washington, Adams, Jefferson.* New Haven, CT: Yale University Press, 2003.

Waldstreicher, David. *A Companion to Benjamin Franklin.* Oxford, UK: Wiley-Blackwell, 2011.

———. "Founders Chic as Culture War." *Radical History Review* 84 (Fall 2002): 185–194.

———. *Runaway America: Benjamin Franklin, Slavery, and the American Revolution.* New York: Hill and Wang, 2004.

Walker, Clarence E. *Mongrel Nation: The America Begotten by Thomas Jefferson and Sally Hemings.* Charlottesville: University of Virginia Press, 2009.

Warner, Michael. *The Letters of the Republic: Publication and the Public Sphere in Eighteenth-Century America.* 1990, Reprint, Cambridge, MA: Harvard University Press, 2006.

Warren, Mercy Otis. *History of the Rise, Progress and Termination of the American Revolution.* 2 vols. Indianapolis: Liberty Classics, 1988.

Watson, Thomas E. *The Life and Times of Thomas Jefferson.* New York: Appleton, 1903.

Wayans, Marlon. *Scary Movie.* Burbank, CA: Dimension Home Video, 2000.

Weems, Mason. *A History of the Life and Death Virtues and Exploits of General George Washington.* New York: Grosset and Dunlap, 1927.

———. *The Life of Benjamin Franklin.* 1829. Reprint, Philadelphia: Hunt, 1845.

Weinberger, Jerry. *Benjamin Franklin Unmasked: On the Unity of His Moral, Religious, and Political Thought.* Lawrence: University of Kansas Press, 2005.

Weld, Horatio Hastings. *Benjamin Franklin: His Autobiography.* New York: Harper, 1856.

White, Deborah Gray. *Ar'n't I a Woman: Female Slaves in the Plantation South.* Revised edition. New York: Norton, 1999.

White, Kevin. *The First Sexual Revolution: The Emergence of Male Heterosexuality in Modern America.* New York: New York University Press, 1993.

———. *Sexual Liberation or Sexual License? The American Revolt against Victorianism.* Chicago: Dee, 2000.

Wiencek, Henry. *An Imperfect God: George Washington, His Slaves, and the Creation of America.* New York: Farrar, Straus, and Giroux, 2003.

————. *Master of the Mountain: Thomas Jefferson and His Slaves*. New York: Farrar, Straus, and Giroux, 2012.

Wilkins, Roger. *Jefferson's Pillow: The Founding Fathers and the Dilemma of Black Patriotism*. Boston: Beacon Press, 2001.

Wills, Garry. *"Negro President": Jefferson and the Slave Power*. Boston: Beacon Press, 2003.

Wilson, Lisa. *Ye Heart of a Man: The Domestic Life of Men in Colonial New England*. New Haven, CT: Yale University Press, 1999.

Wilson, Woodrow. *George Washington*. New York: Harper, 1896.

Wood, Gordon S. *The Americanization of Benjamin Franklin*. New York: Penguin, 2005.

————. *Revolutionary Characters: What Made the Founders Different*. New York: Penguin, 2006.

Young, Alfred F. *The Shoemaker and the Tea Party: Memory and the American Revolution*. Boston: Beacon Press, 1999.

Young, Alfred F., Gary B. Nash, and Ray Raphael, eds. *Revolutionary Founders: Rebels, Radicals, and Reformers in the Making of the Nation*. New York: Knopf, 2011.

Zagarri, Rosemarie, ed. *David Humphreys' "Life of General Washington."* Athens: University of Georgia Press, 1991.

Zall, Paul M. *Benjamin Franklin's Humor*. Lexington: University Press of Kentucky, 2005.

————. *Franklin on Franklin*. Lexington: University Press of Kentucky, 2000.

INDEX

Note: Page numbers in italics refer to illustrations.

Abbott, John Stevens Cabot, 105–106
Adams, Abigail, 90–96; and absences of
  John Adams, 90–92, 93–94; courtship of,
  83–84, 90, 95; depiction of, in *John Adams*
  (miniseries), 77, 78; on Franklin, 102; full
  life of, 91–92; letters of, 79, 84, 88, 90–91,
  94–95, 186n56, 187n65; marriage of, 79,
  90–96; in popular culture, 77–78, 92–95,
  187n83; statue of, 94
Adams, Charles Francis, 84
Adams, John, 8, 77–96; as amorous
  Puritan, 84–89; appearance of, 77–78,
  85; children of, 17, 78, 79; courtship of,
  83–84, 90, 95; death of, 79; depiction
  of, in *John Adams* (miniseries), 77, 78;
  early memories of, 82–84; and European
  culture, 80–81, 82–83, 87; faithfulness
  of, 78, 86, 94; on Franklin, 81, 82–83,
  87, 102; on Hamilton, 81, 120, 127;
  heteronormative desires of, 87; as ideal
  husband, 92–93; judgment of others by,
  80, 81, 82–83, 84, 148; letters of, 79, 81,
  87, 90, 91, 94–95; lifetime of, 79–82;
  long absences of, 84–85, 90–92, 93–94;
  marriage of, 79, 90–96; moral purity of,
  78–82; in popular culture, 77–78, 92–95,
  187n83; portrait of, *77;* in preface to *Sally
  Hemings,* 72; as Puritan descendant, 79;

and Hannah Quincy, 85, 86, 87, 88–89;
  statue of, 94
Adams, John Quincy, 17, 82
Adultery: by Hamilton, 122–123, 124–125,
  128–137, 141; by Jefferson, 60–61
"Advice on the Choice of a Mistress"
  (Franklin), 99–100, 104–105, 111
Affair(s): by Hamilton, 122–123, 124–125,
  128–137, 141; by Jefferson, 60–61; by
  Morris, 148–155, 157–159
Alexander Hamilton (documentary), 119,
  135–137
Alexander Hamilton Post 448 of the
  American Legion, 139
American Experience (television series), 95, 119
American Legion, Alexander Hamilton Post
  448 of the, 139
Ames, Ezra, 161
Amory, John K., 41, 178n135
Appearance: of Adams, 77–78, 85; of
  Franklin, 98, 116; of Jefferson, 62–63;
  of Morris, 144–147, 156–157, 160–163,
  162, 196n23; of Washington, 19, *20,* 31,
  33–36, *35*
Appleby, Joyce, 72, 181n83
Arnold, Benedict, 2, 18
Autobiography (Franklin), 100, 102, 103, 105,
  109, 111–112, 165

Bachelor(s): Franklin on, 100–101, 105; Jefferson as, 61, 63; Morris as, 8, 144, 145, 150, 151–153, 155–158
Backscheider, Paula R., 170n6
Bailey, Ralph Edward, 127, 132
Banner, Lois W., 4
Barrell, William, 186n56
Bayard, Thomas F., 105
Beecher, Henry Ward, 129, 137
Benemann, William, 140
Berlant, Lauren, 170nn7–8
Biographies, popular, 4–6, 171–172n19
Bland, Mary, 25
Bloch, Ruth, 115
Body. *See* Appearance
Bottorff, William, 75
Boutell, Lewis Henry, 126
Boyd, Julian, 59
Brady, Patricia, 34
Brillon de Jouy, Anne-Louise d'Hardancourt, 109–110, 113–114, 116
Brodie, Fawn, 58, 68, 69, 125, 182n105
Brookhiser, Richard: on Adams, 93; on Hamilton, 136; on Morris, 159, 160–161, *162*, 198n61; on Washington, 34, 40
Brown, William Wells, 64
Burnard, Trevor, 170n7
Burr, Aaron: duel with Hamilton, 8, 120, 121, 128, 141; vs. Morris, 145, 160; sexual depiction of, 7
Burwell, Judy, 51
Burwell, Rebecca ("Belinda"), 49–53, 60, 74, 76
Bush, George W., 45

Callender, James, 47–48, 65–67, 122, 127, 182n105, 183n128
Carr, Peter, 65, 70, 182n107
Chadwick, Bruce, 38
Chamberlain, Mellen, 83
Chappel, Alonzo, 161, *162*
Chaumont, Jacques-Donatien Leray de, 101, 110
Chernow, Ronald, 119–120, 128, 135–136, 137
"Choice of a Mistress" essay (Franklin), 99–100, 104–105, 111
Church, Angelica, 124, 125, 194n83
Clark, Mary Higgins, 31–32
Class. *See* Elite; Middle class
Clinton, Bill, 4, 71, 137, 166

Clotel; or, *The President's Daughter: A Narrative of Slave Life in the United States* (Brown), 64
Cogan, Jacob Katz, 123
Common-law marriage of Franklin, 112. *See also* Franklin, Benjamin: common-law wife of
Conant, Charles, 126
Corbin, Alice, 51
Cosway, Maria: and Sally Hemings, 58, 63, 66, 67, 180n66; Jefferson's romance with, 57–60, 74, 76
Crain, Caleb, 138
Custis, Martha. *See* Washington, Martha
Custis, Martha Parke ("Patsy"), 34, 38

Dandridge, Martha. *See* Washington, Martha
Davenport, Ann Cary, 153–158
Davies, David, 183–184n3
de Flahaut, Adèlaide, 148–155, 157–159, 198n61
de Flahaut de la Billarderie, Alexandre-Sebastien, 148
D'Eon, Chevalier, 101, 108
Desexualization: of Adams, 85; disability and, 147; of Founding Fathers, 1–2, 169n1; of George Washington, 11–13
Desmond, Alice, 31, 33
Diggins, John Patrick, 87–88, 94
Disability of Morris, 144–147, 156–157, 160–163, *162*, 196n23
Dudley, E. Lawrence, 108
Durand, Asher B., *77*
du Simitière, Pierre Eugène, *143*

East, Robert A., 92–93
Ebony (magazine) on Jefferson-Hemings relationship, 66, 68
Eighteenth century: affairs in, 148; common-law marriage in, 112; disability in, 147; inequality of men and women in, 73; love letters in, 26–27, 57, 59, 90, 95; misogyny in, 63, 115, 131, 159; Puritanism in, 79–80, 89; salon culture in, 155–156, 160; sex scandals of, 13–17; sexual openness of, 99, 100; sterility vs. impotence in, 41
Eisenbach, David, 3
Elderly image of Founding Fathers, 2, 169n1
Elite: Adams as, 83, 85; Founding Fathers as, 6, 7, 9; Franklin as, 117; Hamilton

as, 134; and masculinity, 152; Morris as, 147, 148, 149, 160; sexual culture of, 6; George Washington as, 13, 32, 39; Martha Washington as, 16

Ellis, Joseph: on Adams, 95; on Jefferson, 59, 71, 74, 179n23; on Washington, 33, 36

Elson, Ruth Miller, 18, 102

Fairfax, George William, 22

Fairfax, Sally, 21–22, 25–29, 31, 33

Faithfulness: of Adams, 78, 86, 94; of Franklin, 112–113; of Jefferson, 55, 57; of Washington, 18, 28, 29

Falstaff, John, 147

Farquhar, Michael, 4

Fauntleroy, Betty, 176n92

Federalist chic, 169n1

Femininity: of Abigail Adams, 92; of Maria Cosway, 58; of Chevalier D'Eon, 108; of Martha Jefferson, 54; of Thomas Jefferson, 62; of Monticello, 52; of salon culture, 149; of Washington, 36

Ferling, John, 36, 85–86, 93

Fischer, David Hackett, *14*, 33–34

Fissell, Mary, 146

Fitzpatrick, John C., 28–29

Fleming, Thomas: on Adams, 88–89; on Founding Fathers, 3; on Franklin, 98, 111; on Hamilton, 137; on Jefferson, 59, 61, 183n128; on Washington, 33, 34, 38

Fleming, Will, 52

Flexner, James Thomas, 40

Flynt, Larry, 3

Ford, Henry Jones, 135

Ford, West, 42

Founders chic, 144, 169n1

Founding Fathers: ambivalence about relevance of private behavior of, 167–168; conclusions about, 165–168; crafting of self-images of, 165; curiosity about "real" lives of, 2; desexualization of, 1–2, 169n1; exceptionalism of, 165–167; familiarity with sex lives of, 4; filling in gaps in information about, 4–5; mythic proportions of, 166–167; in national identity, 3, 170nn6–7; nineteenth-century view of, 6, 165–166, 167; public view of, 170n7; as role models, 167, 199n6; romanticized view of, 167; sexual personalizing of, 5; stories about sexual escapades of, 3, 170–171nn8–10; studies

on intimate lives of, 3–4, 171n11; tabloid press at time of, 6; twentieth-century view of, 6–7; twenty-first-century view of, 7

Franklin, Benjamin, 7, 8, 97–117; Adams's disapproval of, 81, 82–83, 87; appearance of, 98, 116; *Autobiography* of, 100, 102, 103, 105, 109, 111–112, 165; common-law wife of, 100, 103, 105, 106, 107–108, 109, 112–113, 115; and Chevalier D'Eon, 101, 108; early lie told by, 103, 106, 108; early memories of, 102–106; earthy sayings of, 108–109; as faithful husband, 112–113; as first great American, 106, 117; as foxy grandpa, 97–98, 117; and French beauties, 101–102, 103–104, 110, 113–117; vs. Hamilton, 98, 100; in his lifetime, 99–102; illegitimate son of, 98, 101, 103, 105, 106, 112; infidelities of, 103–104; intrigues with low women by, 106, 112; mixed reputation of, 102–106, 188–189n20; and National Hall of Fame, 104; portrait of, *97;* ribald essays of, 99–101, 111; scandals involving, 101; as self-made man, 102, 111; as sexual modern, 97–98, 106–113; view of women of, 109–111, 115; as womanizer, 98, 104, 110–111, 113, 115, 116

Franklin, William, 98, 101, 103, 105, 106, 112

Freeman, Douglas Southall, 28, 31

Freemason(s), Washington as, 16, 173n9

Freud, Sigmund, 6, 27, 63

Furstenberg, François, 18

Garrison, William Lloyd, 64

Gaustad, Edwin S., 115–116

Gay: Hamilton as, 137–140; Washington as, 140

Gelles, Edith B., 91–92, 187n65

Gender: in biography, 166; and Hamilton affair, 123, 129–130, 131; and national identity, 5, 9. *See also* Femininity; Masculinity

General George Washington at Trenton (painting), *35*

Gentleman Revolutionary: Gouverneur Morris, the Rake Who Wrote the Constitution (Brookhiser), 159, 161, *162,* 198n61

Giamatti, Paul, 77, 183–184n3

Gladfelder, Hal, 146

Godbeer, Richard, 138

Gordon-Reed, Annette, 68, 69–70, 74
Gouverneur Morris Esq'r, Member of Congress
 (portrait), *143*
Grant, John, 88

Hagood, Wesley O., 4
Hall, H. B., *97*
Hamilton, Alexander, 8, 119–142; Adams
 on, 81, 120, 127; affair of, with Maria
 Reynolds, 121–122, 125, 128–134;
 birth out of wedlock of, 119–120, 121,
 125–128; blackmail of, 121–122, 133,
 136; depictions of affair of, 123, 128–134,
 137, 191–192n11; documentary about,
 119, 135–137; vs. Franklin, 98, 100; in his
 lifetime, 120–123; as homosexual, 137–
 140; and Jefferson, 56, 62, 124–125, 129,
 134, 136; legacy of, 140–142; as lothario,
 123–125; marriage of, 121, 131–133, 135–
 136; as outsider, 119–120, 128; portrait
 of, *118;* public confession of affair of, 121,
 122–123, 130, 134–137, 141–142; virility
 of, 131, 132, 135, 140; and Washington, 8,
 13, 120, 122
Hamilton, Allan McLane, 126–127, 133–
 134
Hamilton, Elizabeth Schuyler ("Betsey" or
 "Eliza"), 121, 131–133, 135–136, 140
Hamilton, James, 121, 127
Hamilton, John C., 125
Hart, Gary, 86
Hartley, Mrs., 25
"Head and Heart" letter, 59–60
Helvétius, Madame (Anne-Catherine de
 Ligniville d'Autricourt), 113, 114–115
Hemings, Elizabeth, 73
Hemings, Madison, 64–67, 70
Hemings, Sally, 8, 63–73; accounts rejecting
 story of relationship with Jefferson,
 66–68, 180n66, 182n107; alleged sale
 of daughter of, 64; appearance of, 73;
 Callender's account of, 47–48, 65–67,
 182n105; and Maria Cosway, 58, 63, 66,
 67, 180n66; descendants of, 45; DNA
 testing of descendants of, 70–71; early
 rumors published about, 47–49, *48;*
 Madison Hemings's account of, 64–66;
 and Martha Jefferson, 47; and Jefferson
 as lovers, 68–69, 71–73, 75, 183n128;
 and Jefferson's legacy, 74, 75–76; and
 Jefferson's marriage, 57; late-twentieth-

century reexamination of relationship with
 Jefferson, 68–69; life of, 47; at Monticello,
 47, 66, 73; in Paris, 58, 65, 66, 67, 69,
 72–73; political cartoon of, 49, *50;* public
 acceptance of relationship with Jefferson,
 46, 69–73; relationship with Jefferson, 46,
 47–49, 63–73; and secrecy of Jefferson, 62;
 song about, 48–49
Hemings, Tom, 47, 66
Hemingses of Monticello, The (Gordon-Reed),
 57, 69–70
Heroism, ideology of, 172n21
Heteronormativity, 170n7; of Adams, 87; of
 Washington, 25
Heterosexuality: of Adams, 78, 84; of
 Franklin, 111, 115, 116; of Hamilton, 138,
 140; of Jefferson, 76; of Washington, 42
Hirst, Francis, 60
Historical consciousness, 171–172n19
Historical fundamentalism, 170n6
Historical memory, 171–172n19
History of the United States for 1796
 (Callender), 122
Hitchens, Christopher, 53, 60, 61, 73
Hoar, George F., 104
Homosexual. *See* Gay
"Hooped Petticoats and the Folly of Fashion"
 (Franklin), 100
Houdon, Jean-Antoine, 161
Howells, William Dean, 106–107
Hughes, Rupert, 27–28
Humphrey, David, 23

Idealized image: of Franklin, 111; of
 Hamilton, 122; vs. intimate realm, 1–9; of
 Morris, 155; of Washington, 23, 31–32, 36
Ideology of heroism, 172n21
Illegitimate child(ren): of Franklin, 98, 101,
 103, 105, 106, 112; Hamilton as, 119–120,
 121, 125–128; of Jefferson, 64–68, 70–71,
 76
Impotence vs. sterility of Washington, 40–41
Infidelity of Hamilton, 119–120, 121,
 125–128
Intimate realm vs. idealized image, 1–9
Irving, Washington, 21
Isaacson, Walter, 97–98, 116
Isenberg, Nancy, 6

Jay, John, 80, 101–102, 145, 146
Jefferson, Maria ("Polly"), 66, 72

Jefferson, Martha, 53–57; character and appearance of, 53, 54, 56, 179n28; courtship and marriage of, 53–57, 68; daughters of, 55, 63, 67, 68; death of, 46, 55, 56, 57; and Sally Hemings, 47; and Monticello, 47, 54–55, 56, 57; and secrecy of Thomas Jefferson, 62; and Betsey Walker, 60

Jefferson, Thomas, 8, 45–76; alleged sale of daughter of, 64; appearance of, 62–63; and Rebecca Burwell, 49–53; as chaste widower, 46, 55, 57, 59, 62–64, 68, 74, 76; and Maria Cosway, 57–60; daughters of, 55, 63, 67, 68; death of, 46; descendants of, 17, 45; and design and architecture of Monticello, 52, 63, 68, 179n23; DNA testing of descendants of, 70–71; and Hamilton, 62, 124–125, 129, 134, 136; "Head and Heart" letter of, 59–60; and Sally Hemings, 46, 47–49, 64–73; Madison Hemings's account of, 64–66; in his lifetime, 46–47; intact legacy of, 74–76; marriage of, 53–57, 179n28; as multicultural hero, 7, 46, 74, 75–76; political cartoon of, 49, *50;* portrait of, *45;* secrecy about private life of, 62–64; slave children of, 64–68, 70–71, 76; song about, 48–49; stories told during lifetime of, 46–49; virility of, 56, 62; and Betsey Walker, 47, 60–61

Jefferson in Paris (film), 69

"Jefferson's Daughter" (poem), 64

John Adams (miniseries), 77–78, 183–184n3

Johnson, Eastman, 12

Jordan, Winthrop, 63, 68

Kale, Steven, 149

Kammen, Michael, 2

Kirschke, James, 158–159, 160

Knott, Stephen, 129

Knudson, Jerry W., 182n105

Kramer, Larry, 140

Lafayette, Marquis de, 139, 140

Laurens, John, 124, 138–139, 140

Lavien, Rachel, 121, 127

Lee, Henry ("Light-Horse Harry"), 47

Lemay, Leo, 113

Lepore, Jill, 170n6

Leutze, Emanuel Gottlieb, 11–12, *14, 15*

Lewinsky, Monica, 137

Lewis, Meriwether, 181n83

Liberator (newspaper) on Jefferson-Hemings relationship, 64

Linn, William, 53, 55

Linney, Laura, 77, 184n3

Livingston, Kitty, 194n83

Lodge, Henry Cabot, 25, 126, 131

Lopez, Claude-Anne, 98, 109, 110, 113–114, 116–117

Louis XVI (King), 110

Lovelace, Robert, 159

Lovell, James, 92, 93, 187n65

"Lowland beauty," 20, 21, 25, 27

Lyman, T.P.H., 53

Lystra, Karen, 17

Madison, Dolley, 7, 37, 177n127

Madison, James, 7, 17, 37, 136, 177n127, 199n6

Malone, Dumas, 61

Manliness. *See* Masculinity

Marriage: of Adams, 79, 90–96; of Franklin, 100, 103, 105, 106, 107–108, 109, 112–113, 115; of Hamilton, 121, 131–133, 135–136; of Jefferson, 53–57, 179n28; of Morris, 145, 151–152, 158, 161, 163; of Washington, 13, 21, 23, 30–31, 36–42

Marshall, John, 19, 21

Masculinity: of Adams, 77, 78, 92, 95–96; of Founding Fathers, 2, 7, 167; of Franklin, 99, 115–116; of Hamilton, 120, 131, 132, 135, 140; of Washington, 8, 17–18, 23–24, 25–29, 42

May, Elaine Tyler, 30

McCoy, Samuel, 84

McCullough, David, 77, 86

Memory, selective national, 2

Men, love between, 171n11. *See also* Gay

Mencken, H. L., 79

Middle class: Franklin and, 107, 117; and racism, 30; Maria Reynolds as, 123, 133, 137; Victorian virtues of, 104; view of Morris by, 157

Middlekauff, Robert, 114, 116

Miller, John C., 68, 125, 139

Minnegerode, Meade, 84, 90

Miscegenation, 68, 76

Misogyny, 63, 115

Mitchell, Broadus, 132

Monroe, James, 17, 121–122, 131, 132–133, 134

Monticello: design and architecture of, 52, 63, 68, 179n23; Sally Hemings at, 47, 73; Jeffersons as newlyweds at, 54–55, 56, 57; and legacy of Jefferson, 76; slaves at, 64–65, 66

Moore, Betsy, 51

Moore, Charles, 29–30, 31

More, Paul Elmer, 108

Morgan, Edmund, 57

Morris, Anne Cary, 151–152

Morris, Gouverneur, 8, 143–163; achievements of, 144, 145; body of, 144–147, 156–157, 160–163, *162*, 196n23; vs. Burr, 145, 160; as chaste bachelor, 151–153; Davenport transcriptions of diaries of, 153–158, *154;* diaries of, 147–151; in his lifetime, 145–147; John Jay on, 80, 145, 146; marriage of, 145, 151–152, 158; portraits of, *143*, 161, *162;* as rake, 8, 159–160, 161–163, *162;* rediscovery of, 158–160; and Washington, 18, 161

Morris, Robert, 144, 146

Morse, Benjamin, 105

Morse, John Torrey, 54, 65, 83, 84, 130

Mulford, Carla, 115

Murray, Joseph A., 136–137

National Constitution Center, 4

National Hall of Fame, 104

National identity: Founding Fathers in, 3, 170nn6–7; sex in, 2–3, 170n7

National memory, selective, 2

Nature (magazine) on Jefferson-Hemings relationship, 70–71

New York Herald (newspaper), love letter by George Washington in, 22, 26, 28

Nicholas, Sally, 51

Nineteenth century: biographies in, 5–6, 21; childlessness in, 30; depictions of Adams in, 83–84, 86; depictions of Founding Fathers in, 6, 165–166, 167; depictions of Franklin in, 102, 103, 104–106, 108, 109, 111, 115; depictions of Hamilton in, 120, 125–126, 130–131, 138; depictions of Jefferson in, 49–52, 54, 57, 60, 62, 69; depictions of Morris in, 144, 150–152, 163; depictions of Washington in, 18–25, 38; Victorian morality of, 6

Nock, Albert Jay, 52

Observations on Certain Documents . . . (Hamilton), 122

"On Early Marriages" (Franklin), 105

Onuf, Peter, 62

Page, John, 51–52

Painting of President John Adams, A, 77

Paris: Adams in, 80–81, 83, 85, 87, 88; Franklin in, 98, 101–102, 103, 109, 110, 111, 113–117; Jefferson in, 57–60, 65, 66, 67, 69, 72, 73; Morris in, 146, 147–155, 157–159

Parton, James, 51, 54–55, 106, 129–130

Pasley, Jeffrey L., 169n1

Payne, Dolley. *See* Madison, Dolley

Peale, Rembrandt, *45*

Personalization of public past, 4

Philipse, Mary, 20, 21, 22, 25, 30

Physique. *See* Appearance

Pike County Republican (newspaper) on Hemings family history, 64–65

Pine, Frank Woodworth, 108

Pittsburgh Courier (newspaper) on rumored son of George Washington, 42

Popular biographies, 4–6, 171–172n19

Popular historymaking, 171–172n19

Popular memory, shaping of, 5–6, 171–172n19

Port Folio (magazine) on Jefferson-Hemings relationship, 48–49

Portrait of Alexander Hamilton, 119

Portrait of Benjamin Franklin, 97

Posey, Thomas, 24, 26

Private lives of public figures, 1–9, 167–168

Prussing, Eugene, 28, 134

Public image and private sexual conduct, 1–9, 167–168

Puritan(s), 79; Adams as, 8, 79–80, 81–82, 83, 84–89; and Franklin, 100, 107, 111, 113, 117; and Hamilton, 122; and Morris, 148, 152; and Washington, 37

Quincy, Hannah, 85, 86, 87, 88–89

Race and racism: in biographies, 166; and Jefferson-Hemings relationship, 47–49, 64–73, 75, 76; and reputed illegitimate son of Washington, 42; Theodore Roosevelt on, 30

Randall, Henry Stephens, 49–50, 54

Randall, Willard Sterne: on Hamilton, 137, 194n83; on Jefferson, 53, 59–60, 180n66; on Washington, 32, 33, 176n92

Randolph, Ann Cary, 145, 158

Randolph, Sarah N., 50–51, 53–54

Read, Deborah, 100, 103, 105, 106, 107–108, 109, 112–113, 115

Renwick, Henry Brevoort, 125–126, 129

Renwick, James, 126, 129

Reynolds, Maria: affair of, with Hamilton, 121–122, 125, 128–134; blackmail by, 121–122, 133, 136; characterization of, 123, 130, 131, 133–134, 136; and Elizabeth Hamilton, 132–133; Hamilton's acknowledgment of affair with, 134–137; and Monroe, 121–122, 132–133

Richmond Recorder (newspaper) on Jefferson-Hemings relationship, 47–48, 66

Romantic: Adams as, 77, 78, 87, 90–96; Franklin as, 109, 110, 111, 113, 115; Hamilton as, 123–125, 138–139; Jefferson as, 46, 51, 57–59, 61, 62, 63, 64–73, 74; Morris as, 148–151, 156, 157, 158–159, 161–162; Washington as, 23, 25, 27–28, 32–36

Roosevelt, Theodore, 30, 152–153, 156

Rush, Benjamin, 7

Russell, Phillips, 107

Sally Hemings (film), 71, 72–73

Salon culture: and Franklin, 98, 101–102, 109, 110, 113, 115–116; and Morris, 148–149, 152, 155–156, 160

Savage, Edward, *24*

Scary Movie, 46

Scharff, Virginia, 71

Schlesinger, Arthur M., Jr., 87

Schuyler, Elizabeth. *See* Hamilton, Elizabeth Schuyler ("Betsey" or "Eliza")

1776 (musical), 56

Sex: in national identity, 2–3, 170n7; and quest for relatable past, 1–9

Sex scandals of eighteenth century, 13–17

Sexual personalizing of Founding Fathers, 5

Shea, George, 130

Skelton, Martha. *See* Jefferson, Martha

Slave children: of Jefferson, 64–68, 70–71, 76; of Washington and Madison, 199n6

Slavery: Founding Fathers and, 7; and Jefferson-Hemings relationship, 6, 47–49,

64–76, 166, 167; Madison and, 199n6; Washington and, 39, 199n6

Smertenko, Johan, 124, 125, 127–128, 131

Smith, Abigail. *See* Adams, Abigail

Smith, Page, 94

Sparks, Jared, 19–21, 151, 152

"Speech of Polly Baker" (Franklin), 100

Spitzer, Eliot, 78

Stagg, Kevin, 146

Stanton, Elizabeth Cady, 104

Statue of Washington and Family (sculpture), *39*

Steinberg, Alfred, 85

Stepchildren of Washington, 23, 29–30, 38–40, 43, 177n127

Sterility vs. impotence of Washington, 40–41

St. George, Judith, 87

St. Louis Daily Globe-Democrat (newspaper) on rumored son of George Washington, 24

Strong, Frank, 106

Stuart, Gilbert Charles, *11*

Sumner, William Graham, 126, 138

Swiggett, Howard, 63, 155–157

Talleyrand-Périgord, Charles-Maurice de, 148, 158

Tansill, Charles: on Founding Fathers, 3; on Franklin, 109, 110–111; on Hamilton, 132, 134; on Jefferson, 59, 61; omission of Adams in book by, 87

Tea Party, 170n6

Thomas, Evan, 169n1

Tilton, Elizabeth, 129, 137

Time (magazine) on Franklin, 113, 116

Tise, Larry, 104, 105, 109

Todd, John Payne, 177n127

Trumbull, John, 34, *35, 118*

Tucker, George, 50

Turner, David M., 146

Turner, Frederick Jackson, 106

TV Guide on *John Adams,* 77

Twentieth century: depictions of Adams in, 84–85, 90, 91–92; depictions of Franklin in, 107–111, 113, 117; depictions of Hamilton in, 125, 126–128, 129, 131–133, 135, 137–139, 141; depictions of Jefferson in, 46, 51–53, 55–61, 62, 63–64, 65–68, 71, 74–76; depictions of Morris in, 144, 155–157, 161, 163; depictions of Washington in, 17, 25–32; Founding Fathers in, 6–7; sexual revolutions of, 6–7

Twenty-first century: depictions of Founding Fathers in, 7; depictions of Franklin in, 98, 111; depictions of Morris in, 159, 161; depictions of Washington in, 32–42

Unger, Harlow G., 43
"United States of Amnesia, The" 2
Upper class. *See* Elite

Van Doren, Carl, 107–108
Vidal, Gore, 2, 32
Virility. *See* Masculinity

Walker, Betsey, 47, 59, 60–61, 66, 74, 76
Walker, Clarence E., 73
Walker, John, 47, 60
Warren, Mercy Otis, 82
Washington, Augustine, 33
Washington, George, 7–8, 11–43; body of, 19, *20,* 31, 33–36, *35;* childlessness of, 16–18, 23, 29–30, 40–43, 177n127; courtship and marriage of, 13, 21, 23, 30–31, 38; as desexualized statesman, 11–13; as domestic ideal, 17–25, *24;* early romances of, 20, 21, 23, 25–29, 176n92; estate of, 22; and Sally Fairfax, 21–22, 25–29, 31, 33; faithfulness of, 38, 177n124; as father of nation, 17, 18, 38, 42–43; as Freemason, 16, 173n9; and Hamilton, 8, 13, 120, 122; happy family life of, 20–21, 29–32, 38–40; as homosexual, 140; importance of discussing personal life of, 2; love letters of, 20, 21–22, 26–27, 28–29, 33, 38, 175n58; and "Lowland beauty," 20, 21, 25, 27; manliness of, 8, 17–18, 23–24, 25–29, 42; and modern marriage, 36–42; and Morris, 18, 161; and Mary Philipse, 20, 21, 22, 25, 30; portraits of, *11,* 11–12, *14, 15, 24, 35;* as role model, 18–19, 23; as romantic man, 23, 25, 27–28, 32–36; rumored sons of, 24, 26, 41–42; and sex scandals of eighteenth century, 13–17; slave children of, 199n6; statues of, *20,* 39, *39;* stepchildren of, 23, 29–30, 38–40, 43, 177n127; sterility vs. impotence of, 40–41; story about sexual escapades of, 3, 170–171n9; as symbol of United States, 32; and twentieth-century happy family, 29–32; virtues of, 19

Washington, Martha: and childlessness of George Washington, 16–17, 23, 29–30, 40–41; children of, 23, 29–30, 38–40, 177n127; courtship and marriage of, to George Washington, 13, 21, 23, 30–31, 38; and estate of George Washington, 22; and Sally Fairfax, 22; on Hamilton, 124; happy family life of, 20–21, 29–32; letters between George Washington and, 38; and modern marriage, 36–39, 40–41; portrait of, *24;* statue of, 39, *39;* George Washington's love interests prior to, 25–29, 33; wealth of, 36–37

Washington Crossing the Delaware (painting), 11–12, *14, 15*
Washington Family, The (painting), *24*
Washington's Crossing (Fischer), *14,* 33–34
Wayles, John, 53, 73
Wayles, Martha. *See* Jefferson, Martha
Wealth: of Franklin, 102; of Elizabeth Schuyler Hamilton, 121; of Morris, 152; of Martha Washington, 13, 20, 31, 36
Weekly Anglo-African (newspaper) on alleged sale of Jefferson's daughter, 64
Weems, Mason L. ("Parson"), 2, 18, 19, 22, 105
Weinberger, Jerry, 111
Widower: Franklin as, 113; Jefferson as, 46, 55, 57, 59, 62–64, 68, 74, 76
Wikipedia on Morris, 161–163
Wilson, Woodrow, 25
Womanizer: Franklin as, 98, 104, 110–111, 113, 115, 116, 136; Jefferson as, 67
Wood, Gordon S.: on Franklin, 97, 101, 112, 117; on Washington, 17, 33, 37
Woodhull, Victoria, 129–130

Zall, Paul, 98

THOMAS A. FOSTER is an Associate Professor in the History Department at DePaul University. He is the author of *Sex and the Eighteenth-Century Man: Massachusetts and the History of Sexuality in America* and the editor of three books, most recently *Documenting Intimate Matters: Primary Sources for a History of Sexuality in America*.